The Environment
of the
First-Line
Police Supervisor

THE ENVIRONMENT
OF THE
FIRST-LINE
POLICE SUPERVISOR

ROBERT C. TROJANOWICZ
Michigan State University

Prentice-Hall, Inc., Englewood Cliffs, New Jersey 07632

Library of Congress Cataloging in Publication Data

TROJANOWICZ, ROBERT C
   The Environment of the First-Line Police Supervisor.

   Bibliography: p. 297
   Includes index.
   1.–Supervision of police personnel. I.–Title.
HV7936.S8T76   658.3'02   79-21358
ISBN 0–13–282848–0

Editorial/production supervision and interior design by Alice Erdman
Cover design by A Good Thing, Inc.
Manufacturing buyer: John B. Hall

Printed in the United States of America

10 9 8 7 6 5 4 3 2 1

PRENTICE-HALL INTERNATIONAL, INC., *LONDON*
PRENTICE-HALL OF AUSTRALIA PTY. LIMITED, *SYDNEY*
PRENTICE-HALL OF CANADA, LTD., *TORONTO*
PRENTICE-HALL OF INDIA PRIVATE LIMITED, *NEW DELHI*
PRENTICE-HALL OF JAPAN, INC., *TOKYO*
PRENTICE-HALL OF SOUTHEAST ASIA PTE. LTD., *SINGAPORE*
WHITEHALL BOOKS LIMITED, *WELLINGTON, NEW ZEALAND*

In memory of Russell W. Moss
and John R. Reid

Contents

Chapter 3

Chapter 4

Chapter 5

Chapter 9

Preface

The factors that affect the role of the police sergeant range all the way from the community's attitude toward the police in general, through the organizational style of the particular department, to the training of the individual officer whom the sergeant has to supervise.

This book is written for the first-line police supervisor, the sergeant, as well as for those who aspire to become first-line supervisors and those who do not but are interested in the topic.

Much of the material found in the book is based on an extensive study of three major midwestern police departments. This study was conducted by interviewing 300 police officers of all ranks, observing their actions, and administering questionnaires. The research was specifically aimed at the first-line police supervisor; it focused on the perceptions of the role of the sergeant as viewed by the sergeants themselves, the officers they supervised, and the people who supervised the sergeants. The study was patterned after one done by Neal Gross, entitled, "Explorations in Role Analysis: Studies in the School Superintendent Role." The forced-answer questionnaire was adapted from the Gross study.

Even though this book is the result of exhaustive library and field research, the research findings are introduced only when appropriate to make a point and illuminate the many facets of the role of a sergeant in a contemporary police department. Experts in the field of police and organizational administration were selected to write four of the nine chapters. Their names appear at the beginnings of their chapters, each of which was specifically prepared for this book. The authors are Dr. Kenneth E. Christian, Dr. Steven Edwards, Chief Richard Gleason, Prof. Stephen G. O'Brien, and Mr. Sydney White.

In addition, I would like to acknowledge the assistance of the following people: Wesley Hoes, James Heyden, Robert Weisman, Stephen Cline, Dr. Christopher Sower, Dr. John M. Troyanovich, Dr. Samuel L. Dixon, Roger W. Watson, Robert G. Leonik, Donna C. Hale and Dr. George T. Felkenes.

Robert C. Trojanowicz

The Environment
of the
First-Line
Police Supervisor

Overview and Rationale of the Book

The first-line supervisor in any organization has a difficult job. Descriptions often given to such a person have been "man in the middle," "mediator between management and labor," "father confessor," and "the forgotten man." And if these descriptions are accurate, the first-line *police* supervisor has an even more difficult job than most others. His responsibilities range from thorough knowledge of the technicalities of his job to the role of trainer and "coach" to his subordinates.

The variables associated with the sergeant's job are numerous and diverse. This book attempts to capture the many facets of first-line police supervision.*

CHAPTER HEADINGS AND SUMMARIES

The following chapter headings and summaries will give the reader an opportunity to determine the overall direction of the book.

---

*Authors note: I am totally aware of the growing numbers of women in American police departments, and of the excellence of their work. In writing this book, however, the guest authors and I have found it unwieldy to continually try to use expressions such as "he or she." It is for this reason that you will find the male pronouns used almost exclusively and they refer to women police officers as well as men.

Chapter 2, "Organizational and Supervisory Styles," describes how the first-line police supervisor, like his counterparts in other organizations, has to "walk the tightrope" of organizational functioning in an attempt to satisfy both superiors and subordinates. The sergeant is often immersed in the dynamics of the organization, confused about how to act and react. This chapter discusses the various organizational styles that the sergeant may be exposed to and describes supervisory leadership styles, to illustrate the mismatch that may occur when the sergeant attempts to use a leadership style that is incongruent with the particular organizational orientation.

Downs, for example, discusses types of behavior of supervisors and others in organizations. He identifies the types as *climbers, conservers, advocates, zealots,* and *statesmen.* [1] Each has a particular style of behavior in the organization. The *climbers* attempt to maximize their power, income, and prestige by seeking promotions, through aggrandizement, and by jumping from department to department to make opportune use of timing and "connections."

Conservers, as the name implies, take a conservative orientation to organizational functioning. They jealously guard what they have and, because they are "shaky" and insecure, they resist change and are reluctant to take chances. Unlike the climber, the conserver wants to preserve the status quo. Even though they don't actively seek promotions as climbers do, conservers are often promoted because they are predictable and don't "rock the boat."

The *advocate* has difficulty seeing and becoming committed to the goals of the organization. He vigorously and aggressively pushes for anything that will give his department more resources, power, prestige, and notoriety.

> Like climbers, they provide a dynamic force in bureaus. However, they are simultaneously more conservative and more radical than climbers. They are more conservative because their loyalty leads them to oppose changes that might benefit them personally but injure their organizations. They are more radical because they are willing to promote views that might antagonize their superiors if doing so will help their organizations. [2]

Zealots are even more narrow-minded than advocates. They become so committed to a particular program or policy that they have difficulty "seeing the forest from the trees" and being objective about their endeavors. They do not make good administrators because of their limited view of problem areas.

---

[1] Anthony Downs, *Inside Bureaucracy* (Boston: Little, Brown and Co., 1967), pp. 92–111.
[2] Ibid., p. 109.

Unlike climbers and advocates, zealots are not really interested in "capturing" functions from other social agents, or inventing new functions, unless to do so benefits their sacred policies. However, they are tremendously desirous of procuring more resources for developing those policies. Therefore, zealots are not extensive "imperialists"; rather they agitate for extremely intensive expansion of a few policies.[3]

Statesmen are probably the only persons who are altrustic in orientation and who attempt to do what is good for the organization and the public, even at the expense of personal loss. It is difficult to remain a statesman for long, however, because when the competitive struggle begins for resources, such a person often loses out because of his willingness to compromise and mediate for the good of the organization.

Chapter 2 will introduce the reader to several other leadership styles, to show the many different kinds of supervisory behaviors in police organizations and to demonstrate that even though "pure" styles may be rare, the sergeant usually has a distinguishable orientation to managing his subordinates.

Chapter 3

Regardless of the organization's style or their own supervisory leadership orientation, sergeants have unique problems associated with their supervisory role. Chapter 3, "The Sergeant: The Man in the Middle," focuses on the pressures and pulls on a first-line police supervisor. No matter how hard the sergeant tries, superiors and subordinates will never be totally satisfied. This is the "middleman" dilemma.

Furthermore, it cannot be assumed that the first-line police supervisor's tasks and responsibilities are synonomous with those of his counterparts in business and industry. The sergeant's job is much different from that of the foreman. Table 1-1 shows summary comments from interviews with more than 300 police officers, including many first-line supervisors, regarding the differences between the roles of the sergeant and the foreman.

There was general agreement throughout the ranks that the sergeant's job is much more complex than that of his foreman counterpart. The sergeant has to deal with the public, must make complex on-the-spot legal decisions, and is constantly involved in the training of his subordinates. In addition, the sergeant is also a police officer and, unlike the foreman in business and industry, when necessary has to perform line functions.

Also, the line officer identifies more with the sergeant than does the assembly-line worker with his foreman, because most police officers aspire

[3]Ibid., p. 110.

TABLE 1-1

Is the Sergeant's Role Different From the Foreman's Role?

Patrolmen	Detectives	Sergeants	Lieutenants	Command
In police work:	In police work:	In police work:	In police work:	In police work:
Sergeant has more power and influence	Sergeant doesn't have to supervise as closely	Sergeants have more freedom	Sergeant's job is more complex	Supervisees are not in one place
Decision making is more complex and critical	Sergeant has to be more flexible	Sergeant does not have an answer for every situation	Sergeant likes the line man's job, whereas the foreman doesn't want to be a line man	Difficult to measure productivity
Police have contact with public	Sergeant has to be innovator	Leadership is better in police departments because of military model	Sergeant has less control over supervisees	Sergeant has to be more versatile
Sergeant has more unfamiliar situations	Sergeant has to know his job better	Sergeant has two roles—officer and supervisor	Sergeant has more responsibility	Sergeant has to make immediate decisions
Sergeant takes a more personal interest in supervisees		More turnover on shifts	Sergeant has to be more versatile	
Sergeant is more critical to his employees		Output more difficult to measure	Sergeant has larger span of control	
Sergeant has to be concerned with such things as appearance		Not as many guidelines	Sergeant is more of a trainer	
Sergeant has to exert more control		Sergeant has to be concerned about community reaction		
Sergeant doesn't have to supervise as closely		Officers can be more subversive of supervision		
		More comradeship		

Note: Responses are listed in the order of importance as stated by the particular group of respondents.

to become sergeants. There is a greater sense of comradeship between the sergeant and his officers because of the element of danger in police work and the resulting need of police officers to depend on each other in tight situations. This closer identification and comradeship can be a positive element in the supervisor–supervisee relationship, or it can complicate the "middleman" role, especially in the area of monitoring and disciplining.

The very nature of police work, its often ambiguous role expectations, and the complex legal environment create many problems for the sergeant. For one thing, output is difficult to measure, so the obstacles to objective personnel evaluation can be monumental. The foreman in an automobile plant can measure output and its quality and then deal accordingly with his people. What is the sergeant to measure—the number of tickets issued? the preventive effect of a traffic stop and a warning to the motorist?

The sergeant's job is not analogous to that of the foreman in business or industry for many other reasons. The sergeant does not have the foreman's advantage of geographic control. The sergeant's subordinates may be several miles away; they are almost always at least out of eye contact. This in itself makes supervision difficult, necessitating the use of imaginative leadership techniques.

Because police organizations are semimilitary in orientation, another of the sergeant's concerns is the appearance of the officers. An overemphasis on the "spit-shine look" can cause antagonism from them, but a disregard of the uniform code by the sergeant will precipitate consternation from superiors —another example of the uniqueness and difficulty of the role of the first-line police supervisor as "middleman."

Chapter 4

"The Sergeant as Leader," the topic of Chapter 4, extends much of the discussion presented in Chapter 3. Identification of leadership styles and the ramifications of particular styles are only part of the picture. To be effective leaders, sergeants need to use the styles that best fit their personalities, their departments, and the particular units they happen to be assigned to. A sergeant in charge of physical training in the recruit academy will use a different style from one who is assigned as a supervisor in the investigative division. In addition, regardless of style, there are techniques that can be useful to the sergeant when controlling, monitoring, disciplining, counseling, training, and relating to subordinates. This chapter looks at leadership from many perspectives and identifies key elements in the leadership process.

From the interviews mentioned above with police officers, it was evident that officers want a supervisor they can talk to, rely on, and get answers to their questions. They get especially irritated when their supervisor is over critical, "picky," and unwilling to take the time to offer constructive suggestions for problem solving.

Officers also resent "oversupervision." The sergeant is expected to orient, train, counsel, coach, and give advice but, conversely, will create an atmosphere of antagonism if he or she "oversupervises" and will not allow subordinates the latitude to operate.

Oversupervision also manifests itself when the sergeant is perceived as interfering with calls. Officers mention that the ineffective sergeant tends to do this, getting only half the information and expecting the officer to get the rest without knowing what has been received in the first place. This not only irritates the officer, it upsets the citizen who has to give the same information twice.

There was consensus that there are two basic kinds of sergeants, those that are *administration*-oriented and those oriented to *field* operations, with variations in between. The administrative type goes "by the book," knows the technicalities of the job, but is somewhat inflexible. The field type relates well with the officers, is more flexible, but can get sloppy in technicalities and procedures. Selection and training could help the administrative type to be more flexible and personable and the field type to be more knowledgeable in the technical aspects of the job.

However, not all sergeants have to operate in the same manner or fit into the same mold as long as they fulfill the basic requirements of the job. Thus, it is important that the sergeant as leader have a well-defined role, with responsibilities outlined and authority limits delineated.

Continually, throughout the interviews with the officers, the statement was made that the effective sergeant needs to "be all things to all people." Specifically, the sergeant must not only know everything related to the technical aspects of the job, but be sensitive to the feelings of both subordinates and citizens.

Table 1-2 shows the most frequent responses of the 300 interviewees to the question, "What are the traits of an effective sergeant?" As you can see, the responses are consistent throughout the ranks. In all ranks, the respondents felt that the effective sergeant has technical job knowledge but at the same time has concern for officers and is sensitive to them as human beings. The sergeant is expected to be a decision maker and to be able to discipline when necessary.

The officers interviewed were also asked to rank, from 1 (the most important) to 7 (the least important), the supervisory duties mentioned by Whisenand.[4] The rankings they gave are shown in Table 1-3.

As you can readily see, planning and keeping paperwork up to date are

[4]Paul M. Whisenand, *Police Supervision, Theory and Practice,* 2nd ed. (Englewood Cliffs, N.J.: Prentice-Hall, 1976).

TABLE 1-2

What Are the Traits of an Effective Sergeant?

Patrolmen	Sergeants	Lieutenants	Command
Can be relied on by officers to answer questions	Is "all things to all people"	Is able to listen	Has ability to get along
Can relate and communicate	Is a friend and counselor, not aloof	Is aloof but not standoffish	Is a "square shooter"
Is friendly but able to discipline	Is able to discipline	Is "all things to all people"	Is not aloof or "buddy-buddy"
Is "all things to all people"	Is fair and honest	Is a disciplinarian	Is "all things to all people"
Can get along with officers	Is able to listen and get along with people	Is a good judge of character	Can make decisions
Is a leader	Is friendly but not "buddy-buddy"	Is aggressive in decision making	Is aggressive
Is not a "nitpicker"	Is empathic and compassionate	Projects a positive attitude to officers	Is qualified
Is fair and understanding	Understands his or her role	Understands the sources of problems	Has good moral character
Complements officers	Can make decisions and use good judgment	Has been in the military	Has confidence
Is compassionate and empathic	Is even-tempered and flexible	Is a good teacher and communicator	Is able to both defend and punish officers
Gives officers flexibility and latitude	Is a good teacher	Is self-confident	Is firm but fair
Is a good role model	Is tactful	Is able to answer questions	Does not socialize with officers
Does not oversupervise	Projects an image of leadership	Is fair	Is a trainer
Need not resort to force	Is military-oriented	Can communicate and verbalize	Is loyal
Backs officers up	Is a positive thinker		Is level-headed
Is a self-starter, with an organized life	Is able to see overall objectives		Is a good role model
Knows strengths and weaknesses of officers	Is a positive role model		Is a counselor
Is aggressive but not overbearing	Is a person officers can rely on		
Is not a "company man"			
Doesn't belittle officer in front of others			
"Pitches in" when needed			

Note: Responses are listed in the order of importance as stated by the particular group of respondents.

TABLE 1-3

Rankings of Sergeant's Duties

Functions of the Police Sergeant	Patrol Officers and Detectives	Sergeants	Lieutenants and Command Officers
Implementing and reporting new procedures from above	5	5	5
Controlling and monitoring supervisees	4	3	2
Leadership ability	1	1	1
Effectiveness in decision making	2	2	4
Helping develop supervisees	3	4	3
Planning	6	6	6
Keeping paperwork up to date	7	7	7

viewed by everyone, regardless of rank, as the least important of the seven items listed. This probably reflects the low priority planning is given in police departments in general, regardless of the level of the supervisor. Police departments have a history of ineffective planning and of operating on "crisis by management," for several reasons. The primary one is the community's perception of the police as a reactive force; the public seems to believe that officers should be rewarded only for activities like apprehending an armed robber, arresting a drunk driver, or responding to a disagreement between neighbors. Therefore, since planning and research are not perceived as a valued activity by either the public or the politicians who distribute the economic resources, the police department is forced to direct its energies to areas where it will be supported and rewarded—to "crime fighting."

As pointed out earlier, the line officer identifies with the sergeant because most officers aspire to that position. Conversely, the sergeant often identifies with the line officer because they are both police officers, and this can lead to the sergeant's being overinvolved in line activities. As one sergeant stated, "Road work gets into your blood." This situation has implications regarding the planning aspect of the supervisor's job. In some cases, sergeants are promoted to that position because they were effective line officers; but once they have that rank, everyone—including the sergeants themselves—realizes that they do not have the traits or the desire to perform the duties of a supervisor: controlling, directing, dealing with paperwork, and overseeing rather than "doing." They let "doing" take priority, which takes time away from planning and paperwork. This, coupled with the community's expectation of reactive enforcement, further contributes to the low priority most departments and sergeants give to the planning function and the negative attitudes some sergeants have toward doing paperwork.

Just as there was consensus about the low rating given planning and paperwork, *leadership* was considered by all the ranks the most important aspect of the sergeant's job. The areas of disagreement in the importance of the seven functions were primarily in the second rank. Sergeants and the ranks below them felt that effectiveness in decision making was the second most important responsibility of the sergeant; lieutenants and the ranks above saw control and monitoring of subordinates as the most necessary after leadership. This is understandable, in view of the fact that one of the most frequent criticisms of sergeants by their supervisors is that they are too close to their officers, which hinders effective controlling, monitoring, and disciplining. Sergeants usually counter this criticism by saying that closeness and friendship do not affect their ability to perform these functions. The problem, they say, is that they are not backed up when they do discipline one of their officers, and it is this lack of support by department administrators that subverts the discipline and monitoring process and hinders the sergeant in being an effective leader.

Ultimately, the sergeant's leadership success or lack of it is reflected in his or her ability to motivate subordinates. Boxx and Simon have summarized the most often cited theorists on motivation (see Table 1-4). The propositions range from satisfaction of the supervisee's need to feel safe in the work environment to opportunities for psychological growth.

In addition, most contemporary theorists state either directly or indirectly that one of the most, if not *the* most, important factor that relates to worker motivation is the basic belief of the worker's organization—and his first-line supervisor in particular—in human dignity. Because the relationship between the sergeant as leader and the officers will be strained without the acceptance of human dignity, Dalena has developed a "bill of rights" for workers and supervisors:

Bill of Rights for Workers: The supervisor should have:

1. An ability to take as well as give during a heated argument. Then, an ability to forget it.

2. Honesty and forthrightness. If something has to be done, tell it straight. Don't say it's because "someone" ordered it.

3. A willingness to take our past records into account before punishing for a mistake.

4. A willingness to let workers do the work. Workers resent a working foreman [sergeant] more than anyone realizes.

5. Exercise the mind before the mouth.

6. Compassion, empathy, trust, thoughtfulness, tolerance, tenacity.

TABLE 1-4

Motivation of Subordinates

Theorist	Propositions
Maslow	Five levels of needs: physiological, safety, social affiative (belongingness), self-esteem, and self-actualization
Herzberg	A. Maintenance factors (working conditions, salary status, and job security)
	B. Motivational factors (achievement, recognition, possibility of growth, work itself, and responsibility)
McGregor	The need for the supervisor to understand his employees and create opportunities by identifying worker potential, removing obstacles, encouraging growth, and providing guidance
Argyris	Management must offer its workers the opportunity to grow and allow personal needs to be satisfied.
McClelland	All workers have a desire to achieve, and training programs can teach and develop this need.
Likert	The effective supervisor has to be interested in his supervisees. When supervisors and workers have common interests and needs and are supportive of each other, then organizational goals will be facilitated.

Source: W. Randy Boxx and Alex J. Simon, "Is 'Mr. Right' the Wrong Man for the Job?" in Management for Supervisors: Readings and Cases, P. Preston and T. Zimmerer, eds. (Englewood Cliffs, N.J.: Prentice-Hall, 1978), pp. 122 and 123.

7. An ability to communicate; carry policy down, but carry feedback up, too.

8. A commitment to punish the laggard. Workers don't condone their actions.

Bill of Rights for Foremen [sergeants] in their relations with their bosses:

1. A salary at least 10% higher than the highest paid worker in the unit.

2. An emphasis on work accomplished, not on work that didn't get done —and for a good reason. If this emphasis isn't there, the foreman is forced into a position of fabricating excuses.

3. An *effective* means of processing complaints or grievances. This is probably the foreman's biggest need.

4. More than just the right to blow his cool to his bosses. Instead, he should be encouraged to provide accurate feedback from workers and to fight for what he believes is right.

5. Worker input to help determine the foreman's merit raises.
6. A minimum of paperwork.[5]

The sergeant's leadership encompasses many variables and is the most important factor related to worker productivity and satisfaction. Underlying the sergeant's relationship with subordinates is treatment of them with respect and dignity. Chapter 4 emphasizes the many characteristics of leadership.

Chapter 5

No book on the role of a sergeant in a police department would be complete without a discussion of the "nuts and bolts" of the operational side of that role. The sergeant has many duties and functions, ranging from the periodic inspection of his supervisees, to giving advice about a legal matter, to counseling a subordinate who has an alcohol problem. Chapter 5, "The Operational Role of the Sergeant," complements the other chapters in illustrating the many functions, often considered routine, that are necessary for organizational achievement.

Much of the job description of the police sergeant has been borrowed from business and industry. As pointed out earlier, the sergeant's job is unique, and generalizations from business and industry aren't always relevant or applicable. But Katz has grouped the skills of administrators into three categories, and these groupings have relevance for first-line supervisors.

An administrator is one who (a) directs the activities of other persons and (b) undertakes the responsibility for achieving certain objectives through these efforts. Within this definition, successful administration appears to rest on three basic skills, which we will call *technical, human,* and *conceptual.*[6]

By *technical* skills, Katz is referring to the procedures and techniques to perform the job. A structural engineer must be familiar with the type of soil needed to effectively construct a building and the requirements for withstanding stress and strain. The effective police sergeant will need to be well versed in the law and knowledgeable in the equipment that supervisees are using. Technical knowledge is the basic minimum requirement for any first-line supervisor, regardless of his organizational affiliation.

The need for *human* skills is evident when it is considered that the

---

[5]Donald T. Dalena, "Foreman—The Worker's Point of View," *Industry Week,* Penton IPC, Cleveland, Ohio, 1975.

[6]Robert L. Katz, "Skills of an Effective Administrator," *Harvard Business Review,* (September–October 1974), pp. 90–102.

greater part of the supervisor's time is spent communicating with supervisees. This is even more the case in police work, because the public is being served; and unlike private industry, where the assembly-line worker doesn't have his machine or the automobile part he is working with talking back to him, the line police officer is dealing with human beings, who are often in an irritated or upset state. The police sergeant has to be able to communicate with the officer, suggesting methods to use in talking to the citizen who is in such a state, as well as with the citizen who wants to speak with a supervisor.

> As *technical* skill is primarily concerned with working with "things" (processes or physical objects), so *human* skill is primarily concerned with working with people. . . . The person with highly developed human skill is aware of his own attitudes, assumptions, and beliefs about other individuals and groups; he is able to see the usefulness and limitations of these feelings. By accepting the existence of viewpoints, perceptions and beliefs which are different from his own he is skilled in understanding what others really mean by their words and behavior.[7]

Although technical skills are obviously necessary for an effective first-line supervisor, it is human skills that will make or break the supervisor. The sergeant who cannot relate to, communicate with, and demonstrate at least a minimal amount of human skills with supervisees, the general public, and his or her supervisors will soon find that technical skills are of little use. The supervisees won't ask for help and may even do their best to avoid contact, the citizen will want to speak with a "higher authority," and superiors will lose confidence in the sergeant's ability to carry out supervisory functions.

The third area that Katz mentions is the *conceptual* skill of the supervisor. This is the ability to see the "big picture," to be able to relate the functions and purpose of the unit to the overall goals of the organization.

Even though competition for resources between units can be healthy, overcompetitiveness can be dysfunctional for overall organizational goal achievement. Destructive competition between, say, the patrol and investigative divisions in a police department can lead to antagonism and even a lack of information sharing. The effective patrol sergeant, for example, can conceptualize the problems the patrol officers can create for the investigative division if they don't properly secure the crime scene.

> In a very real sense, conceptual skill embodies consideration of both the technical and human aspects of the organization. Yet the concept *skill*, as an ability to translate knowledge into action, should enable one to distinguish between the three skills of performing the technical activities (technical skill), understanding and motivating individuals and groups (human skills) and coordinat-

[7]Ibid., pp. 91.

ing and integrating all the activities and interests of the organization toward a common objective (conceptual skill).[8]

An effective sergeant is able to combine and relate all these skill areas to the supervisory situation. For example, at a crime scene, the patrol sergeant can impart the technical requirements for securing the area, communicate the directives in a helpful, concerned manner to subordinates, and be able to anticipate what will be helpful for the investigative officers in their follow-up investigation.

The ineffective sergeant will not know the proper techniques for securing the crime scene, will be abrasive or uncommunicative to subordinates and the public, and will care little about those who will have to do the follow-up investigation.

Carroll and Anthony have listed several specific duties of the first-line supervisor. All of them involve either technical, human, or conceptual skills. The following are those most applicable to the police sergeant, with the first group relating to what the sergeant's superiors should expect of him.

Management Expectations: The supervisor should:

Plan the work of his department

Coordinate the department's work with other departments

Train employees when needed

Make work assignments

Interpret and implement management policies

Understand and communicate to his employees all aspects of company operations

Maintain both morale and discipline

Send recommendations for change upward

Motivate departmental members as best he can

Establish a warm and trusting working climate within the department

Handle employee problems promptly

Be fair in all departmental matters

With respect to *his own employees,* the supervisor should:

Explain to employees all matters connected with their job

Train employees when needed

Assume a role of counselor on occasion

Distribute all department amenities fairly

Discuss proposed changes before they take place

Provide sound policies for employee personal problems

Orient new workers

[8]Ibid., p. 94.

Develop good morale

Stand up for employees when they are being treated arbitrarily
from above[9]

The list above astutely outlines the duties of the first-line supervisor. Dividing supervisory responsibilities into two categories, management expectations and responsibilities to employees, is useful in illustrating that even though there is some overlap between the two responsibility areas, by and large there are different pressures and pulls on the sergeant because he is the middleman between management and the line officers.

Management expects sergeants to plan work schedules, make assignments, and coordinate the activities with other departmental units. The training division, for example, may need additional assistance, so a patrol officer must be assigned to that special duty. At the same time, the sergeant is expected to be fair and distribute all departmental assignments and amenities fairly. The point is that not only do routine assignments need to be made; there has to be a sensitivity to supervisees' skills, ambitions, and needs. If the sergeant does not deal fairly with line officers in making assignments or other activities, tension and conflict may ensue, affecting the work environment and ultimately the services provided to citizens.

Interpreting and implementing management policies and understanding and communicating to the officers all aspects of the departmental operations are primary functions of the sergeant. The sergeant is the link between the officers and management; the title of "middleman" is more than just rhetoric. He has to be an effective middleman if the department is to operate smoothly and effectively. By making suggestions for improvement himself as well as funneling his officers' ideas upward, the sergeant can involve the officers at least indirectly in the decision-making process and make them feel an integral part of the department.

An aspect of police supervision that is often neglected is the *training* function that the sergeant performs. Almost every contact the officer has with the public is a ready-made opportunity for the sergeant to be a trainer and a "coach." When the officer senses that the sergeant is a constructive advisor, employee motivation and morale will be improved. In this regard, Carroll and Anthony's listing of responsibilities not only emphasizes the supervisor's relationship to management but also focuses on the supervisor's responsibilities to supervisees.

[9]Archie B. Carroll and Ted F. Anthony, "An Overview of the Supervisor's Job," *Personnel Journal*, March 1976.

Chapter 6

Chapter 6, "Supervisory Promotional Practices," details past and present selection training and assessment practices and provides helpful suggestions for future consideration when selecting sergeants, training them to be effective supervisors, and assessing them to ensure productive long-term functioning.

Police departments in contemporary society are very complex, thereby complicating the job for the sergeant, who now needs resources and knowledge and can no longer merely refer to past experience. Technological advancements and legal precedents make it impossible for the sergeant to operate as in "the good old days."

As Chapter 6 points out, too often police departments rely on the "good man" theory. A "good man" is a jack of all trades, can do anything and everything, and will rise to a supervisory level on his own, if he is left alone. Formal assessment and training are carried out for the sergeant only when there is grant money available, or when an enlightened chief recognizes the importance and complexity of the sergeant's role.

Formal promotion procedures to the rank of sergeant are often haphazard, inconsistent, or even nonexistent. Where there are formal procedures, there is often no job analysis preceding the formulation of the examination.

Career development is also emphasized in this chapter, and a model for career development is presented.

Chapter 7

The purpose of this book is to provide the reader with as broad and complete a perspective as possible of the many variables associated with the role of the sergeant in a police department. Such a book would be incomplete without a cross-cultural comparison. Chapter 7, "A Cross-Cultural Comparison of the Role of the Sergeant," discusses and compares the role, selection, training, and general functioning of the British police sergeant with those of the sergeant in the United States. In addition, the governmental, social, and geographic context of the British sergeant is taken up, as well as an analysis of the British police structure, the origins of the rank of sergeant, and its development. The limits of the British sergeant's authority are outlined, along with his role in police organizations and the conditions of his service. A summary at the end of the chapter presents a cross-cultural evaluation and thoughts for the future. The comparisons vividly point out the similarities in the first-line supervisory role, regardless of culture, but also the uniqueness of the problems faced by the American sergeant.

It has been said that 90 percent of the supervisor's time is spent handling personnel problems within the unit. The problems often occur because of stress in the employees' personal life or organizational environment. Likewise, extensive problems of supervisees cause stressful conditions for the sergeant. Chapter 8, "The Management of Stress," identifies conditions, both organizational and personal, that cause stress and suggests techniques for helping people cope with stressful situations. An astute sergeant is able to identify stress and use the situation as a training and counseling opportunity to help supervisees become more effective in their organizational functioning and happier in their personal lives.

As Chapter 8 points out, the first-line police supervisor has a twofold responsibility for the management of stress. First, sergeants should learn awareness of the sources of stress in their own lives and how these can be eliminated or controlled so as not to impair their effectiveness on the job, or the quality of their personal and home lives. Second, they should learn to recognize and deal with job stress affecting their subordinates. The two aspects are closely interrelated, since many of the same stress variables affect both officers and their supervisors.

Chapter 9

The final chapter, "The Sergeant as a Reflection of His Department and Community," culminates the discussion of the constellation of factors that affect the functioning of the first-line police supervisor. The importance of support from the department and the community is emphasized. In addition, a process is presented that facilitates the construction of a workable role definition for the sergeant in the community. Without a well-defined role that can be translated into a job description reflecting the needs of the particular community and the legal requirements of the department, the sergeant will have no meaningful *reference points* with which to guide his supervisees, nor will there be a gauge by which to evaluate the sergeant's effectiveness or ineffectiveness. In the role development and construction process, it is mandatory that the groups most directly affected by the sergeant's functioning have input. The most important groups are the community residents, the police department administrators, the line officers, and the sergeants themselves. A complete and inclusive role definition and job description that reflect the needs of the community as well as the goals of the police department will provide the sergeant with reference points that will facilitate the supervisory process.

There has been much recent discussion in criminal justice about the *role* of the first-line police officer. The process usually "breaks down" when the element of discretion is introjected into the discussion, with the advocates for a flexible police role arguing that the effective police officer is one who has discretion and is able to use it when appropriate. When this argument becomes convincing then there is little progress toward standardizing the role definition by specifically putting the line officer's role expectations down in "black and white".

Hence either of two extremes is taken—leave the role definition loose recognizing that discretion is a real and necessary part of the line officer's role or on the other extreme standardize the line officer's role to the point where a clerk could do the job.

A meaningful and workable compromise is to adequately define the role of the line officer's supervisor, the sergeant. In this way there are guidelines for police action as viewed from the immediate supervisor's perspective. The line officer still has discretion but within the sergeants sphere of supervisory influence. With an adequate role definition the sergeant is able to monitor, oversee, coach, advise, suggest, answer questions, and counsel. Because the sergeant, as a supervisor, is not "caught up" in the day to day activities like the line officer he has a more expansive perspective to see the "big picture," reflecting community needs, yet adhering to the legal mandates of his department.

The key, then, is not overdefining the role of the line officer but adequately identifying the factors that relate to effective supervision of the line officer. Chapter 9 details a process to accomplish the construction of a role definition for the sergeant.

CHAPTER TWO

Organizational and Supervisory Styles*

All organizations have purposes and goals, and police departments are no different. Attainment of the goals requires workers, and whenever there is more than one worker, there usually has to be someone to oversee the work activity to make sure of goal achievement. The sergeant in a police department, as the first-line supervisor, is the person charged with the responsibility of monitoring, controlling, disciplining, organizing, coordinating, and directing the work of the line officers.

The individual worker is not always totally content in his work environment; to most workers, the job is merely a means to an end—monetary compensation that can be ultimately translated into goods for survival and personal and family satisfaction. The sergeant, depending on his effectiveness and the support of his community and department, can help make the workplace not only tolerable but even enjoyable. He can be the catalyst that motivates subordinates to be productive and competent, the vital link that translates directives, policies, and procedures into meaningful action.

The sergeant's role as first-line supervisor is even more critical in the light of the often ambiguous role of the police and the many external pressures exerted on the department by politicians, special-interest groups, and the general citizenry. The sergeant may not often feel these pressures directly, but the top administrators do, and the effects as they are transmitted downward through the organizational levels to the sergeant can be intense.

*Note: This chapter was written with the assistance of John M. Trojanowicz.

As one sergeant stated, "The intensity becomes greater as the directives go down the chain of command."

Thus, pressures emanate from both the external environment and the internal organization. Added to this is the factor of organizational style within the department. The organizational style will affect the sergeant's personal leadership style, and the leadership style will determine, in great part, the effectiveness of the sergeant's supervisees. In other words, the variables of organizational and leadership style are linked together, and they manifest themselves in the way the first-line supervisor—the sergeant—relates to his supervisees and their problems. This chapter will present and discuss several organizational and supervisory leadership styles.

MANAGEMENT STYLES

The influence of the worker on the organization has been altered over the years. In the early 1900s, the worker had little freedom and input. With changing times and the increased influence of unions and other organized work groups, the worker has obtained more privileges and economic rewards, even if input has still sometimes been minimal.

In police organizations, it has usually been the police sergeant who has felt the effect of such changes, from both management and workers. He has had to be flexible, adjustable, and adaptable to changing societal and organizational conditions.

For a perspective on the influence of differing organizational styles on the operation of the organization and on the attitude of the worker, the classical, human relations, and structuralist approaches will be presented. The three approaches were the result of studies in industrial organizations, but they are applicable in police organizations because management styles in police departments have been adapted from business, industry, and the military.

The Classical Theory of Scientific Management

This theory is based on the premise that man's primary motivation is economic or materialistic. The organization and its individual members are seen as striving for the same goals, and thus, no great conflict should logically exist between management and workers. Consistent hard labor and efficiency result in benefits to both management and labor in the form of higher profits, which result in higher pay and greater fringe benefits.

This attitude results in an organizational structure that largely reflects the managerial perspective: clearly defined division of labor, with highly specialized personnel and a distinct hierarchy of authority. The expectations of management regarding work output are based on what is scientifically established as physically possible: What can an individual produce in a given time with the tools or machinery at his disposal? Pay is tied as closely as possible to output, with piecework wages being the ideal.

The classical organization breaks down the various procedures of production into individual movements, each performed by a different person, who, because he specializes in one task, can develop and maintain maximum efficiency with a minimum investment in learning and intellectual and physical effort—and who can be easily replaced. Most of this idea relates directly to industry, but in view of how highly specialized some police departments are, the classical approach becomes relevant.

Because the span of each worker's activities is severely limited, coordination of effort becomes the primary function of management, which organizes itself into a hierarchy in the shape of a pyramid. Every five or six workers require a first-line supervisor, every five or six first-line supervisors need a second-line supervisor, and so on up to the center of control at the top of the pyramid. Visualize a police organizational chart and you will see the relevance.

In the classical organization, labor can be divided by purpose or goal; all workers with the same goal are grouped together in a single unit. In police work, such units would be the patrol division, the investigative division, special operations, and so on.

Another means of dividing labor is by clientele; all workers dealing with the same kinds of people are grouped together in the same unit—for instance, in police work, the juvenile division. Geographical area is another way to divide labor; the state police patrol the highways, for example, whereas the sheriff's department has jurisdiction over county roads and their adjacent territory, and the municipal police department is responsible for the safety of people within the city limits.

It is obvious from the foregoing discussion that classical theorists are primarily concerned with the formal organization, with organizational charts, titles, ranks, and formal communication systems—orders, directives, memoranda, regulations, policies, and procedures. Moreover, with their emphasis on material rewards, the classicists also focus primarily on one type of organization member, the type that Robert Presthus terms "upward-mobile" and that Downs classifies as the "climber."[1] These people eventually come to monopolize power positions and obtain a majority of the organization's rewards.

Presthus characterizes "upward-mobiles" as those who are unflaggingly optimistic, who like their work, and who are proud to be members of their

[1]Robert Presthus, *The Organization Society* (New York: Random House, 1962), pp. 164–204; Anthony Downs, *Inside Bureaucracy* (Boston: Little, Brown and Co., 1967), pp. 92–112.

organization. They accept the organization as the best of all possible worlds and are thus able to promote organizational goals without personal conflict. In other words, they are able to carry out whatever the organization demands of them because the value of doing so exceeds their own personal values, whether moral, political, or familial. They are able to both defer easily to the authority figures above them and act as authority figures to their subordinates. They are able to perform in these seemingly conflicting roles because of an uncommon sensitivity to the needs and desires of others, which enables them to successfully manipulate others. They rationalize their manipulativeness and lack of spontaneity as the necessary price for organizational success.

The "upward-mobile" has an extraordinary drive for power, yet he also demonstrates behavior that is viewed as dependent: He needs the security of the organization. "Commanding presence, effective staging, long-range views, an air of infallibility, the ability to dignify commonplace observations —these are typical upward-mobile postures."[2] The "upward-mobile" finds it impossible to admit to any form of weakness. He shows what might even be a relatively genuine personal attachment to his superiors, but he regards his inferiors impersonally, as mere instruments. He is an archconformist and is impatient with dissent and controversy. He is often anxious about rank and the symbols of prestige because he realizes that he needs self-promotion as well as discipline in order to rise in the organization. The "upward-mobile" stresses efficiency, strength, self-control, and dominance and possesses an abiding and profound respect for authority, with which he identifies and that therefore does not threaten him.

The Human Relations Theory

Although the classical theorists with their managerial perspective had such people in mind in their views on worker motivation, the "upward-mobile" as defined by Presthus is truly in his element in the organization described by "human relations" organizational theorists. Downs's "climber" would be equally comfortable in either type of organization.

Theorists of the human relations approach—Elton Mayo, John Dewey, Kurt Lewin, and others—posited that, unlike the classical approach:

1. The level of production is set by social norms, not by physical capacities.
2. Noneconomic rewards and sanctions significantly affect the behavior of the workers and largely limit the effect of economic incentive plans.
3. Often workers act or react not as individuals but as members of groups.
4. The formal leader may not exercise as much control over the group as an informal leader does.

[2]Presthus, *Organization Society,* p. 173.

5. Communication between the ranks is essential; worker participation in decision making is important, and democratic leadership is seen to be more effective than authoritarianism.[3]

According to this theory, workers who perform either above or below the level of the group incur group sanctions. These methods are so effective that most workers prefer the acceptance of their peers to economic gain. Management in the "human relations" organization, therefore, deals not with individuals but with groups, employing methods such as group discussions, collective decision making, and democratic leadership that concerns itself with the problems of the workers as well as those of the work.

The Structuralist Theory

Although the classical and human relations schools were in most features almost diametric opposites, they shared in common the belief that individual needs and desires are sufficiently similar to organizational goals as to preclude inevitable conflict. The one saw utopia realized in the maximization of economic opportunity; the other thought it is achievable by maximizing emotional fulfillment. A third school of thought, the structuralists, forwarded the notion that a certain amount of alienation of the workers from the organization, and the resulting conflict, are inevitable and can even be desirable.

Structuralist thinking represents a synthesis of the ideas of the classicists and the human relationists. The structuralists see as inevitable certain strains between organizational needs and personal needs, between rationality and emotionality, between conformity and individualism, between formal and informal relations, between supervisors and subordinates, among and between ranks and divisions. The structuralists view the organization as a dynamically interacting community. Its various subcomponents obviously share some important interests, otherwise the organization could not survive. In relation to these, a good deal of cooperation can be expected. In other important areas, however, the interests of the organization compete against those of the individual. The efforts of management to induce workers to produce, for example, is basically alienating to the worker. He works to secure food, clothing, and shelter, and he gains a certain emotional satisfaction in belonging to and being accepted by a viable group. But he cannot have any deeply intrinsic interest in his work, since he controls neither the means of production nor the product. Moreover, the high degree of specialization required by modern mass production denies him the personal satisfac-

[3]Amitai Etzioni, *Modern Organizations* (Englewood Cliffs, N.J.: Prentice-Hall, 1964), pp. 32–39. See this book for an excellent discussion of the subject.

tion and pride of accomplishment that the medieval artisan knew when he completed an article from start to finish. As a result, Eli Chinoy suggests, "workers spend much of their working day in a semi-conscious delirium, dreaming about their major source of satisfaction, the postwork day."[4]

Structuralists suggest that the inevitable conflicts of organizational life be faced squarely and allowed to surface so that they can be dealt with realistically. This approach results in adjustments and compromises that enable the organization to heal its wounds as they occur, rather than allowing them to go untended until its health is so badly undermined as to endanger its survival.

The structuralists would recognize most workers not as the "upward-mobiles" or "climbers" for whom the classical and human relations organizations provide a benevolent and satisfying environment, but rather as the type that Presthus designates the "indifferents."[5] The "indifferents" are those workers who view organizations as systems expressly designed to frustrate the individual. Since the "indifferent" identifies with neither organizational goals nor the rewards that come with their achievement, he refuses to compete for those rewards. He regards his work as merely a means for obtaining off-the-job satisfactions. He cooperates to the extent necessary to ensure his economic security but rejects the idols of the "upward-mobile" and the "climber," success and power. His indifference might be either the result of his own frustrated attempts to climb the social ladder or a function of his class. Working- or lower socio-economic class people, for example, often enter the labor market with such low expectations that their basic orientation to work is one of indifference. This accounts at least partially for the fact that the progeny of elite classes are so disproportionately represented in positions of power in organizations.

Far from being an object of pity, the "indifferent" is the most "normal" of individuals. Since his expectations are realistic, he is spared the status anxiety, the success striving, and the need to conform that plague the "upward-mobile" and "climber." Moreover, he separates his work from a more meaningful personal area. Since he expects nothing from the organization, the "indifferent" is not intimidated by its sanctions and its discipline, so he is able to retain a significant degree of autonomy and individual identity. And since he makes no emotional investment in the organization, he also seeks no emotional fulfillment in it, rendering him immune to the emotional frustrations of the work environment. One can readily see the possible problems an upwardly mobile police sergeant would have in trying to control an "indifferent."

Probably the most unfortunate of the types found in organizations,

[4]Etzioni, *Modern Organizations,* p. 42.
[5]Presthus, *Organization Society,* pp. 205, 256.

because of his high level of conflict, is the "ambivalent."[6] The "ambivalent" often becomes neurotic, since his creativity and self-esteem conflict with the high degree of conformity demanded by the bureaucratic organization, be it a police department or a factory. He is torn by ambivalence: Although he cannot, on the one hand, reject the organization's promise of success and power, he also cannot play the roles required to compete for them.

> The "ambivalent" is typically intensely intellectual and socially inhibited. His rational mind questions and probes, making it impossible for him to accept authority at face value. His idealistic, independent, and individualistic personality brings him into conflict with bureaucratic demands for conformity, loyalty to the organization and its leaders, and respect for the "party line." . . . He knows enough about risk and uncertainty to conclude that decision-making at best is highly tentative. If solutions were known, there would be no need for decisions. He regards truth as relative and changing.[7]

He is, consequently, too self-centered to be a good organization man. He tends to be more intelligent than those who, because they can accept the simplicity of organizational demands, achieve positions of power in organizations. His situation is rendered even more difficult by the fact that such people perceive him as a distinct threat to the status quo, which favors them. Moreover, even the "indifferents" recoil from the "ambivalent"; his challenge to the status quo threatens them as well, since their accommodation to the organization is characterized by their acceptance of it.

Given this situation, the "ambivalent" cannot help but view both his superiors and most of his peers as dangerous and inimical to him, which severely inhibits his relations with them. Further inhibiting is his tendency to express his aggressions directly and verbally rather than camouflaging them or expressing them subtly and indirectly. Since he seeks the truth and the ultimate in honesty, he does not develop the personal discipline required to perform the ritualistic behavior commonly regarded as tactful. Besides criticizing authority, he also admits to his own personal fears and inadequacies. This brand of honesty threatens the authoritarian principle upon which organizations are premised and thus only incites further the hostility of the bureaucratic environment against him.

Furthermore, he cannot help but regard people as individuals rather than as instruments, the way the "upward-mobile" and the "climber" do. Since he idealizes personal relationships, it is impossible for him to make the kinds of decisions regarding individuals that organizational demands require.

[6]Ibid., pp. 257–86.
[7]Ibid., pp. 266, 267.

He demands self-realization; he wants to count, to put his ideas into practice. Yet in big organizations such demands are usually honored only through subordination of individual claims. . . . While the upward-mobile is sustained by status rewards and great expectations, and the indifferent accommodates by limiting his aspirations, the ambivalent is chronically disturbed. While upward-mobile anxiety seems to reflect mainly a *fear of failure,* the latter's fear mirrors *ethical conflict,* arising, for example, from bureaucratic claims for exploitative roles. Although incapable of playing the roles required for success, he badly needs success to validate his intensive need for recognition. Although majority values must be honored, he is temperamentally incapable of accepting them. . . . [However] the ambivalent type plays a critical social role, namely that of providing the insight, motivation and the dialectic that inspire change. The upward-mobile honors the status quo and the indifferent accepts it, but the ambivalent is always sensitive to the need for change.[8]

The "ambivalent" is somewhat analogous to the college-graduate police officer, who presents unique challenges for his sergeant. Not only will the effective sergeant have a conscious supervisory style; he may need several styles, depending on the particular officer. (Chapter 3 expands on the college graduate versus the noncollege graduate in police organizations.)

ORGANIZATIONAL CONTROL

The structuralists have shown that conflict between organizational and individual needs is inevitable. Therefore, in order for an organization to achieve its goals, it will have to exercise control over those of its members whose needs do not conform with those of the organization. Since the "upward-mobiles" and "climbers" tend to identify strongly with organizational goals and procedures, they require a minimum of control. Their behavior is designed to achieve the rewards of the organization; thus, the promise of these rewards is sufficient incentive to ensure conformity. This is, of course, a form of control; it is sometimes referred to as normative control and is the most effective and least alienating of the various forms. However, it is effective only with those who have a deep commitment to organizational goals, such as Jesuit priests, career marines, or dedicated members of political parties, especially those of the extreme left or right. Presthus's "ambivalents" and "indifferents" and Downs's "conservers," "advocates," "zealots," and "statesmen" have to be kept in line by controls. Usually, utilitarian types of control will suffice: suspensions, fines, cuts in pay, threats of dismissal, and the like. Although utilitarian control is unpleasant and also often alienating, it is not nearly as alienating as coercive control, by which the person is physically forced to conform by the use of a gun, fists, a whip, or a lock. The

[8]Ibid., pp. 281–82, 258.

type of organization determines to a great extent the kind of control that is appropriate. A prison, for example, uses coercive control, corporations and police departments a combination of utilitarian and normative control; a religious order relies almost exclusively on normative control.

Leadership is related to control in several ways. A leader may be able to control because of the position he holds in the organization or because of his official status. This is referred to as "official" leadership. Another person may be able to control others because of personal magnetism or charisma even though he holds no official title; he would be termed an "informal" leader. A "formal" leader would enjoy both the official position and the personal esteem of his followers.

A supervisor in a modern American police department no longer has the option of coercive control, although there was a time in the not too distant past when the first-line supervisor could "lick any man on the job" and literally owed his position to his ability with his fists. In most modern situations, the supervisor has to control subordinates either with utilitarian mechanisms or with normative pressure. Even the use of utilitarian controls is severely limited by union contracts.

Probably the most common form of control in police departments today is a process in which there is implicit bargaining between the supervisor and his subordinates (the "psychological contract," which will be discussed in Chapter 9). Although such arrangements are seldom stated and almost never admitted to, most subordinates will perform at an acceptable level, set by both the work group and by the supervisor, if the supervisor treats them with consideration and dignity and allows them a reasonable degree of autonomy and discretion.

Another vehicle for controlling subordinates is competition. By granting the symbols and benefits of the organization to those who conform to his conception of excellence, the supervisor can sometimes increase the level of performance of subordinates. The giving of awards in police departments is an example. Competition between groups within the larger organization has been shown to be a more effective motivator than competition between individuals, however, since the latter is often more disruptive than productive. In police departments, there may be competition between shifts in the patrol divisions, or between the patrol division and the investigative division.

The best control is the satisfaction that a person derives from his or her work. The best insurance of this is the process by which people are hired for certain jobs. Obviously, not everyone is equally suited for all types of work. If the selection process is designed to determine who is most suitable for the position in question and is able to eliminate those who are unsuitable, the whole problem of control is greatly alleviated—

although it can never be eliminated, simply because not all members will willingly put forth their best effort for all supervisors under all conditions at all times. Although the phenomenon of job satisfaction is basically internal to the individual, the sergeant can contribute to it by making the work environment conducive to goal achievement. It might be much more satisfying to a police officer, for example, to respond to an incident, investigate it completely, and see it through to its closing rather than merely "putting out the fire" and then passing the case on to a team of investigators to see it through. Being part of a socially well integrated team also enhances job satisfaction. People who enjoy working together will normally do a better job.

Sayles and Strauss have determined that the following worker needs must be met if the work is to be intrinsically satisfying:

1. Workers need to feel that their work requires skill, that it is important, and that they enjoy a certain amount of autonomy in its accomplishment.
2. They need the understanding and the praise of their supervisors and to know where they stand in the latter's eyes.
3. They need the acceptance and the attention of their peers.
4. They need self-confidence.[9]

SUPERVISORY LEADERSHIP STYLES

Style of supervisory leadership is another important factor in job satisfaction. Probably the best exposition of the leadership styles tried and tested in the United States is represented by Table 2-1. The authoritarian style is associated with the classical approach, and the democratic style is analogous to the human relations approach. The laissez-faire style is merely a "do-your-own-thing" approach.

McGregor uses a different typology to explain supervisory style. He calls his approach Theory X and Theory Y. He says the traditional classical organization, with its centralized decision making, superior–subordinate pyramid, and external control of work is based on Theory X, a set of assumptions about human nature and human motivation that includes the following:

1. Work is inherently distasteful to most people.
2. Most people are not ambitious, have little desire for responsibility, and prefer to be directed.
3. Most people have little capacity for creativity in solving organizational problems.

[9]Leonard R. Sayles and George Strauss, *Human Behavior in Organizations* (Englewood Cliffs, N.J.: Prentice-Hall, 1966), pp. 13–18.

TABLE 2-1

Leadership Styles

Authoritarian	*Democratic*	*Laissez-Faire*
1. All determination of policy by the leader.	All policies a matter of group discussion and decision encouraged and assisted by the leader.	Complete freedom for group or individual decision, with a minimum of leader participation.
2. Techniques and activity steps dictated by the authority, one at a time, so that future steps are always uncertain to a large degree.	Activity perspective gained during discussion period. General steps to group goal were sketched, and when technical advice was needed, the leader suggested two or more alternative procedures from which choice could be made.	Various materials supplied by the leader, who made it clear that he would supply information when asked. He took no other part in work discussion.
3. The leader usually dictated the particular work task and work companion of each member.	The members were free to work with whomever they chose, and the division of tasks was left up to the group.	Complete nonparticipation of the leader.
4. The dominator tended to be "personal" in his praise and criticism of the work of each member; remained aloof from active group participation except when demonstrating.	The leader was "objective" or "fact-minded" in his praise and criticism, and tried to be a regular group member in spirit without doing too much of the work.	Infrequent spontaneous comments on member activities unless questioned, and no attempt to appraise or regulate the course of events

Source: "Definition of Leader Roles" (pp. 26–27) (under your title "Characteristics of the three treatment variables") from AUTOCRACY AND DEMOCRACY by Ralph K. White and Ronald Lippitt. Copyright © 1960 by Ralph K. White and Ronald Lippitt. Reprinted by permission of Harper & Row, Publishers Inc.

4. Motivation occurs only at the physiological and security levels.[10]

A belief in these assumptions leads management to a specific style:

1. Management is responsible for organizing the elements of productive enterprise —money, materials, equipment, people—in the interest of economic ends.
2. With respect to people, this is a process of directing their efforts, moving them, controlling their actions, modifying their behavior to fit the needs of the organization.
3. Without this active intervention by management, people would be passive—even resistant—to organizational needs. They must therefore be persuaded, rewarded, punished, controlled—their activities must be directed.[11]

This approach is analogous to the authoritarian style and classical approach. McGregor felt that motivation would be difficult to maintain with the Theory X approach.

His Theory Y attitude is that:

1. Expenditure of physical and mental effort in work is as natural as play, if the conditions are favorable.
2. Self-control is often indispensable in achieving organizational goals. External control and threat of punishment are not the only means for achieving goals.
3. The capacity for creativity in solving organizational problems is widely distributed in the population.
4. Motivation occurs at the affiliation, esteem, and self-actualization levels, as well as the physiological and security levels.
5. People can be self-directed and creative at work if properly motivated.[12]

In Theory Y, management is still responsible for organizing the work environment, but a different view of the workers is taken. According to McGregor:

1. The motivation, the potential for development, the capacity for assuming responsibility, the readiness to direct behavior toward organization goals are all present in people. Management does not put them there. It is a responsibility of management to make it possible for people to recognize and develop these human characteristics for themselves.
2. The essential task of management is to arrange organizational conditions and

[10]Douglas McGregor, *The Human Side of Enterprise* (New York: McGraw-Hill, 1957), pp 23–30; and Paul Hersey and Kenneth H. Blanchard, *Management of Organizational Behavior: Utilizing Human Behavior* (Englewood Cliffs, N.J.: Prentice-Hall, 1969), p. 41.
[11]Ibid.
[12]Ibid.

methods of operation so that people can achieve their own goals best by directing their own efforts toward organizational objectives. This is a process primarily of creating opportunities, releasing potential, removing obstacles, encouraging growth, providing guidance.[13]

The Managerial Grid

Another way of visualizing and describing supervisory styles is by means of the managerial grid developed by Blake and Mouton.

The supervisor's style is placed on the grid where a visual representation can be made. The supervisor is rated from 1 to 9 in two areas: concern for people and concern for work group performance. A score of 9,9 would be both a concern for people and concern for work performance; a 1,1 score would be the other extreme, a low concern for both people and work performance. Other scores would vary somewhere between 1 and 9. For example, if concern for people is high but concern for work-group performance is low, the numerical score would be about 9,1. If the supervisor fits Downs's "conserver" style, he would be rated around 5,5, in the middle of the grid.

The most effective supervisor is one who has concern for people and at the same time is able to get the group to perform effectively. A supervisor score in this case would be 9,9. Another prominent style would be that of the authoritarian supervisor, who has little concern for people, just for work output and performance—a 1,9. The 1,1 supervisor has "retired" in his position. He avoids making decisions, avoids conflicts, and generally does little more than he has to. He is for all intents and purposes a nonexistent supervisor.

SELECTING A SUPERVISORY STYLE

Tannenbaum and Schmidt have suggested a useful approach to use when choosing a supervisory leadership style. They state that the problem of the modern manager or supervisor is to know when to be democratic yet to retain control and authority over subordinates.[14]

As mentioned earlier, traditional or classical management theory had little concern for employee input or worker participation in decision making. The contemporary supervisor is often in a dilemma:

[13]Ibid.
[14]Robert Tannenbaum and Warren H. Schmidt, "How to Choose a Leadership Pattern," *Harvard Business Review*, May–June 1973, p. 2.

Often he is not quite sure how to behave; there are times when he is torn between exerting "strong" leadership and "permissive" leadership. Sometimes new knowledge pushes him in one direction ("I should really get the group to help make this decision"), but at the same time his experience pushes him in another direction ("I really understand the problem better than the group and therefore I should make the decision"). He is not sure when a group decision is really appropriate or when holding a staff meeting serves merely as a device for avoiding his own decision-making responsibility.[15]

Figure 2-1 is helpful in illustrating that the supervisor does not have to choose between an authoritarian and a democratic style. There is a wide range of possible behavior, depending on the situation and the subordinate being supervised.

Tannenbaum and Schmidt summarize their propositions by stating:

In summary, there are two implications in the basic thesis that we have been developing. The first is that the successful leader is one who is keenly aware of those forces which are most relevant to his behavior at any given time. He

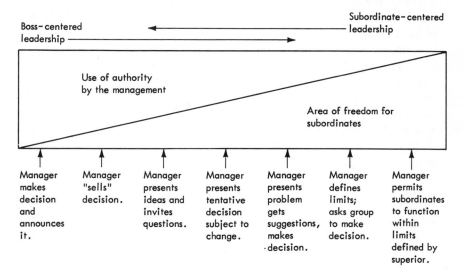

Figure 2-1 Continuum of leadership behavior

Source: Robert Tannenbaum and Warren H. Schmidt, "How to Choose a Leadership Pattern," *Harvard Business Review,* May–June 1973, p. 3.

[15]Ibid.

accurately understands himself, the individuals and group he is dealing with, and the company and broader social environment in which he operates. And certainly he is able to assess the present readiness for growth of his subordinates.

But this sensitivity or understanding is not enough, which brings us to the second implication. The successful leader is one who is able to behave appropriately in the light of these perceptions. If direction is in order, he is able to direct; if considerable participative freedom is called for, he is able to provide such freedom.

Thus, the successful manager of men can be primarily characterized neither as a strong leader nor as a permissive one. Rather, he is one who maintains a high batting average in accurately assessing the forces that determine what his most appropriate behavior at any given time should be and in actually being able to behave accordingly. Being both insightful and flexible, he is less likely to see the problems of leadership as a dilemma.[16]

The quotation above has much applicability to the police sergeant. There are times when the style of leadership needs to be autocratic, such as in a civil disturbance. When an order is given, it must be followed without question, for the safety of the entire group and to accomplish the mission. In most other police actions, such as public service activities (settling a domestic dispute), the sergeant can use a more democratic, counseling, or coaching style of supervisory leadership.

As Tannenbaum and Schmidt stated, the supervisor often does not know when to be democratic and when to be decisive. And the use of the military model in police departments often complicates the situation and confuses the sergeant. The military model is appropriate to battlefield conditions, where split-second decisions have to be made and every soldier has to act in a disciplined manner and comply with the order. Almost all missions are group-oriented, and teamwork is mandatory. In police work, most actions do not require the coordinated effort of several officers. The police officer is usually an independent decision maker, and his behavior, although sometimes requiring split-second decisions, also involves a methodical evaluation of the total situation. Most of the time, the officer has a wide area of discretion within which to operate and does not require the centralized guidance used in the military, where authoritarian leadership contributes to goal achievement. The police officer's actions and reactions are usually the result of his own independent evaluation and the use of his discretion, rather than of direct orders from his sergeant. What he generally needs from the sergeant is help—counseling and coaching—rather than authoritarian directives.

In the past, many police officers had military backgrounds and could effectively adapt those military principles that were applicable to the civilian

16Ibid., p. 10.

police department and reject those that were not useful. Today, most officers have not been in the armed forces, but because they have been told that a police department is a semimilitary organization, sergeants may attempt to use military principles without having a proper feel for when they are applicable, thus perverting them to the detriment of the department while at the same time antagonizing subordinates.

The point is that it is not an either–or proposition. Some military principles are applicable in certain circumstances and in others are completely inappropriate. In situations like riot control and barricaded gunmen, military principles are very helpful. In cases of domestic disputes or groups of boisterous but nondelinquent juveniles, the use of military principles can only aggravate the situation. In giving advice to supervisees, a sergeant has to know when to suggest a structured military orientation and when to use the more democratic, independent style.

There are many different styles of leadership (also see Chapter 4), and the successful sergeant is one who can adapt to changing situations and select the technique that is most appropriate, because "leadership style is inextricably bound up in the leader's ultimate success or failure."[17]

PRACTICAL EXAMPLES—AN ANALYSIS OF SUPERVISOR STYLE BY A POLICE OFFICER

The following are "real-world" examples from the experience of a police officer. They are presented as a vehicle for translating the theoretical discussion above into practical application.[18]

SERGEANT HARDCORE

During recruit training, he was classified as Class Advisor. He was responsible for 35 trainees.

Background Data

Age	30 Yrs	Marital Status	Divorced
Total Service	5 Yrs	Children	None
Patrolman	3 Yrs	Education	B.S. (Criminal Justice)
Sergeant	2 Yrs	Veteran	Yes

[17]Hersey and Blanchard, *Management of Organizational Behavior,* p. 95.
[18]Examples are taken from Robert G. Leonik, "The Sergeant," Michigan State University, 1978.

Perceptions of Man

Man is a back-stabbing animal who cannot be trusted. God made man centuries ago, but it took Samuel Colt to make all men equal. The only way to learn something is "by the numbers." Paramount to all, never admit that you made a mistake, because it is a sign of weakness and not "macho."

Observation

He used to be in the Marine Corps. From day one, I never liked the man, although I respected him for his expertise. On our first meeting, he appeared with spit-shined shoes *(I mean looking glass shined),* perfectly pressed trousers, military pressed shirt, almost bald head (he still claimed to be in need of a trim), and a swagger stick.

He was 100% serious all the time and appeared to be a fantastic police officer who was one step this side of God.

Everything about him was by the numbers. He would not allow for mistakes, and if you said you were sorry, he would turn red and yelp, "Never say you are sorry. It's a sign of weakness!" He was the only sergeant in the academy like that. Everybody else seemed normal in appearance (hair, uniform, and shoes, no swagger stick).

He displayed open dislike for the black members of the class and succeeded in getting four out of six to resign. In class, you either kept your mouth shut or he made a fool of you. He also displayed open favoritism toward all the veterans in the class, especially marines. He rewarded them by placing them in positions of responsibility (class commander and squad leaders).

He was second on the lieutenant's promotion list and was scheduled to be promoted within the year. Instead, he was forced to resign. While he was involved in a softball game with his marine recruits, one of them suffered an injured foot. When it came time to write the report (which was required for all injuries occurring to trainees), he altered the time so it appeared that the accident happened on departmental time, thereby saving the trainee the hospital costs. The charge was falsification of a departmental document. This was the the only publicized charge; there were others, including sex with female members of the class.

His favorite analogy was, "The department is an iron mistress that rules with an iron fist. You can't be loyal to a wife, because the department always comes first." He epitomized the "upward-mobile" or "climber" type.

Conclusion

He was definitely a Theory X authoritarian type. Even though he was educated (college graduate, in upper 10% of his class), he displayed an open dislike for other graduates. (You weren't educated until you fought in a war or killed somebody in the line of duty.) True, in the academy situation a structural approach is needed to an extent, but his open display of favoritism for the few destroyed the motivation of the others. A manager, supervisor, or instructor he was not. He proved that an education does not in itself make a good supervisor.

Although it may be a proper style for training (not educating) a large group of people in a short period of time, this style proved not very practical in the long run, because it gave the recruits a misperception of what police work is all about.

SERGEANT LOW PROFILE

My first assignment was to the Internal Investigations Division, where I was assigned to Sergeant Low Profile.

Background Data

Age	36 Yrs	Marital Status	First
Total Service	15 Yrs	Children	3
Patrolman	9 Yrs	Education	GED
Sergeant	6 Yrs	Veteran	Yes

Preceptions of Man

Basically a Theory Y democratic, human relations approach. Views man as a rational animal capable of making his own decisions. He will work as much as he wants to, and does not like to be pushed. The supervisor should provide the opportunity and set the example.

Observation

I was a little bit afraid of Sgt. LP when I first met him. He was very serene and easygoing. At this point, I would guess that since I am naturally high-strung, his quietness was just different. Besides, it was my first day on the job.

This assignment was plainclothes. My first day on the job was spent with a police cadet also assigned to the same division. (He was 19 years old and had approximately one year of service as a cadet). Basically, I got a tour of the offices and was excused early.

Day 2 was a little different. My hours were 8:00 A.M. to 4:00 P.M., which was bad for my bus schedule, as I was to discover. Anyway, I arrived approximately five minutes late. When I walked in, Sgt. LP gave me a very stern look, stated, "If anybody asks, you have been severely reprimanded!" and then went about his work. I cowered with fear all day, afraid I was in trouble. However, I was advised by my cadet friend that he was not serious, but just wanted me to have an answer in case somebody else in the command should have noted my tardiness.

He assigned me to case preparation. This job entailed assembling case documents regarding charges of police brutality, for presentation before the complaint evaluation board. He showed me just once, asked if I had any questions, and then went back to his desk. I didn't fully comprehend the responsibility I actually had preparing these documents. However, he identified my motivation (to be left alone), and then I proceeded to set a new record for cases completed. During the first two weeks, I prepared 35 cases, and subsequently put myself out of a job! I attribute much of my success to Sgt. LP. He identified my strengths, individualized supervision, and let me do my job.

It was important to me that he was always there if I had any questions, not only regarding assignments, but relating to any aspect of police work. Having no conception of what was expected of me and a lot of apprehension, I asked a lot of questions. He would take as much time as was needed to fully explain his answer. What made it even better was the way he used practical or actual situations for answers, giving me the situation, asking what I would do and why, then giving his critique. He never made fun of me, but was always very patient.

His greatest words of wisdom were, "Always give people a choice (don't dictate, you'll get hurt); always maintain a low profile; don't let the job get to you; and a good officer not only avoids sin, but also the near occasion of sin."

Conclusion

My time spent with this sergeant was the most beneficial of my entire tenure with the department. He was a man I respected and could go to (and did, until I left) at any time, for advice or with problems. He always took the time to explain things fully. His style was perfect. His basic assumptions were Theory Y, with communication both up and down the chain of command. He was always available, but I was on my own. He never pushed. He was a person to respect.

SERGEANT DOUBLE DIPPER

I was then placed in the patrol division and assigned to a district known as the "country club." In addition to the large number of parks, it was also the largest district in the city. I was assigned to a uniformed patrol squad consisting of 13 members.

Background Data

Age	39 Yrs	Marital Status	First
Total Service	16 Yrs	Children	4
Patrolman	10 Yrs	Education	GED
Sergeant	6 Yrs	Veteran	Yes

Perceptions of Man

Basically a Theory X type, he was a curious combination of several styles. He thought man was motivated strictly by money: Money is everything. An education is useless because you can always buy somebody (lawyer, banker, accountant) to do your thinking for you. As a subordinate, it was a cardinal sin to do anything that would cause him to make a decision or, worse yet, stay overtime.

Observation

It took me only one night to determine his style. My first night on the street (midnight shift), the sergeant put me in a two-man car with his "blood brother." This officer stated that there was going to be a burglary at the warehouse we were parked in front of, and to keep my eyes open. Five minutes later, he was fast asleep and snoring. About two hours had passed when I observed a set of headlights approaching. I tried to wake my partner up, but he told me to buzz off and went back to sleep. I was amazed when the car pulled alongside and it was my sergeant. I saluted him, but he just looked at me funny and then took off his coat, pulled out a pillow, and also went to sleep. One hour later, both of them woke up and went up to the warehouse door. I was dumfounded when the sergeant pulled out a set of keys, entered the building, punched a few clocks, and then went back to sleep.

I found out that the sergeant and my partner had a private security and painting business on the side and that he selected and hired men from the squad to work for him. Although the painting jobs were spread out all over the county, the buildings they guarded just happened to be in the area he was responsible for. Thus, they were paid twice for protecting the same property.

Needless to say, the "select" men of the squad were given the best assignments, with the dregs being given to those of us less fortunate. In addition, I also discovered that our sergeant bought his stripes and was known to perform certain extra functions for command staff. The only reason "our leader" had wanted to make sergeant was for the money and the power to schedule his friends so they could work for him in private business. He would sleep on duty, get up and paint after the shift, and provide his friends with the private security jobs so that they would be indebted to him. They would show their appreciation by doing exactly what he wanted and also cover up for him. All he asked for was two car stops, one ticket, and no surprise breakins on his territory each day. That was the extent of the police function in the squad. Don't do anything to cause him to lose sleep, stay late, or have to make a decision.

What he succeeded in doing was stifling everybody under him. I was the only college graduate in the squad. After he found out I was a "rabble rouser," he stuck me in every dirty job that came along (school crossing, posting No Parking signs, dog and cat calls, and so on). This was successful in reducing my motivation for about one month. Then I decided to fight back.

I reacted, however, in a very positive way. I really wanted to "stick it to him" because I felt he was stunting my development as a police officer. There was only one way I could do both: write search and seizure warrants (departmental regulations stipulated that he must go on each one), do good police work, and make some arrests. Of course, this required a lot more motivation on my part, because I had to learn all the rules inside and out (on my own time) and still act dumb in front of the sergeant. I felt this was a more appropriate alternative than merely "putting in my time" and shortchanging the public.

This continued for my entire length of service under this supervisor. I consistently led the squad in arrests (good felonies), and yet I was still being chastised because I wasn't writing as many tickets or making as many car stops as the rest of the squad. On repeated occasions, he tried to cajole me into working for him. He said that I could make more money (I was actually making out pretty good in court overtime) and therefore be happy—not that I would be a better officer. After this failed, he tried peer pressure, which also failed. The result was that I found myself a loner, having the most contact with the state's attorney and local judges, due to my search and seizure warrants (I averaged over five per month). This approval and praise by the court officials provided my motivation and helped neutralize the rejection I felt from my police peer group.

This sergeant was neither a good officer nor a good supervisor. He had a very limited knowledge of the rules and regulations of the department. He knew just enough to get by.

Conclusion

It was a very difficult year for growth as a police officer. Unconsciously and inadvertently, the sergeant succeeded in motivating me despite his methods. His technique was to beat me into the ground, but I used the situation to become self-motivated. Although he was operating at a low level, had a negative attitude toward subordinates in general, had little love for the police department, and was mainly interested in "extracurricular" matters, he succeeded in forcing me to get out on my own and be more self-reliant. Not only did this improve my self-confidence, but it taught me a lot about myself and helped me to become a good police officer. I really don't know what will happen to the other officers in the squad. (Incidentally, there had been no transfers in or out of the squad in over five years; I was the first to come and the quickest to leave.) From a managerial standpoint, both the formal and informal goals of the sergeant and the organization were compatible, because he was allowed to survive. Unfortunately, the methodology was very unethical and, thankfully, a very isolated incident, at least to the best of my knowledge.

SERGEANT STRAITJACKET

After leaving the "country club" I was assigned to the Tactical Division Swat Team. The squad consisted of 3–4 man teams with a total of 12 members.

Background Data

Age	31 Yrs	Marital Status	Separated
Total Service	6 Yrs	Children	1
Patrolman	5 Yrs	Education	B.A. (Criminal Justice)
Sergeant	1 Yr	Veteran	Yes

Perceptions of Man

Subordinates must be watched carefully or they will make mistakes and make the supervisor look bad. If the supervisor looks bad, he won't get promoted. If the supervisor is not always on the subordinates' backs, they will goof around. The sergeant is the boss, and that's all there is to it. Basically, he was Theory X, an authoritarian style with very constrictive oversupervision.

Observation

After leaving the garden spot of the city, I was assigned to the ghetto. To my chagrin, the first thing I found out was that my new sergeant had been a patrolman under my old sergeant. He was given the word that I was a "rabble rouser".

He was always watching me and tried to be wherever I was. Everytime I had a good call, he would show up, handle the call, then give me the report to write (or dump it on me). He did know the rules inside and out. However, he was an upwardly mobile "climber," his only goal was to get promoted. He wanted it so bad he could taste it.

This really made things difficult. He would not let anybody do his job and had no faith or trust in his subordinates. On the other hand, his subordinates had no faith or trust in him. Nobody would go on a sniper call with him in command. Instead, there was a more experienced patrolman who would take charge. Morale was very low in the squad.

However, he couldn't be everywhere all the time. So we developed our own intrasquad code for when something was going down, so that the sergeant would not be there. This worked very well, and helped to improve the morale. Despite the sergeant, we were a pretty tight-knit group, highly motivated with good morale.

Despite his antics, I was still promoted to police agent. For a time, this was a motivator, but once again, I was on my own. Peer pressure and approval were positive motivators, because the tactical squad was an elite assignment. Unfortunately, the sergeant was really stifling. He was eventually transferred, and not promoted. He was so conservative that he wouldn't allow himself or his supervisees the latitude to do more than an average or mediocre job.

Conclusion

He was a very ineffective supervisor. Owing to his desire for promotion, he refused to delegate any responsibility for fear somebody might make a mistake, which would be a reflection on him. Although peer influence and acceptance were motivating factors, the sergeant was successful in preventing any long-term positive motivation.

CONCLUDING ANALYSIS OF THE SERGEANTS' STYLES

As was expected, each supervisor exhibited a different style (or non-style) of management, with varying degrees of efficiency.

Sgt. Low Profile, in my opinion, was the best supervisor of all. First, the setting (plainclothes) was the most relaxed and conducive to a motivating work environment. (Headquarters is a brand new building with comfort control and piped-in music. And, it was his idea to have the music, because of his human relations theory approach.) Second, his style of supervision was very low-keyed. That is, he would tell you what he wanted to achieve. How you arrived at it was up to you; you could either do it the "usual" way or invent your own. There was a lot of responsibility delegated, and he wasn't always peeping over your shoulder, oversupervising, fearing that mistakes would be made. He would be a 9, 9 on the managerial grid—showing concern for both people and output.

But most of all, he cared about me and how I was progressing. Although he only had two subordinates, he still had responsibility for maintaining the administrative section of the division (he did have civilian secretaries). This could be the main reason he had so much time to spend with me (questions and practical situations). Our relationship lasted for my entire tenure, and even after I resigned, I still returned for advice on personal matters and he always had the time. Most of his success was probably due to his built-in knowledge and empathy for people and a genuine caring. A lack of formal education was made up for by practical knowledge of human behavior and life in general. A large factor was that he was happy as a sergeant, and had no desire to be promoted, an attitude reflected in his demeanor.

Sergeant Double Dipper shouldn't even be considered as a supervisor. On the managerial grid he would be a 1,1—"retired in position." His style was also closely akin to the laissez-faire approach. However, even though it was achieved inadvertently, he succeeded in motivating me. Although the motivation developed mostly out of spite and a genuine dislike for being relegated to being a peon, I overcame this obstacle and pushed myself to greater heights. I learned more about the law, people, and myself in that one year than during my entire formal education. Negative supervision can be as much a motivator as positive supervision. It depends on the individual supervisee.

Sergeant Hardcore was a good instructor for a military-type setting, for instructing a large number of people in a broad area of subjects in a relatively short period of time, but that was about the extent of his usefulness. His downfall was his open display of favoritism and prejudice. This totally destroyed his credibility and ultimately led to his resignation. People just didn't trust him. And all this occurred despite his formal, liberal education. He would be difficult to place on the managerial grid because of his inconsistent behavior and obvious psychological problems.

Sergeant Straitjacket was probably the second worst sergeant I encountered. He was always looking over your shoulder and watching lest a mistake be made that would tarnish his record and destroy his chances of getting promoted. Despite his education, he would be a 1,9 on the managerial grid —little concern for people, high concern for work performance so he could get ahead. He forced us to come up with ways of "playing the game" and beating his system. Not all of us fought, some capitulated and became a part of his system.

CHAPTER SUMMARY

None of the styles discussed will be appropriate or even feasible in all theoretical situations. A stressful, fast-moving emergency situation—a civil disorder or a natural disaster, for example—will probably require authoritarian leadership. In a situation that is less pressing yet requires teamwork, like team policing, the democratic style will probably work best. In dealing with highly trained professionals who work alone, like the planning and research unit, the laissez-faire style will probably prove most acceptable. As Golembiewski states, "The research literature does not consistently support any one leadership style."[19] Theory X is appropriate in one case, Theory Y in another.

Organizational style is determined by the organization's view of human motivation. The classicists and Theory X – oriented people believe that man's primary motivation is economic, thus there need be no conflict between the needs of the individual and those of the organization. If proper incentives are provided, productivity norms can be determined by the physical limitations of the worker and his equipment, work tasks can be specialized for efficiency, and supervision can be provided by a pyramid-shaped hierarchy consisting of one supervisor for each five or six subordinates. "Upward-mobiles" and "climbers" will probably function better than other types in a classical organization. They will probably function best, however, in a "human relations" type of organization, because it provides the best arena for their skill in manipulating others.

"Human relations" and Theory Y organizational theorists posit that man is primarily motivated by social rather than materialistic needs and therefore reacts to management and the work situation more as a group member than as an individual; that his level of productivity is determined largely by the standards set by his fellow workers, and he is more responsive to the informal group leader than to the boss with the title. As a result of these theories, "human relationists" espouse a democratic organizational style. But they share with the classicists the belief that conflict between individual and organizational needs is not inevitable.

[19]Robert T. Golembiewski, "Three Styles of Leadership and Their Uses," *Personnel*, XXXVIII, No. 4 (July–August 1961), 35.

A third school of thought, the structuralist, maintains that a certain amount of alienation of the workers from the organization and the resulting conflict are inevitable and can even be desirable, because they keep each other "honest." They suggest that conflict be faced squarely and allowed to surface so that it can be dealt with realistically. The structuralists would view most workers not as "upward-mobiles" but as "indifferents," who accommodate to their work but whose primary satisfactions are derived from activities off the job.

Probably the most unfortunate of the types that one finds in organizations is the "ambivalent." He is in a constant state of frustration because, although he accepts the organization's promise of success and power, he cannot play the roles required to compete for them. It is he, in his state of constant agitation, who initiates change in an otherwise static milieu. He is also a candidate for stress-related problems (see Chapter 8).

Since organizational and individual needs often conflict, the organization has to ensure the cooperation of the individual by the use of controls. These range from physical brutality to intense indoctrination.

A leader may be able to control his subordinates because of the position he holds in the organization, because of his own personal magnetism or charisma, or a combination of both. Probably the most common form of control employed today results from implicit bargaining between the supervisor and his subordinates. Competition serves as another form of control. The best assurance of top performance, however, is the satisfaction that a person derives from his work. The sergeant can make a significant contribution toward the job satisfaction of his subordinates by a skillful manipulation of the variables of the work situation and by his style of leadership.

The sergeant has to understand his own style so that he can contribute to greater worker satisfaction and productivity. He has to create an atmosphere that facilitates goal achievement while at the same time helping make the workplace at least tolerable for the individual worker. An acceptable work environment can contribute to the personal and professional growth of the police officer.

CHAPTER THREE

The Sergeant
as the
Man in the Middle

It has become trite to call the first-line supervisor the "man in the middle." In reality, there is much truth to the statement, especially as it applies to the first-line police supervisor. This chapter will discuss several problem areas that arise from the often conflicting pressures and pulls on the sergeant from both line officers and the department management.

THE ENVIRONMENT

I have already alluded several times to the contemporary sergeant's complex environment and the many challenges facing him. He is an important link between his subordinates, the department administrators, and the community. The achieving of departmental goals is dependent on his effectively and appropriately communicating and interpreting policies, procedures, orders, and all those intangible organizational expectations that are not put down in writing. He is in fact a socializing agent, especially to the younger officers.

The sergeant of the past had a more clearly defined role and in many respects an easier time of it, because the police department was even more classically oriented than it is today. An autocratic style of leadership was expected and even accepted. Contemporary social changes, including the union movement, contributed to more complex grievance procedures and personnel policies. The sergeant, as the first-line supervisor, is expected to adjust and adapt.

Police department administrators often mouth the rhetoric of improving human relations within the organization by using behavioral science principles to motivate the line officers and providing a general work environment that is conducive to improving morale. In reality, however, attitudes about employees and what motivates them have changed little in some organizations over the years, and comments like, "I worked shift work for 20 years and I didn't get a divorce," or, "It took me 15 years to make sergeant, I wasn't impatient like the young guys," are common in modern police organizations. Not that such statements may not be true. However, times are different now, and pressures from young supervisees are more intense, so the sergeant ends up caught in the vise between department administrators who want to operate as in "the good old days" and younger supervisees who "want to do their own thing" and achieve personal and organizational rewards as quickly as possible; reluctance to change from administrators, and impatience with the status quo from supervisees.

An effective sergeant has *conceptual* skills that enable him to see the overall goals of his department and how his unit fits into goal achievement. This conceptual ability to see the "big picture," however, may precipitate criticism from his supervisees if they feel that he does not "go to bat" enough for them when they make requests. They become impatient when their sergeant responds to a request by saying, "It can't be done because it conflicts with organizational policy and will complicate another unit's functioning." The effective sergeant is sensitive enough to know when to press his superiors for change, and when the timing isn't right.

Producing change in a police department is not an easy task. Policing by its nature is conservative, because police departments are commissioned to enforce the law as it is currently codified. They cannot change the laws; it is not their function. The basis of police work is the law, and our society is built on laws. But preserving the status quo with regard to police legal matters is often carried over to the department's general organizational orientation in nonlegal matters, such as procedures, policies, and orders, which also take on a status quo aura. This carryover creates frustration, especially for the younger line officers. And the sergeant is sandwiched between those officers' desires for changes in policies and procedures and the department administrators' orientation to "do it the way it has always been done."

This situation is only one example of the sergeant's dilemma of being the man in the middle. The astute sergeant is able to determine which areas cannot be changed because of their legal basis and then transmit this fact to his supervisees. Conversely, in department policy and procedure areas, where directives originate from a nonlegal basis and the sergeant feels they are unworkable and should be changed, he can transmit his concern to his superiors and press for change.

THE ADVANTAGES AND DISADVANTAGES OF BEING A SERGEANT

Why would a person want to be a sergeant, with all the attendant headaches of the job, often operating in an environment and under conditions in which neither superiors nor subordinates can be totally satisfied?

In the survey described in Chapter 1, in which 300 officers were interviewed, all the ranks except command officers rated economic gain and prestige as the greatest advantages of being a sergeant. (See Table 3-1.) Being the "man in the middle" was the most often identified problem area. The lack of a well-defined role that can be translated into a job description for sergeants contributes to this problem. A detailed description of the sergeant's functions, duties, responsibilities, and authority would reduce many of the "middleman" repercussions. A well-defined role, however, is precisely what the manipulative police administrator and community political interest groups don't want, because it would reduce their areas of "flexibility." Ambiguous role definitions are conducive to scapegoating, and the sergeant is the most frequent target because he is the least powerful management person in the organization.

All ranks except command officers, again, also alluded to the lack of backing and support from the administration as a major problem for the sergeant. Several patrol officers and detectives stated that they did not want to become sergeants because of the "grief" (lack of backing and authority) and the overall paucity of rewards, plus the extra, nonpaid time the sergeant has to put in. Many officers, including sergeants, said the only reasons they wanted to be sergeants were the increased pay and shift preference. They were not motivated by the challenge of supervising people and overseeing their work.

Few police organizations have personnel systems that reward the highly productive and motivated officer except by promotion to a higher rank. Promoting an officer to a supervisory position just to reward him for having been a good line officer when his interest is not in supervision is, as one sergeant stated, like "taking a 30-game winning pitcher and making him the manager." The department loses a good line officer and may gain an inadequate sergeant.

Much emphasis has been placed on employee motivation for goal achievement when, in fact, as Reeder mentions, the key is supervisor motiva-

TABLE 3-1

What Are the Advantages and Disadvantages of Being a Sergeant?

Patrolmen		Detectives		Sergeants		Lieutenants		Command	
Advantages	Disadvantages	Advantages	Disadvantages	Advantages	Disadvantages	Advantages	Disadvantages	Advantages	Disadvantages
More money	Man in middle	No advantages	Bad for family	More money	No compensation for overtime	Money	Man in middle	More decision-making power	No well-defined role
Prestige and respect	Poor hours and pay	More money	Man in middle	Prestige and respect	Man in middle	Prestige	Responsibility for officers	Pride in achievement	Man in middle
Stepping stone	Lack of authority and backing	Prestige	No authority	Stepping stone	Shiftwork	Responsibility	Lack of backing	Opportunity to direct and lead	Job pressure
Ability to assist and train	Putting in more time	More flexible working hours		Sense of accomplishment	Responsibility for men	Pride in achievement	Putting in extra time	Prestige	Losing comradeship of officers
Being in charge	More responsibility and grief	Less work		Being a teacher and trainer	Less desirable leave days	Extra privileges	More responsibility	Money	
Getting to make good calls	Having to defend administration policies—a buffer			Helping correct problems and make changes	Scapegoat role	A chance to train			
More leeway in decision making	Boredom			More freedom	Interference and second guessing from administration and lack of backing	A step to a higher rank			
More influence	Pawn of the administration			Influencing officers	Lack of direct involvement in decision making	More power and privileges			
More responsibility	Having to discipline friends			Picking calls you want to make	Inequity between patrol and investigative divisions	Less routine functions			
None	Lack of respect			Having knowledge of what's going on and making input	Suspicion and rejection by officers				
More administrative duties	Losing contact with the public			Supervising rather than doing the job	Social and marital problems				
Greater discretion	Too large a span of control			Increased responsibility					
Better leave days	Politics in promotion			Opportunity to lead					
Less routine police work	Too much paperwork			Link between officers and administration					
Better retirement	Too many insignificant duties								
Less report writing	No job description								

Note: Responses are listed in the order of importance as stated by the particular group of respondents.

47

tion. Understanding what motivates a sergeant is as important as understanding line officers' motivation.

> A person is motivated to become a supervisor because he or she wants to be in a position to make decisions that count, that make a difference in what happens. In organizational life, it is the way a person makes his mark in the work and assures himself of the importance of his own existence. Furthermore, it is an added source of satisfaction that other people recognize from whence the decisions spring; that people are aware of the fact that you are, indeed, making a mark. . . . But what do the modern employee motivation techniques do to that picture? They destroy a good deal of the sheen. You, the manager, are supposed to let your employees participate in the decision-making process by proposing alternatives, criticizing various approaches, and in some cases, making the decisions themselves. When this happens, the decisions that are made can no longer be identified as being yours and yours alone. Even if they turn out to be very good decisions, you no longer get all of the credit for them. The mark you have made in the world can no longer be clearly identified as your mark.[1]

So, on the one hand, participatory management by line personnel, which many have thought important for organizational functioning, may be counterproductive for the first-line supervisor. But on the other hand, neither the sergeant nor the line officer have much input into police department policy. They have at least this in common.

The 300 officers interviewed, regardless of rank, agreed that sergeants had little or no input into departmental policy in their organizations. When sergeants are told they are the "grease that makes the organization wheels roll," or the "cement that holds the department together," but then are given little opportunity to contribute to important department operations, their feeling that they are important to the organization is blurred. Sergeants need to be listened to, because they have to "sell the program" to their officers. Having input makes them more committed to enforcing orders, procedures, and departmental directives. If their input cannot be trusted then they should not be supervisors.

When the sergeant doesn't feel he has input, he will be reluctant to solicit it from his supervisees. The findings of the 300 interviews unanimously show that sergeants don't usually encourage input from their officers because, "I do not have input—why should my supervisees?" or, "It's not a part of my job description," or, "It is not appropriate in a semimilitary organization, where communication should be from the top down, not vice versa." (See Table 3-2)

[1]John A. Reeder, "The Best-Laid Plans of Mice, Men and Behavior Scientists," in *Management for Supervisors: Readings and Cases,* Paul Preston and Thomas M. Zimmerer, eds. (Englewood Cliffs, N.J.: Prentice-Hall, 1978), p. 39.

TABLE 3-2

Do Sergeants Encourage Their Officers to Suggest New Procedures Or Changes?

Patrolmen	Detectives	Sergeants	Lieutenants	Command
No, sergeants feel that since they don't have input, the administration won't listen to the officers either. Sergeants encourage input, but the procedure is so elaborate that it discourages officers. It depends on the sergeant. The paramilitary structure isn't conducive to getting suggestions. Sergeants will listen, but it doesn't go any further. They don't ask, but they are open to suggestions.	Sergeants don't see it as a part of their job. Some sergeants do. It wouldn't do any good anyway.	It depends on the sergeant. It is not encouraged or actively sought. Sergeants try, but the officers don't think anything will be done anyway. Sergeants actively encourage input.	It depends on the sergeant. It depends on the shift lieutenant. They don't solicit input. Since the sergeants don't feel they have input, they don't encourage it from their officers. They encourage input. Investigative sergeants encourage it more than patrol sergeants. Sergeants don't see it as a part of their role.	Sergeants don't encourage input—they don't see it as part of their job. It depends on the sergeant.

Note: Responses are listed in the order of importance as stated by the particular group of respondents.

This last is another example of the perversion of a military principle—that the organization knows what is best for the line officers. The less effective sergeants use the military model as an excuse for not soliciting input, apparently feeling that asking the opinions of their officers is a sign of weakness that shows up the sergeant as not having all the answers.

In truth, however, effective military commanders are trained to incorporate all relevant information and input regardless of its source; it may be from a forward observer in a combat situation who is only a private. To reiterate, if police administrators are going to use the military model, they had better understand it and not pervert the principles, using them only to facilitate manipulation and self-interest.

THE SERGEANT AS MOTIVATOR AND MORALE BUILDER

Everyone has heard stories about noted morale builders—Vince Lombardi's half-time locker-room talks, John F. Kennedy's speeches to the Senate, General Patton's battlefield encouragements, and many others. These make excellent stories, but in reality, how much influence can the sergeant have on the behavior of his supervisees in contemporary police departments?

The sergeant, like any first-line supervisor, cannot motivate someone who is lazy and incompetent. But he can influence, to varying degrees, most of the people he is supervising if his department has at least minimal entrance standards. "Locker-room speeches" and "annihilate-the-enemy" tirades do little to produce long-term results.

Furthermore, the police sergeant can do little to ameliorate the attitudes of an apathetic public toward crime, reduce the criticism that the police officer takes as the government symbol of authority, or win the battle with the self-interested politician who envisions the local police department as servants for his survival through political favoritism.

Positive motivation and good morale extend beyond locker-room speeches and "glad-handing" techniques. Morale and motivation are the result of the sergeant's day-to-day communication, counseling, advice, and ready accessibility. As "man in the middle," the sergeant can be the linkage that blunts the realities of a politically active community and a sometimes aloof and possibly incompetent police administration.

The effective sergeant as man in the middle can sense when something is happening at management levels and when his supervisees are reacting to organizational and community politicking. For example, a police administrator was receiving dual directives from his city council. On the one hand, his department was being criticized for not having positive community relations; on the other, he was also being chastised for not emphasizing parking-ticket writing, since the city was losing revenue. The chief's frustration was transmitted downward in the organization to the sergeant level.

The sergeants on one shift were astute enough to know that the situation could cause problems, so they instructed their officers to be especially sure their parking-ticket writing was appropriate and not indiscriminate. The sergeants on the other shifts transmitted their frustration to their officers, with the result that the officers overreacted by writing many more tickets than normal, and even in situations where they knew the public would complain to the administration. Parking tickets were issued even on cars that were immobilized because of a recent flood. It was the officers' way of getting back at their administrators for making the work environment intolerable.

After the ticket epsiode, the department's administrators discussed the situation with the sergeants whose shift did not become involved in the excessive ticket writing. The sergeants explained why the other shifts reacted the way they did—namely, political interference and the department administrators' reluctance to face the problem squarely with the city council. The problem was alleviated when the chief backed up his officers by telling the council that indiscriminate, excessive ticket writing, even though it produces more revenue, causes problems with the community.

The situation illustrates that it is possible for the sergeant to influence his supervisees both positively and negatively. The sergeant who is sensitive to what is happening in his organization can forestall many problems. It should be mentioned, however, that any positive effect the sergeant can have on his supervisees' motivation will be only short-term if the department does not eventually handle the situation appropriately. Even the effective sergeant has only limited positive influence on his people. If organizational conflict, inconsistency, and disruption occur on a long-term basis, the officers' (and sergeants') frustration will pop out someplace.

Motivating the line officer is difficult enough even when the sergeant has the support of his superiors and there is minimal outside political and interest-group interference. A factor associated with motivation but even more elusive and difficult to define and deal with is *morale.*

Smith and Wakeley define morale as:

> . . . the worker's intrinsic interest in what he is doing as measured by his work effort, initiative and satisfaction. An individual or group has high morale when there is a high level of involvement in the task to be done, great effort expended and considerable happiness with the work itself. Low morale exists when the individual or group acts and feels apathetic, uninvolved, and indifferent about the work and its outcomes. Morale lies in the interaction between a worker and his work. That is, one employee may be interested and another

uninterested in the same work, and some work may be more interesting to all workers than other work.[2]

To be sure, morale and motivation of the worker are related to more factors than merely the effectiveness of the sergeant. The sergeant has to have the support of top management and be rewarded accordingly when his supervisees do a good job. There is much that top management can do to motivate the sergeant, and it is ultimately top management that sets the tone for the department. Comella suggests the following, relative to what department administrators can do to motivate and support the first-line supervisor. He feels management leaders must:

1. Set high standards by their own competence, drive, and performance.
2. Encourage competition.
3. Distribute rewards proportionate to work performance.
4. Give the most challenging jobs to the most capable people, not those with the most work status.
5. Create work rules and policies that will not stifle initiative, creativity, and leadership—the fewer administrative details needed to accomplish a given function, the better.
6. Delegate authority and responsibility where it is appropriate and deserved. The further down on the work ladder that decisions are made, the more efficient the enterprise will be.
7. Allow personnel the maximum freedom possible in pursuing and accomplishing the various elements of their work.
8. Define work responsibility and accountability clearly.
9. Deal harshly with attempts to "play politics" in work activities.
10. Keep employees informed.
11. Handle grievances in an equitable fashion.[3]

These actions and attitudes are the minimum that the sergeant should expect from his superiors. When these conditions exist, they will facilitate the sergeant's ability to motivate his people, which will in turn contribute to increased worker morale and reduce some of the problems the sergeant encounters as "man in the middle."

[2]Henry Clay Smith and John H. Wakeley, *Psychology of Industrial Behavior,* 3rd ed. (New York: McGraw-Hill, 1972), p. 24.
[3]Tom Comella, "Call to Leadership," *Automation,* Penton Publishing Company, Cleveland, Ohio, June 1967.

AUTHORITY, RESPONSIBILITY, AND ACCOUNTABILITY
OF THE SERGEANT

The designation of the sergeant as the "man in the middle" relates directly to the authority and responsibility he has and the system of accountability his organization has established for him.

One of the complaints most often heard from sergeants is that they do not have authority commensurate with their responsibilities. The 300 survey respondents had a variety of opinions to the question, "Do sergeants have enough authority to make decisions?" (See Table 3-3.) Sergeants, detectives, and patrol officers usually responded that sergeants do not have enough authority, whereas lieutenants and above generally felt that sergeants have the authority but are unwilling to use it in many cases. In the final analysis it depends on the individual sergeant.

Suggestions were offered, such as allowing the sergeants to do more

TABLE 3-3

Do Sergeants Have Enough Authority To Make Decisions?

Patrolmen	Detectives	Sergeants	Lieutenants	Command
Lieutenants and above make the major decisions.	Sergeants don't have authority commensurate with their responsibility.	It depends on the lieutenant the sergeant is working for.	They have a lot of decision-making power and authority if they want to use it. They should make more decisions.	They have the authority, but some sergeants don't use it.
They don't have authority commensurate with their responsibility.	They make day-to-day decisions, like leave days, but not policy decisions.	Sergeants aren't allowed to make enough decisions—they don't have authority.	They are afraid to make decisions because of administration "second-guessing" and lack of backing.	Sergeant is afraid to make decisions because of "Monday morning quarterbacking."
Sergeants should have more authority so that the officers would respect them more.	Lieutenants make most of the decisions.	Sergeants make field decisions but not policy decisions.	Most decisions are made at higher levels.	Sergent makes decisions on legal questions but not in the policy area.
It depends on the lieutenant.	All major decisions are made by the staff (captains and above).	Sergeants are afraid to make decisions because they won't be backed.	They make field decisions but not policy decisions.	Sergeants don't want to take responsibility.
Sergeants don't use their authority because they know they won't be backed.	Sergeants don't want to make waves with the administration.	Too much interference from the administration.	They have the authority, but they don't know what the peramiters are.	They don't have authority.
Sergeants have enough authority to make field decisions.	They have authority, but they don't want to use it.	Sergeants will make decisions but will keep the lieutenant informed.	They make too many decisions.	They just have authority in field situations.
Sergeants don't want to make waves.	Some sergeants have too much authority.	They have enough authority.	The promotion system doesn't determine a man's decision-making ability.	Sergeants have authority when the lieutenant isn't there.
Sergeants should have much more authority in field decisions and in the discipline area.	Lieutenants and above interfere too much.	Good backing from the lieutenants but not from the staff.	Sergeants don't have authority because the administration doesn't want to relinquish authority.	
Investigative sergeants have more leeway.	Captains get overinvolved so they can have material at staff meetings.	The sergeants have authority, but they should be consulted more.	The sergeant's authority depends on the lieutenant he is working for.	
Most of the decisions sergeants make, patrolmen should be making.	Detective sergeants have authority only in their own squads.			
	Sergeants oversupervise, but they don't have authority.			
	The sergeant's role isn't as strong as it used to be.			

Note: Responses are listed in the order of importance as stated by the particular group of respondents.

roll-call training rather than merely making perfunctory announcements. It was also felt that they should have most of the say on uniform wear, since they have to wear the same uniform as their officers. In addition to allowing the sergeants more input on matters such as uniform wear and equipment use, the respondents said sergeants should have a greater role in settling grievances. This is one of the major responsibilities of the foreman in a factory.

There were several critical comments, especially from the sergeants, relative to their perceived lack of authority. For example, they felt that the attitude is, "If you make the right decision, sergeant, I am behind you 100 percent. If you are wrong, you are on your own," or, "Sergeant, when you make the right decision, you are lucky; when you make the wrong one, it's your posterior."

In many cases, sergeants felt the major problem was that they did not have a well-defined role, that even though their responsibilities may be detailed, their limits of authority are usually unstated or vague. When sergeants are not given backing and authority (whether real or perceived), they will quite naturally align themselves with their officers, creating problems of supervisor morale and complicating the monitoring, controlling, and disciplining process.

It was suggested that one of the reasons sergeants are not given more authority is that the upper command wants to be involved in the day-to-day police activities—as mentioned earlier, "police work gets into your blood." By getting involved in the routine line activities, lieutenants and above have an excuse for not getting the paperwork done (which many dislike anyway) and not giving more attention to the planning function. The resultant lack of authority of the sergeant, as perceived by both the sergeants and their supervisees, is related to the sergeants' lack of input into departmental policy, discussed earlier. Even though on the organizational chart the sergeant is listed as a part of management, he is often no more than a "super patrol officer."

The authority question is another example of how military principles are not effectively translated to the civilian police department. The sergeant in the military has a well-defined job description and knows his limits of authority. Seldom would a captain in charge of a military police company be involved in line activities so that he could be a part of the "big bust." But top-management personnel in civilian police departments often involve themselves in daily activities. The difference is probably due to the fact that military officers have usually entered at the officer level rather than having been noncommissioned military police, so the daily line activities have never "gotten into their blood."

The sergeants' lack of authority and minimal input into departmental policy are symptoms of the usual reactive rather than proactive policies in police departments. As mentioned earlier, police departments are usually rewarded for reacting to problem situations rather than planning for preventive activities.

In summary, in order for the sergeant to be effective, not only does he have to be given authority commensurate with his listed responsibilities; he has to have consistent direction and expectations from his immediate superior so that the system of accountability is workable. A loosely run police department that has ambiguous role definitions and excessive outside interference will usually not have an effective system of accountability. The sergeant may be directly accountable to his immediate supervisor as illustrated on the organization chart, but he may in fact be "second-guessed" all the way up the chain of command to the chief and informally supervised by someone other than his immediate superior.

An ambiguous system of accountability will not only cause morale problems among departmental personnel; it will undermine the organizational authority system and contribute to "game playing," "brownnosing," and departmental politics.

THE SERGEANT AND DISCIPLINE

One of the most difficult, and often the least desired, function of a sergeant's job is disciplining. (Chapter 5 expands the discussion of disciplining.) By the very nature of the sergeant's job, he is expected to monitor, oversee, control, and, if necessary, discipline his supervisees. A police officer requires more than training—he needs constant evaluation, being complimented when he performs effectively, being told and corrected when he makes a mistake, and being disciplined when he repeatedly disregards policies or procedures or when his infraction is serious.

Sergeants dislike the role of disciplinarian, for the obvious reason that it is distasteful to chastise grown people for not doing the job, but also because of the abundance of documentation required, owing to the appeals and grievance procedures that are frequently initiated after disciplining takes place. The less obvious problems with discipline relate to the sergeant's lack of authority: In some organizations, the sergeant is not backed up by his superiors, and thus the disciplinary procedure becomes emasculated. Favoritism, inconsistency, and unnecessary interference by superiors can destroy the effectiveness of a disciplinary procedure. Interference in the early stages of the discipline process makes the sergeant the unimportant and ineffective "man in the middle."

A well-thought-out and consistent disciplinary procedure is mandatory in police departments. Tamm mentions the following as the immediate objectives of the disciplinary process:

1. To produce a change in thinking and actions on the part of the individual to bring his efforts into line with departmental standards
2. To improve the performance of the group as a whole by deterring its members from engaging in disapproved practices
3. To raise and maintain the prestige of the department by going on public notice that compliance is uniformly insisted upon from all members of the force[4]

This list carries a fourfold thrust: behavior change, performance improvement, prevention, and increase in public confidence. Listing the objectives of discipline, however, is much easier than knowing when to discipline, how much discipline to administer, and under what conditions.

Police departments, because of their usual classical, semimilitary orientation, base their philosophy of discipline on traditional principles of punishment. Some of these are:

1. Punishment should be proportional to the offense.
2. The end effect of punishment is deterrence of others who have not "sinned."
3. Punishment should be used as an example for others in the organization.
4. When a single individual cannot be identified as the perpetrator, the entire group should be punished.
5. The severity of the punishment should be accelerated with each additional occurrence.
6. The announcement of punishment and its administration should be given the maximum possible visibility and exposure, in order that the deterrent effect shall be maximized.[5]

Even though some of these may be worthwhile principles, they are still based on a negative view of human nature. In any group, a certain percentage of workers will need to be disciplined and, as the research with the 300 officers illustrated, effective police officers expect their deviant peers to be disciplined for infractions. It was even stated by several officers that the disciplinary procedure is not severe enough and that all officers ultimately suffer when the deviant ones are not dealt with immediately, because when the situation gets out of hand, restrictions are placed on all. The resultant effect will be oversupervision and a view of the officers as merely children who have to be constantly watched.

The bare minimum that should be expected is clear disciplinary procedures. Bramblett lists the following principles as necessary for the effective maintenance of discipline:

[4]Quinn Tamm, "Discipline and Performance Appraisal," *Police Chief,* International Association of Chiefs of Police, Vol. 29, No. 9 (1962), 6–7.
[5]George S. Odiorne, "Discipline by Objectives," in Preston and Zimmerer, *Management for Supervisors,* pp. 259–60.

1. Make instructions simple and understandable.
2. Know the rules.
3. Move in promptly on violations.
4. Get all the facts.
5. Permit employees an opportunity to explain.
6. Decide what actions to take.
7. Take disciplinary action.
8. Maintain the "hands-off" policy (never physically touch an employee unless in self-defense).
9. Observe contractual procedures in disciplinary situations.
10. Make records.[6]

The 300 officers interviewed were asked how policies and orders were enforced in their organizations. (See Table 3-4.) Such enforcement was perceived as a problem area by the respondents. On the one hand, several officers felt that some sergeants were too lax in enforcement; on the other hand, it was also felt that the sergeants were not backed up by the administration when they did enforce orders. The end result was the avoidance of situations that should be handled or the inconsistent enforcement of orders, depending on the sergeant, the officer in violation, the shift lieutenant, the political climate, and the type of infraction. Also, as mentioned above, it was felt that deviant officers should be confronted immediately and action taken promptly, rather than putting off such problems until they become more serious and a departmental directive is issued that affects everybody.

Another problem perceived by many of the officers, including the sergeants themselves, was that new policies, procedures, and orders are enforced very strictly at first, then enforcement slacks off and becomes lax. They felt that if the order, policy, or procedure is important enough to be enforced, it should be enforced consistently and evenly all the time. If it is not important enough, it should not have been introduced, because its lack of enforcement encourages laxness in other, more important areas.

Checking reports of their officers can also be touchy for sergeants. Officers tend to feel that the sergeant is too "picky" if he wants to check every report; on the other hand, if he does not check any reports or checks them in a perfunctory manner, he is perceived as lazy, unconcerned, and uninterested in departmental and officer improvement. The effective sergeant learns to spot-check the competent officers, make suggestions and "coach" when mistakes are made, and monitor closely—even if it means looking at every report—those officers who are considered problem employees. In other

[6]Earl R. Bramblett, "Maintenance of Discipline," *Human Resources Management,* Vol. 1, No. 1 (Autumn 1961), 10–14.

TABLE 3-4

How Are Orders Enforced?

Patrolmen	Detectives	Sergeants	Lieutenants	Command
By sergeants and lieutenants on the shift.	There is no effective enforcement.	Sergeants mostly, but also the shift lieutenant.	Sergeants usually, but sometimes the staff interferes.	Sergeants enforce via the chain of command.
Enforcement is too lax.	The chain of command is supposed to be used but isn't.	Sergeants enforce procedures but not major infractions.	The sergeants enforce orders.	Sergeants don't like the role of enforcers.
From sergeant all the way up to chief.	The sergeant enforces.	There is a lack of enforcement by the sergeants because they feel they won't be backed by the administration.	Sergeants have difficulty in disciplining the officers.	There needs to be better communication of orders, etc.
The sergeant usually disciplines.	The sergeant doesn't know where he stands.		Disciplining stays within the shift.	Chain of command isn't used effectively.
It depends on the sergeant as to whether he disciplines.	Sergeant and shift lieutenant enforce orders.	Everyone from sergeant up to chief gets involved in enforcement.	The chain of command isn't used effectively.	Sergeants and the shift lieutenants enforce them on their own shifts.
Lieutenants do the disciplining.		The chain of command is used up but not down.	The person who does the disciplining depends on the seriousness of the infraction.	
Sergeants are supposed to, but they don't because they aren't backed.				
Discipline is erratic. It depends on the friendship between the sergeant and the officer.				
Sergeants have the most immediate role, but not the major role.				

Note: Responses are listed in the order of importance as stated by the particular group of respondents.

words, he individualizes supervision and takes appropriate individual action when necessary.

There were a variety of responses to the question, "If departmental orders are not followed, why not?" (See Table 3-5.) The responses ranged from "Because they don't make sense" to "Because the officer forgot."

Most respondents felt that if orders are not followed, there is usually a reason other than the violator's having a belligerent attitude. The effective sergeant should regard a situation in which orders are being violated by several officers as a warning signal of possibly serious departmental problems. The sergeant can use his "middleman" role to evaluate the problem area, transmit his findings to the administration, and help solve the problem.

Difficulty arises, however, when the problem is with the department administration itself—when its members do not want input from the sergeant and would not alter the situation even with it. It is in these situations that the "middleman" role causes trouble for the sergeant. He is expected to support the administration's policy even if it is inappropriate and unworkable, but his officers expect him to transmit their problems with the unworkable policy to the administration. He is unable to satisfy either the administration or his subordinates. This is when morale is affected and it becomes difficult for the sergeant to motivate his people.

In other situations, a line officer may want to transmit his problems with a certain policy to a lieutenant or captain, but because of an unsympathetic or inadequate sergeant, may find that the semimilitary orientation subverts his good intentions. If it is necessary to use the chain of command, he will have to rely on his sergeant to transmit the communication "up the chain," but he knows the sergeant will not do it. If he disregards the chain, he can be criticized; if he doesn't make his problems known, he will be frustrated, and that will affect his morale and motivation.

Some command officers criticized the sergeants for not taking a tougher disciplinary stance with their officers. One captain said, "Military sergeants can discipline their people effectively, and the soldier listens to his sergeant." Again, it is impossible for police sergeants to act like army sergeants, because they are civilians first and police officers second. In the military, this is reversed, and the soldier is under 24-hour control.

The "middleman" role can be used for the benefit of the sergeant's supervisees as well as the betterment of the organization if the sergeant has the ear of the administration. But if he is seen as merely the transmitter of policies, with no input and little feedback expected, then the role will act as a vise, squeezing him from both directions.

The sergeant can use several techniques in disciplining. As middleman, he can project to his officers the seriousness of the need to enforce departmental policies while at the same time empathizing with them if the policy appears to be cumbersome or unworkable. Policies and procedures can be

TABLE 3-5

If Departmental Orders Are Not Followed, Why Not?

Patrolmen	Detectives	Sergeants	Lieutenants	Command
Because they don't make sense and are unreasonable	Unreasonable orders	Could be an unworkable order	The officer is belligerent	Officers don't understand the orders
Because the administration is perceived as being inconsistent	Lack of discipline	Sergeants don't believe in it and troopers pick it up	Depends on how it was communicated	Officers don't agree with the orders
Problems in communication	Poor communication from the top	They want to "test" the system	Lack of discipline	It's a bad order
Lack of enforcement and discipline	There are too many orders	There are too many orders	There are too many orders to keep track of	Poor communication from captain and above
Lack of credibility between the officers and the administration		Officer might not know what the order is—could have been on leave, etc.	It's a bad order or unreasonable	
The order is hazardous to the officer		Poor communication when transmitting order	Some officers are always challenging orders	
Because the sergeants don't agree with the order		Laxity in enforcing orders	The younger officers have to have an explanation and answers	
Inconsistent orders—there are hair regulations but not regulations for persons overweight		Because the chances of getting caught are slim	The order isn't understood	
There are too many rules and regulations		Because they forgot	To circumvent it	
			Discretion in policework contributes to devious maneuvering	
			The order isn't protected	
			Because it doesn't have a bearing on the job	

Note: Responses are listed in the order of importance as stated by the particular group of respondents.

changed, but feedback is necessary from line officers through their sergeant. If the sergeant has influence and his input is respected by administration policy makers, then unworkable policies will be altered.

In addition, it is helpful if the sergeant has had some input into policy development. Even if that input has been minimal, the sergeant will at least understand the policy and be able to communicate it to his supervisees. But if he has not participated in making the policy and does not agree with it, he can still say to his people, "I don't particularly agree with this new procedure, but it is my job to see that it is carried out. I will do my best to transmit to the administration your problems with it and try to get it changed. But until then, I will enforce it." Such a technique allows the sergeant to be honest with his supervisees when asked a direct question. It projects both a commitment to enforcing the rules and a sensitivity to the problems of subordinates. Even if the sergeant is unable to get the rule changed, the officers will know where their sergeant stands instead of seeing him "play both ends against the middle."

The ineffective sergeant will either take an authoritarian stance—"Follow the orders and don't ask questions"—or he will be organizationally subversive and look the other way when an infraction takes place.

DEALING WITH THE UNION

Unionization, like any other activity, has created both positive and negative conditions for police departments. The union can be an effective means to protect the officer from an inadequate and authoritarian supervisor. On the other hand, it can also protect an ineffective officer, making disciplining by the sergeant difficult and sometimes almost impossible.

In many departments, the less effective sergeants have said that they could not effectively monitor or discipline because of the interference of the union. This is often used as an excuse, so that the sergeant need not go through the legitimate process of observing, collecting information, documenting, and knowing the procedures, orders, and policies well enough so that the infraction can be properly cited and dealt with. It is hard work to be a good supervisor. Dealing with problem employees and their infractions is a tedious process. The lazy and incompetent sergeant who does not want to take the time and exert the effort will blame someone or something other than himself—and that something can be the union.

The inadequate supervisor may merely react to situations, or he may press as far as he can until the union intervenes. In either case, his supervision is not consistent and thorough, based on a workable set of principles. This type of sergeant operates on an "eight-to-five" orientation, putting in time and collecting a paycheck. He does not usually feel the intense pressures of being the man in the middle, because he does only what is essential for survival and is not conscientious enough to either represent his supervisees to the administration or effectively carry out the responsibilities given him by his superiors.

In many contemporary police departments, sergeants are unionizing because of the feeling that no one understands their dilemma. They feel they have little input into administrative policy, so they are not really a part of the administration; yet at the same time, the administration does not want them closely associated, at least socially, with the line officers, because this would taint their objectivity and make it difficult for them to enforce the rules. The net result is frustration and the desire to be associated with a group that understands their problems. When the desire for association goes beyond social contact, a union is discussed and sometimes formed. Supervisory unions are unnecessary when sergeants have input into organization policy, are considered a part of the management "team," and are rewarded for their positive contributions.

SPECIAL PROBLEM AREAS FOR SERGEANTS

Performance Appraisal

The sergeant, as man in the middle, has to deal with several special kinds of problems in his role as first-line supervisor. One of the most difficult areas for him is rating his supervisees. A supervisor can very quickly contribute to low morale and reduce motivation by being subjective and showing favoritism in his rating process.

Sometimes the sergeant can feel pressure, either formal or informal, from the administration to rate one of his supervisees higher because the officer is a "fair haired boy," or has influence with the command. Without an objective means to evaluate his personnel, the sergeant will be amenable to manipulation and pressure, causing further problems in his middle-manager role.

Walsh lists the following as the most common rating errors:

1. *Error of leniency.* The error of leniency is by far the most common of all errors in the rating of personnel. Leniency occurs when the supervisor rates higher than the realities of employee performance warrant. The effects of this type of rating are (a) to force ratings so drastically toward the top of the rating scale that they are valueless to management; (b) to create unrealistic employee confidence when improvement in performance is really needed; and (c) to damage morale of the truly outstanding workers, who begin to wonder if it really pays to work diligently when the less proficient employees receives the same rating anyway.

There are a number of pressures on supervisors which tempt them to be lenient—the wish to avoid unpleasant scenes, the feeling that low ratings reflect poor supervision, the desire to retain the friendship of their employees, and often the belief that other supervisors do not rate fairly, and they do not want to penalize their own employees.

2. *Central tendency error.* In any normal distribution, more people will be rated closer to the mean than to any other point on the scale. A rating near the norm becomes a central tendency error only when it does not reflect a true evaluation of performance. It is most likely to occur when the supervisor does not know a worker very well or when he has difficulty in collecting verifiable facts. The normal rating for either very good or very bad performance is unfair to the employee, his co-workers, and management.

3. *Contrast error.* This type of rating error arises from the tendency of some supervisors to rate employees in terms of their own expectations and aspirations. Employees who satisfy the personal needs of the supervisor will generally be rated higher.

4. *Halo error.* The tendency of raters to rate in terms of a very general impression rather than on the basis of specific traits is called a halo error. It occurs when the rater thinks in terms of the good or poor officer and groups all the ratings (categories) for that individual at the high or low end of the scale.

5. *Association error.* This is referred to as the logical error and is similar to the halo-type error. The association error is committed when the rater gives similar ratings to traits which seem to be similar. For example, when the rater assumes that if a person has good judgment, he must also have good presence of mind; if he is attentive to duty, he must also have a high degree of inititiative.

6. *Overweighting error.* There is a tendency for raters to be unduly influenced by an occurrence, either good or bad, involving the ratee near the end of the rating period. This error often occurs when one or more outstanding occurrences near the end of the rating period are out of proportion to the average performance during the entire period.[7]

The effective supervisor is able to adequately measure the performance of his supervisees. For the department to achieve its goals, the line officers have to perform the line functions. They need reference points by which to judge how well they are accomplishing the department's objectives, and rewards to stimulate their motivation so that tasks are not only accomplished but performed at an acceptable level or above.

There are two distinct purposes for conducting performance appraisals. The first of these is related to planning for, monitoring of, and training of the subordinate; while the second purpose concerns the administration of salaries and rewards. These two purposes, both of which are extremely important, put the supervisor into a classic role conflict. Can I be a friend, a confidant, a

[7]Jude T. Walsh, "Performance Rating for Police Supervisor," *Police Chief,* Vol. 41, No. 4 (1974), 51–53.

counselor, and a trainer on one hand, and still be the coach, and the person who holds the purse strings on the other? It is most difficult to be in such a position, since it is difficult to be sure which of these goals merits more attention, and more commitment. This is obviously a decision that each of us must reconcile with our own managerial philosophies. The critical issue, however, is which of these roles the employee perceives the supervisor to be emphasizing. This conflict between being a coach and being a counselor adds to the discomfort and conflict during the performance appraisal.[8]

This again illustrates the dilemma for the first-line supervisor. Too often he has the task of monitoring and assessing the supervisee but has little control over organizational rewards like salary increases or preferred assignments. The one area where he does have influence is in the periodic evaluations that he makes of his officers, because these should have an effect on promotion—which ultimately means more money, status, and other organizational rewards.

In too many departments, however, periodic evaluations and appraisals are mundane, routine activities that get little commitment from the department administration, minimal motivation from the sergeant, and reluctant participation by the officer because "they don't mean anything, the department will promote who they want to anyway."

Some other problems in rating are the following:

Rater uninterest, negligence, or incompetence

Rater emotional bias, subjectivity, and attitude

Emphasis on incidental rather than pattern behavior of employee

Use of periodic appraisal as a substitute for day-to-day supervision

Negative employee attitude toward the system

Lack of counseling skill or interviews by the supervisor

Ineffective or inadequate training of the mechanics of the rating system

Not knowing the employee well enough or insufficient exposure to his performance at the time of rating[9]

It is obvious then that the greatest requirement of any appraisal system is that the department's *administration be committed* to it, use it, and provide the sergeant with the necessary training to employ the appraisal for the benefit of all concerned. The sergeant has little or no influence on salary raises, because of standardized contracts with associations, unions, or civil service. The evaluation can only provide the reference points to measure

[8]Brian L. Hawkins, "Communication: The Key to Effective Performance Appraisal," in Preston and Zimmerer, *Management for Supervisors,* p. 212.
[9]Lyle Knoles and Joseph C. DeLadurantey, "Performance Evaluation," *Journal of Police Science and Administration,* Vol. 2, No. 1 (1974), 33.

performance. The administration, however, has to use it because it believes in it, and not just because the contract demands it. The appraisal system has to be directly linked to the reward system and used to distribute the rewards, such as merit acknowledgments, promotions, and special assignments.

Next, the appraisal system has to have the active participation of the supervisee. The dialogue between the sergeant and the officer provides a vehicle for discussion of the entire work situation, giving the officer the feeling that his input is not only solicited but required for effective organizational operation. Both the officer and the sergeant should be prepared prior to the appraisal interview to discuss specific content areas. This will convey an atmosphere of give and take rather than a routine checklist, ultimately translated into a score that means little or nothing to the officer. The ineffective sergeant appraises by extremes, rating most people either high or low; and the evaluation gets little input or participation from the supervisee, both because the sergeant doesn't ask for it and because the officer feels that it would be a waste of his breath anyway.

Figure 3-1 illustrates a questionnaire that can be given to employees prior to the appraisal interview. Its purpose is to stimulate thinking, self-evaluation, an organization critique, and pinpointing of references that will be helpful in the interview dialogue. It shows the employee that time and effort have been put into the appraisal process, that the organization is serious about how it operates. The employee knows that he will be asked questions and encouraged to discuss his entire situation and his perceptions with his supervisor.

The questions in Figure 3-1 will stimulate a good deal of discussion, because they allude to the adequacy of the role definition and job description (No. 1); how the job tasks mesh with the worker's expectations (2, 3); the amount of support and backing he feels he is getting (4); whether he has input into the organization's operation (5); his evaluation of the organization and its atmosphere (6–11); his goals for the future (12); his accomplishments (13); his areas of weakness (14); suggestions for improvement (15); and finally, what he has contributed to the organization (16–22).

After discussion of these matters, the most salient comments can be easily translated into a written report for future reference, in the form of a narrative summary of what transpired in the interview. The report can be used to identify training needs, areas of strength and weakness, a means of evaluating how the department is carrying out its functions from the perceptions of its line officers, and a readily available record that can be referred to if necessary. The same form can also be used when the sergeant is being evaluated by his superiors.

The following is an example of a typical performance evaluation; it rates the officer on qualities ranging from appearance to promptness.

The form is adequate but should be supplemented with the previously

---

Name | Scheduled Time & Date

Quarterly Review

Please be prepared to discuss the following topics in relation to your scheduled review:

1. Are your duties and responsibilities adequately defined?
2. Do you have enough challenging work?
3. What can you do for (name department) that I haven't given you a chance to do?
4. Do you feel you get the backing and support you need?
5. Are you informed and consulted when you should be?
6. Do you have opportunities to talk problems over freely?
7. Do you have the authority and opportunity to exercise initiative? If so, how have you used it?
8. Do you feel your opportunities are adequate?
9. What could be done to help you do a better job?
10. What kind of place, in general, do you feel this is to work?
11. What other things that you like or dislike about your job would you want to talk about?
12. What are your aims and goals? How do you propose to acquire the knowledge and human-relations skills needed to reach them? How can I help?
13. What have been your outstanding accomplishments for (name department) over the past year?
14. What are your areas that may need improvement and plans for correction?
15. What are your suggestions for improvement of the operation?
16. What are your interests in work assignments for the future?
17. Has your job grown while you have held it?
18. What has happened in your department that would not have happened if it hadn't been for you?
19. Do you feel you are growing in a professional and personal manner as it relates to your career?
20. Assuming the role of the management, would you hire yourself? Why?
21. Do you feel free to speak your mind? Are you a "yes" man?
22. Discuss what you have accomplished in the way of training junior members of the staff.

Figure 3-1 Appraisal questionnaire

Source: William S. Ringler, "Frequent Reviews Improve Employee Relations," *Journal of Systems Management,* 1975, p. 245. [Adapted to a police department]

PERFORMANCE EVALUATION

JOB ASSIGNMENT _____

Name_____ Rank_____ Badge_____ Division
Unit_____
Bureau

Date   Date   Date
Joined_____ Promoted_____ of Birth_____ Rating Date:_____

RATER: IT IS IMPORTANT THAT YOU BECOME THOROUGHLY FAMILIAR WITH INSTRUCTIONS PRINTED ON THE
BACK OF THIS FORM BEFORE EVALUATING AN EMPLOYEE.

Rated By: Rating

_____   _____

_____   _____

_____   _____

Average Rating   _____

                                                        Date
Adjudicated By_____ Rank_____ Rated_____

TO BE SIGNED BY COUNSELING SUPERVISOR

I have interviewed the above-rated person and made him/her aware of the general assessment rating. The subject has also been counselled on the matters needing improvement and commended on those in which he/she excels.

Signature_____ Rate_____ Date_____

Signature Of Employee_____

	BELOW AVERAGE		
	0	2	4

APPEARANCE —

- Uniform
- Physical Condition
- Leather
- Personal Appearance
- Care of Equipment
- Appearance in Court
- Bearing & Demeanor

	0	5	8

WORK PROFICIENCY —

- Quality & Quantity (Specify)
- Attitude
- Work Organization
- Interest
- Enthusiasm
- Ability to Handle Assignments

	0	3	5

WORK KNOWLEDGE —

- Familiarity of Laws
  (Pertaining to Assignment)
- Ability to Handle Assignments
- General Job Knowledge (Explain)
- Technical Preparation
- Federal, State & Local Laws/Ordinances

	0	2	4

PERSONAL ATTRIBUTES —

- Attitude—Work, Community
- Cooperation
- Acceptance of Criticism
- Conduct
- Loyalty
- Moral Standards
- Ability to Relate (Cultures-Races-Creeds)

	0	2	4

JUDGMENT —

- Dependability Under Stress
- Erratic - Non-erratic
- Biased - Unbiased
- Emotional Stability
- Confidence
- Decision Making
- Safety Mindedness

AVERAGE		VERY GOOD		OUTSTANDING
5	6	8		10

12	14	17	19	25

7	9	10	12	15

5	6	8		10

5	6	8		10

		BELOW AVERAGE	
	0	2	4

DEPENDABILITY —

    Court Preparation
    Reliability of Carrying out Duties
    Need for Supervision
    Punctuality
    Sick Time
    Completeness in Reports
    Integrity

	0	2	4

PUBLIC RELATIONS —

    Manner with People
    Attitude
    Contacts with Public
    Friendly
    Considerate
    Courteous
    Sets a Good Example

	0	2	4

PROMOTABILITY —

    Willingness to Learn
    Capacity to Develop
    Leadership Ability
    Accepts Responsibility
    Respect of Fellow Officers
    General Suitability
    Capacity for Decision Making

COMMENTS IN EVERY CATEGORY ARE MANDATORY.

Ratings will be reviewed thru Chain of Command.

Interviewer shall write in employee reaction _after_ interview.

AVOID THE FOLLOWING PITFALLS OF APPRAISAL

(1) "Halo Effect" which is the tendency to over-rate or under-rate a person on the basis of one specific incident or talent. Examine carefully all phases of his work, and determine that all aspects of his performance are on a par with the things it is known he does well.

(2) The tendency to be what you think is kind and uncritical, and rate average on all factors. Study your men, know them, and rate them fairly.

	AVERAGE		VERY GOOD	OUTSTANDING	
5	6		8	10	
5	6		8	10	
5	6		8	10	

TOTAL _____

INTERVIEWERS COMMENTS

GENERAL INFORMATION ON PERFORMANCE EVALUATION REPORTS

The efficiency of a Police Department and its acceptance by the public, depends almost entirely upon the quality of the personnnel. Of the utmost importance is the conduct and integrity of the officer. It is therefore essential that Police personnel are accurately assessed in order that the most suitable are considered for promotion to a higher rank.

Of equal importance, especially during the formative years of a policeman's career, is the assessing and counselling necessary to bring every member to a high degree of efficiency. With this system in practice from the probationary period on, it will be possible to measure the value of each person and the improvement he makes from one assessment period to another.

WHAT IS PERFORMANCE EVALUATION?

Evaluation provides a method of measuring the amount or degree of qualities possessed by our personnel essential in a police officer.

WHY EVALUATE?

A worthwhile motto to use is "Appraise to Improve."

(1) Assessment can be made of a person's progress during any given period.

(2) Evaluation provides reference material for use when making recommendations for promotion and transfer assignment.

(3) With evaluation plus counselling, there is a greater understanding between the Supervisor and the men he supervises.

(4) It brings into sharp focus the duty of a Supervisor, not only to supervise, but to be able to report intelligently on his men.

(5) The man, after evaluation and counselling, knows where he stands. He is complimented on his strong points and made aware of his weak points and how he can improve himself.

WHO IS EVALUATED AND BY WHOM?

All personnel thru the rank of Lieutenant are evaluated by a Supervisor(s) for whom the employee has worked for a period of two months or longer. As a result of the evaluation a Supervisor of each Division, Bureau and Unit will counsel for each man. In the Patrol Bureau, Patrolmen will be evaluated by at least three Supervisors, and a Supervisor will counsel with the employee.

WHERE WILL EVALUATION TAKE PLACE?

Ratings will be conducted in each Division, Bureau and Unit. After the employee has been counselled, the original report will be forwarded as indicated below.

WHEN WILL EVALUATION BE DONE?

Personnel will be evaluated, upon completion of one year of service, every six months following each new assignment. Reports to be forwarded to Personnel & Training Division not later than 10 days after assigned rating date. All probationary evaluations will be conducted at three month intervals, including promotional probation.

HOW WILL EVALUATION BE DONE?

The following are instructions to Raters:

(1) The work record of individuals who are assessed must be compared with persons doing the same type of work in the same bureau. Training Transfer personnel shall be rated with their peers.

(2) Over-assessment or concealment of deficiencies lowers the value of the assessment. The assessor's reputation for judgment is compromised in the eyes of his superiors, and those being assessed are prejudiced, when the assessments are known to be faulty.

(3) The Rater must make a completely impartial and unbiased report, and not allow his personal feelings toward the individual to have any bearing on the markings.

(4) Seldom, if ever, does any one individual possess all traits in their highest degree, or two individuals possess all traits in the same degree.

(5) Each person must be rated on the basis of his or her typical performance.

(6) Each factor must be rated separately. Avoid overall impressions.

(7) A Supervisor will complete the form, and counsel the person rated in a personal interview.

(8) All completed Evaluation Forms will be forwarded through the chain of command to the appropriate Deputy Chief. The Deputy Chief will review and forward to the Personnel & Training Division.

illustrated quarterly review form, because it offers completeness, shows the officer that his verbal input and ideas are important, and extends in scope beyond merely evaluating the individual officer's personal qualities.

The appraisal interview not only encourages dialogue and participation; it forces the sergeant to justify his evaluations and provides backup material for them, since it must focus on the positive as well as negative characteristics of the officer. Too often the evaluator will look only for negatives, to put the officer on the defensive so that the "heat" is off the sergeant.

In any job—and police work in particular, with its wide discretion— the supervisor can identify negatives in an employee by use of "second guessing." Areas of negative evaluation can be used as a focus for training, coaching, and counseling. The officer has a right to know where he stands and what he has to do to meet organizational objectives. The sergeant has the responsibility to be honest with his officers and willing to use the evaluations and appraisal sessions as a teaching-learning situation for the officer's personal growth, for department improvement, and even for supervisory awareness of where problem areas exist.

Performance appraisal is an *ongoing* process; input and officer feedback should not be limited to just the formal interview every few months or year. The sergeant should be on top of the situation all the time, so that corrective measures or compliments can be reinforced immediately after an action. One of the major criticisms of the 300 interviewees was that the only time an officer knows where he stands is at evaluation time, and that it would be much more helpful if the sergeant would keep in touch on a day-to-day basis. Nothing is more devastating to employee morale than being led by one's supervisor to believe one is performing adequately and then being "cut down" at evaluation-appraisal time.

Performance appraisals and evaluations are not magic, nor are they a substitute for constant, day-to-day monitoring, guidance, coaching, training, and counseling. Neither are they meant to show the officer how inadequate he is and how much he has yet to learn. They are one means that the astute supervisory leader can use to assist his subordinates to function more effectively. The sergeant should take pride in being a teacher and a trainer and seeing his people grow. The performance appraisal can provide reference points to measure growth.

The following are summary guidelines for police performance appraisal that can be helpful to sergeants (see Table 3-6).[10] In regard to the *performance rating scale:*

---

[10]Sidney Epstein and Richard S. Layman, *Guidelines for Police Performance Appraisal, Promotion and Placement Procedures,* National Institute of Law Enforcement and Criminal Justice, L.E.A.A., U.S. Department of Justice, National Technical Information Service, 1973, pp. 4–27.

TABLE 3-6

Performance Scale With Distribution[10]

Performance	60 and below	61–70	71–80	81–90	90–100
Dimension	Performs tasks quite marginally	Performs tasks poorly	Performs tasks adequately	Performs tasks very well	Performs tasks in a superior manner
Distribution	3 policemen out of 100 here	17 policemen out of 100 here	60 policemen out of 100 here	17 policemen out of 100 here	3 policemen out of 100 here

[10]Sidney Epstein and Richard S. Layman, *Guidelines for Police Performance Appraisal, Promotion and Placement Procedures*. National Institute of Law Enforcement and Criminal Justice, L.E.A.A., U.S. Department of Justice, National Technical Information Service, 1973, pp. 4–27.

1. Performance-scale dimensions should be based upon specific job behaviors or tasks of police officers in a department.
2. Each performance-scale dimension should be carefully and unambiguously defined.
3. Each performance-scale dimension should be scaled numerically, be defined by a brief phrase, and include expected standards.
4. Each performance-scale dimension should be weighted according to its importance.
5. Narrative material should be prepared supporting all ratings given at the extreme ends of each performance-scale dimension.
6. There should be a summary rating at the end of the rating scale, expressed both accurately and descriptively.
    In regard to the rater:

1. One of the raters should be the immediate supervisor of the ratee.
2. The rater should receive special training before being permitted to rate anyone.
3. The rater must be motivated to make accurate performance ratings.

In regard to rating procedure:

1. Every officer should be rated every six months, and also when he moves to a new assignment that involves a new supervisor.
2. All raters and reviewers should receive training in the rating process. This training should cover, at the minimum, the following:
    a. Ways to minimize personal bias
    b. Standards
    c. Narrative material to support extreme ratings
    d. Feedback review meeting with the ratee
    e. Clarification of the rating scale or other aspects of the rating process
3. All ratings should be reviewed by at least one person at one command level above the supervisor.
4. The ratee should be permitted to see his rating to indicate whether or not he agrees with it.
5. Contested ratings should be handled with a formal process.[11]

Counseling

The effective sergeant's responsibilities extend beyond merely evaluating how well subordinates are fulfilling the tasks required by the department. The performance appraisal and accompanying personal interview can also be a means to identify any personal problems of the officer, including some that

[11]Ibid.

supervisees may consider to be none of their sergeant's business: specifically, mental and drug- and alcohol-related problems.[12] It may be true that what people do on their own time is their own business, but serious personal problems invariably manifest themselves in the way they do their jobs.

Police officers, like any occupational group, can encounter personal difficulties like mental illness, marital problems, and alcoholism. And these usually affect the officer's work performance. So it is not only work-related problems that should be discussed at the appraisal interview but also the officer's intrapsychic conflicts.

Obviously, most sergeants have not been trained to counsel their supervisees in the manner of a trained mental-health worker. But a concerned sergeant who has a positive relationship with his supervisees can identify problem areas, transmit to them that he is available for talks, and be willing to identify a community resource, such as a professional counseling center, if the supervisee needs continuing assistance. Some of the larger police departments even have their own psychologists.

Personal counseling by the sergeant should not be viewed as a very complex process. It is merely a way two or more people can get together to talk about a problem so that the sergeant can give advice if it is solicited. Everyone at some point needs someone to talk to and relate his feelings to. In many cases, just talking about the problem relieves the burden and places the problem in a more realistic perspective. If it continues to create stress for the officer and the counseling or talk sessions seem to be doing no good, the sergeant should seek advice from either his supervisor or a mental-health professional in the community. In some cases, this means referral to a community agency. If such a referral is made, the sergeant should tactfully try to keep on top of the situation, letting the officer know he is available for discussion of the status of the problem situation.

Police commanders have realized for several years, even though they may not have admitted it, that a part of the department's responsibility is concern about the employees' mental health. The sergeant who tells his supervisee to "shape up or ship out" will not make personal problems just magically disappear. They have to be admitted, identified, confronted, and dealt with in a straightforward, concerned, and thorough manner. The sergeant who is an effective supervisor will accept the challenge and do his part in the problem-solving process.

In police departments that get carried away with their semimilitary, macho image, such problems as alcoholism and mental illness may be considered a form of personal weakness. "Every person should be able to handle his own problems—especially police officers, because they are the symbol of

---

[12]For an expanded discussion of counseling the police office see, Claude S. George, Jr., *Supervision in Action: The 'Art of Managing others,* (Reston, Virginia: Reston Publishing Co., 1977).

authority in a decaying society," said a police sergeant. But the same sergeant asked, "Why didn't he tell us he had problems?" after an officer was found dead in his apartment of a self-inflicted gunshot wound.

Compounding the macho, self-sufficient image is the complexity of contemporary society and the many adjustments to it that have to be made by everyone. Alcoholism or mental illness is seldom precipitated by one isolated incident, such as a death in the family. Minor difficulties build up so insidiously that the victim usually does not realize what is happening, and tragically, even his concerned friends, co-workers, and supervisor, if they notice these changes, brush them off as temporary—"he'll get over it." They use his apparently "normal" past behavior as the gauge for the present behavior, feeling that it is just a phase that will pass.

But problems such as these do not often manifest themselves in a dramatic fashion, like a locker-room shootout or a drunk-driving charge. Their onset is usually slow and may be unnoticeable to the unconcerned sergeant. However, the sergeant who feels that his most important assets are his people will notice subtle behavior changes—a formerly jovial officer who becomes even mildly depressed, a once-punctual officer who begins to come to work late and in a disheveled condition, a usually articulate officer who now has problems carrying on a sustained conversation.

It is difficult to confront a friend or supervisee with the fact that something may be going on in his psyche with which he needs assistance. The sergeant who is perceived as fair and concerned about his supervisees will get information transmitted from them, as well as from his own observations, that can act as a basis for approaching the troubled employee.

The confrontation, of course, should not be judgmental, caustic, sarcastic, or deprecating. Confrontation, as it is currently used, means squarely, directly, and honestly discussing the problem with the employee. If the sergeant has a positive relationship with the supervisee, he will be able to talk directly about the problem and volunteer assistance. The help offered may range all the way from just informally talking, using the communication as a cathartic, to referral to a community organization such as Alcoholics Anonymous or a mental-health clinic.

Just as the sergeant should not expect the onset of problems to be dramatic, he should also not expect quick or immediate results in solving them. It usually takes a long time for an illness to manifest itself in a form that shows something needs to be done; likewise, it takes a while for the problem to be resolved by the employee.

The sergeant's middleman role can be an ideal viewpoint from which to identify these problems, confront the issues, and then, with the help of the administration, deal with them. A sympathetic and understanding administration can use several alternatives that will contribute to problem solving. It may grant a nonpaid leave of absence, or a transfer to a unit that is less stressful. In some cases, the job might even be altered to fit the employee who is having a personal problem. Of course, in departments that have "superma-cho" administrators, this will be an unacceptable alternative because of the negative view of the employee; it may be felt that the officer will take advantage of the situation, that "it's not fair to the other employees," or that "if he can't perform all the duties required of the job, he should find some other employment."

The effective supervisor not only will stand behind his people, he will be imaginative enough to identify workable solutions and be committed to doing his part to help solve the problem. In most cases, when the sergeant has done his part and is even willing to give a little extra effort, the adminis-tration will respond favorably.

The College-Graduate Police Officer

A potential problem area for the sergeant is dealing with the college graduate. The ranks of police organizations in the United States are being filled by increasing numbers of these, especially since many departments have followed the lead of federal law-enforcement agencies and are requiring a college degree as a minimum education prerequisite for employment.[13]

In view of the educational escalation of police officers, two practical questions present themselves: (1) How can this new breed of well-educated police officers be retained? and (2) how can they be used most effectively?

As these questions imply, whether a person with a college education is a better police officer may depend to a great extent upon the policy decisions and management styles that are developed within police depart-ments. If a college-educated police officer is actually different from his non-college counterpart, and the rise in educational levels of police officers is imminent, then it seems crucial to identify these differences and develop policies and conditions that can capitalize on them. The sergeant has a key role in this process.

A study by Trojanowicz compared the behavioral styles of college-graduate police officers with those of police officers who had not attended college, developed profiles of these two groups, and provided conclusions and recommendations based on the differences. The information provided is helpful in developing policies, management styles, and conditions that will retain and more effectively employ both college and noncollege police offic-ers and help the sergeant more effectively deal with them.

The research compared samples of officers in a department of approxi-

[13]Robert C. Trojanowicz and Thomas G. Nicholson, "A Comparison of Behavioral Styles of College Graduate vs. Non–College Going Police Officers," *Police Chief,* Vol. XLIII, No. 8 (1976), 56–60.

mately 1,700 sworn officers. At the time of the study, there were 135 college-graduate officers, 126 of whom held the rank of sergeant or below. These 126 were matched with a sample of 126 noncollege officers; using the date of recruit-school attendance and rank. For example, a college-graduate sergeant from the 1964 recruit school was matched with a noncollege sergeant from the same school. A self-administered questionnaire was distributed to the officers, and 60 personal interviews were held.

Even though police officers are more similar than dissimilar when compared to other occupational groups, there were differences on several scales when college-graduate and noncollege-graduate officers were compared. The dissatisfaction of the college-graduate officer was reflected in both the questionnaires and the interviews. The following were the most frequently stated subjects of concern: (1) rejection by peers; (2) lack of encouragement by command officers of continuing education; (3) the need for a reward system that encourages education; (4) a feeling that college graduates should be put in specialist positions where they can use their training and education, rather than in more routine, highly directive activities such as traffic duty; (5) the need for lateral entry and transfers to other departments where experience in police work can be used along with education; (6) the need for more rapid promotions; (7) the opinion that college graduates should be given points on promotional tests or bonuses for education, similar to longevity pay; (8) the need for recognition that a college education gives status and legitimacy to the police profession and helps raise the profession's goals; (9) the feeling that the college-educated officer would help police organizations eliminate the spoils system; (10) a need to separate pay from rank; (11) the fear that as long as traditionalists are running police organizations, there will be no emphasis on a college education; (12) the suggestion of having different levels of police work, with a two-year college requirement for officers operating in the more routine functions like traffic direction, and a four-year college degree required for tasks where decision making and judgment are more critical; (13) the opinion that time spent working for degrees should be applied toward retirement; and (14) a request that mandatory retirement at an earlier age for all police officers be established as policy, so that "new blood" can get into the organization.

There were other suggestions, but these were the ones stated most often. In almost all cases, the interviewees felt that a person, whether college-educated or not, has to have sound judgment and a good moral background and character to be a good police officer. Even though the college graduates did indicate through interviews that there was a need to change traditional organizational procedures so that the college-graduate police officer could be retained and kept satisfied, they also acknowledged that work experience is important and that a college graduate should not automatically expect to be promoted because of educational achievement. It was felt, however, that the college graduate should be given special consideration in many areas.

Profiles. When the profiles of the two samples were compared, the differences were found to be these:

The non-college-graduate officer likes to follow a schedule and a daily routine; moves or counterattacks more rapidly when somebody acts toward him in a belligerent or aggressive manner; considers himself practical, sensible, with both feet on the ground, in contrast to being imaginative, ingenious, and having novel ideas; likes to work closely with his supervisor and have his supervisor make decisions for him rather than consulting with subordinates; would prefer the supervisor to keep a careful watch for deficient performances and to discipline those who fall below the standard; values himself according to how successfully he has conformed to the role requirements of the organization.

The college-graduate officer, on the other hand, is willing to experiment and try new things, as opposed to preferring the established and conventional way; prefers to assume a leadership role, and likes to direct and supervise the work of others; uses a step-by-step method for processing information and reaching decisions; likes to engage in work that provides a lot of excitement and variety, as opposed to work providing a stable and secure future; and finally, values himself by his achievement of the status symbols established by his culture.

Thus we can see that the college-graduate officer is much different from his noncollege counterpart, notably, in preferring less direction from supervisors and a more challenging job—preferences that may in fact cause problems for the organization, since so much police work involves routine activities. The noncollege officer more readily fits into the organization, likes to take direction, and is less of a problem for the organization, mainly because of his acceptance of directive leadership and the goals and objectives of the organization.

Discussion. The significance of these findings is that there are differences between college-graduate and noncollege officers even though they are performing the same function in the organization. The important question to be answered is, How can police organizations change so that the college-educated officer can be retained and employed most effectively without destroying the morale of the noncollege officer in this period of transition? Ultimately, all police positions will be filled by college graduates. In the interim period, however, it is vital to prevent a head-on collision spearheaded by college-graduate officers.[14]

[14]See the report by the National Advisory Commission on Criminal Justice Standards and Goals (Washington, D.C.: U.S. Government Printing Office, 1974).

During this transition period, methods of adaptation can be developed. For example, an engineering-psychology rather than a personnel-psychology approach to personnel development can be utilized.[15] The engineering-psychology approach attempts to alter the organization to adapt to the individual, whereas the personnel-psychology approach fits the individual into predetermined slots. Under engineering psychology, the college graduate can be given duties that stimulate his thinking and imagination, kept away from the more routine functions, and put in positions or specialized units where his education can best be utilized. On the other hand, the noncollege officer, who more readily follows the role requirements of the organization and appears to prefer the more directive and routine activities, can be used effectively in these areas.

The engineering-psychology form of adaptation would effect a change in the administrator's usual orientation to personnel and, in particular, the sergeant's method of relating to his supervisees. Adjusting and adapting to the different profiles of the two groups necessitates individualized supervision and the imaginative use of departmental resources to keep both the college-graduate and non-college-graduate officer motivated. The establishment of policies that encourage increased constructive feedback and more participation by police officers in planning, goal setting, and decision making should improve morale and motivation.

It also seems appropriate to consider actions that might be taken using the personnel-psychology approach. There is an apparent gap between the expectation and realization levels of college graduates in police departments in terms of job satisfaction and rewards. This gap can be narrowed by changing the organization (engineering-psychology approach) and thus raising realization levels, but also by lowering the expectation levels of college graduates and conditioning them for service in the organization (personnel-psychology approach).

As an example, many young people leaving high school immediately enter a law-enforcement program at a college or university. As part of the instruction, they are frequently exposed to case studies or hypothetical high-level police management problems and given solutions that may not translate intact to real-world situations; in some cases, important limiting variables may not be emphasized. Or the instructor may instill expectations of fast promotion and prompt use of high-level management skills, anticipations that will not necessarily be realized. Graduates of such programs may feel that they have the solutions to many of the departmental problems if someone would only listen, and they may become extremely frustrated when they are faced with slow promotions and what they perceive as indifference, if not hostility, when they propose solutions to management problems based on information gained in college courses.

[15]. Edgar Schein, *Organizational Psychology* (Englewood Cliffs, N.J.: Prentice-Hall, 1973).

An educational program in which a prospective police officer attends college for two years prior to employment and is encouraged to return to college when high-level management skills are more appropriate might tend to mitigate this frustration. Such a program should close the expectation/realization gap by not building up unrealistically high expectations at such an early point in a police career. But a combination of lowering expectations and raising realization levels of college-graduate police officers appears to offer the greatest probability of success.

The future of the college graduate in police organization is looking brighter. Many present officers are now attending college, too, and this should help them to empathize with other college-educated officers. The officers interviewed felt that a college degree is beneficial because it makes people more flexible, broadens their horizons, increases their mobility, and helps them to deal with such things as the dynamics of organizational and human behavior.

The officer with the college degree will have to be handled differently by both his sergeant and the department administration if he is to be retained and satisfied. The educated officer is more likely to question decisions that he perceives as illogical and counterproductive, he is not as job-security-conscious as the officer of the past, and his mobility is greatly increased—all of which will force sergeants to do a more effective job of imaginative supervision. The department administration will need to use appropriate job placement to maximize the performance of bright, productive college graduates.

Since a desire to continue educational activities was expressed by many officers, police organizations might alter some organizational policies and procedures to further such activities, perhaps by incentive plans, and to encourage their sergeants to be flexible with shift assignments, vacations, and pass days. At the same time, the organization has a right to expect certain benefits in return. For example, the armed forces grant leaves of absence to attend college, but the serviceman is obligated to stay in the service for a designated "utilization tour" after graduation. The same plan or an altered version could be used in police organizations.

CONCLUSIONS

Some of the problems police organizations have that are related to having officers that are college graduates are these:

1. Suspicion, mistrust, and stereotyping of college graduates is shown by their sergeants, their noncollege peers, and conflict results.
2. College graduates are dissatisfied with traditional police operations, and they question organizational policies and procedures.

3. Career advancement is not opening as fast as some college graduates feel it should, creating feelings of frustration and disenchantment, and often leading to resignations.

4. College graduates who have been trained almost exclusively in theory cannot always relate this theory to the practical requirements of the job. This problem is created largely by college curricula that are not relevant to practical police work. Graduates tend to place all the blame on the police organization rather than looking at the theory itself and coming to a compromise between theory and practice.

5. Nonacceptance of college graduates in some police organizations causes many interpersonal problems and strain, which can affect morale and the effective operation of the department.

On the other hand, there appear to be many positive aspects to having college graduates in police organizations, and the advantages outweigh the disadvantages. For example:

1. Statistics show higher completion rates of basic training programs by college graduates than by noncollege graduates.

2. Having brighter, more sensitive, and more intelligent police officers dealing with the public should serve to upgrade the image of law enforcement over a period of time.

3. The public will be served better by clearer-thinking and better-organized police officers.

4. College graduates will bring more broadminded and innovative thinking to bear, as opposed to the tradition-bound ways of performing various law-enforcement tasks.

5. Graduates will be able to work more effectively with certain segments of society —academicians and peers in the criminal justice system (social workers, judges, attorneys, etc.)—than lesser-educated police officers have done in the past. This should assist in closing the communication gap that has existed over the years between the police and their criminal justice peers in the system.

The police function and role have to be more rationally identified and defined, and then personnel must be given those tasks they can perform best. This means creating more career tracks for personnel with different skills, so that both the organization and the individual can benefit. The differences between college graduate officers and their noncollege counterparts should be recognized and dealt with by police organizations in order to retain the many capable officers who can make a great contribution not only to their own organization but to the law-enforcement profession.

The sergeant as first-line supervisor is the person who can facilitate the use of the college graduate's talents to the greatest benefit of the organization. The sergeant can also do a great deal to encourage college attendance and at the same time individualize supervision so that the competent noncollege-going officer is not disadvantaged. This will necessitate support from his administration; however, his middleman role will be made more difficult by an administration that says a college education is valued but tells the sergeant informally that there should be no special privileges, such as shift changes, for the college-going officer. In such a case, the sergeant is put in a double bind: His organization is on record as encouraging education but does nothing to facilitate it, and the supervisees expect special consideration because they accept the administration's public pronouncements. The sergeant will be caught in the middle between an unsympathetic administration and a frustrated and even hostile supervisee group.

SUMMARY

The sergeant, as middleman, feels the pulls and pressures from both the administration and subordinates. This was the most difficult aspect of the job as perceived by the 300 officers interviewed.

The interviewees were also asked if sergeants were effectively carrying out their responsibilities. The responses, listed in Table 3-7, range widely. One of the more interesting comments was from command, that some sergeants don't want to take responsibility. If this is the case, the administration should certainly find out why, or institute training programs that will help the sergeant be more effective. It may be that the sergeants do not know how to handle the conflicting role expectations of the administration and line officers—that is, how to adapt to their middleman role.

Having an adequate role definition for sergeants reduces some of the middleman conflict, but the nature of the job, of being the lowest department manager, will always create certain problems. For those departments that have no adequate role definition, one place to start is by developing one, so that there are reference points and guidelines to give the sergeant an orientation to fulfilling the requirements of a supervisor. An adequate role definition will also provide the administration with reference points with which to evaluate the sergeant.

Later chapters address the need for adequate role definitions for sergeants so that the advantages of their middleman role can be utilized and its problems mitigated.

TABLE 3-7

Are Sergeants Effectively Carrying Out Their Responsibilities?

Patrolmen	Detectives	Sergeants	Lieutenants	Command
Overall, they are doing the job, given their weak position in the department.	No—the administration wants a passive sergeant, the officers want an aggressive sergeant. He is just a super patrolman.	Sergeants are doing the job.	Sergeants are performing effectively.	The majority are.
No—the administration wants the sergeants to be tougher, the officers want more guidance and concern.	Officers think sergeants are doing the job.	Yes, from the officers' standpoint, but not from the administration viewpoint.	In general, they are, but they are fearful they will get their heads chopped off if they make a mistake.	Half are and half aren't.
The sergeants are too busy "covering their posteriors" with the administration.	The administration doesn't give the sergeant enough latitude.	Most of the sergeants are doing the job.	Sergeants are not doing the job.	Some sergeants don't want to take responsibility.
The administration thinks they are, the officers feel they aren't.	There are too many young inexperienced sergeants.	Half do and half don't.	They are not doing the job because the administration won't let them.	
They do only what they have to, so they don't make mistakes.	The department should get back to having working sergeants.	Sergeants are not doing the job.	Most officers in the department, except captains and above, think the sergeants are doing the job.	
They cannot do a good job under the circumstances.	Sergeants are too "picky."	Yes, from the administration's standpoint, but no, from the officers' viewpoint.		
	The younger officers rely too much on sergeants.			

Note: Responses are listed in the order of importance as stated by the particular group of respondents.

85

CHAPTER FOUR

The Sergeant as Leader

LEADERSHIP: AN OVERVIEW

In reviewing the literature on leadership, one soon realizes that there are as many definitions of leadership as there are leaders in an organization. Brown defines leadership in relation to the animal world and its hierarchical structure:

> The development of the individual leader in human organization stems from the hierarchical pattern sought by all closed groups. The examples of the tendency to hierarchical relationships in animals are well known. A wolf pack has its leader, and so does a herd of cattle, a pride of lions, or a flock of chickens. The process of finding the leader may involve a long series of shifting interrelationships where one individual challenges all others to establish his rank. In other situations the leader may compete with only a few to attain top status. In human society every conceivable way of attaining and holding leadership is known. Whatever the method and no matter how civilized the conditions, the need for leadership and the hierarchical approach to assuring it remain fundamental to the dynamics of organized endeavor.[1]

Leadership, in this context, emerges because in every group there is the tendency to order relationships. Furthermore, the most influential leader

[1]J. Douglas Brown, *The Human Nature of Organization* (New York: AMACOM, a division of American Management Associations, 1973), p. 34.

may not emerge quickly. There can be a long process of shifting relationships and the exchanging of steps in the hierarchical ladder. Leadership is not always permanent; the struggle for dominance is continuous and often brutal in both human and animal groups.

Berne says:

> There are three kinds of leadership, corresponding to the three aspects of the group structure. The responsible leader is the front man, the man who fills the role of leader in the organizational structure. The effective leader, who makes the actual decisions, may or may not have a role in the organizational structure. He may be the man in the back room, but he is the most important person in the individual structure. The psychological leader is the one who is most powerful in the private structures of the members and occupies the leadership slot in their group. All three types of leadership may be invested in the same individual, but there are all sorts of combinations.[2]

Thus, Berne cites three different kinds of leaders. In our discussion, we single out two—formal and informal leaders. The formal leader has the designation and title bestowed on him by the organization but may not necessarily have influence with his subordinates. A police officer may have the formal rank of sergeant but command little respect from his supervises. They may not even ask for his advice but may seek help from one of the experienced patrol officers, who would then be the informal leader.

Bellows feels that leadership involves behavior that is "characterized by both concern for others and the tendency to initiate structure or bring order into a situation by planning and arranging the situation so the work can go forward in a shared direction. This is leadership."[3] If the formal leader can show concern for his supervisees and at the same time get the job done via planning, coordinating, and organizing the work, then this person would be considered the informal as well as the formal leader. In Berne's terms, he would be a combination of the effective, responsible, and psychological leaders.

In regard to the distinction between the formal and informal leaders, or the responsible and psychological leaders, several theorists have pointed out that leadership is not necessarily synonomous with management or supervision:

> Leadership involves an interaction between persons involving an influence attempt by one over the other(s) with certain behavioral end results. It is one of the mechanisms called upon to serve the management function of motivating

[2]Eric Berne, *The Structure and Dynamics of Organizations and Groups* (Philadelphia: Lippincott, 1963), p. 105. (*Note:* Some of the research on leadership was collected by Charles Crouch.)
[3]Roger Bellows, *Creative Leadership* (Englewood Cliffs, N.J.: Prentice-Hall, 1959), p. 299.

a consistently acceptable level of effort toward the achievement of organizational objectives. The manager then is responsible for utilizing leadership in order to achieve organizational effectiveness.[4]

Just as leadership is a tool to be used by the formal manager, so too does the manager-leader have to have the support of his subordinates to optimize management objectives. It does little good for the sergeant as leader to give commands in a civil-disorder situation if no one is going to follow him. Hence leadership is:

> . . . an interaction between persons in which one presents information of a sort and in such a manner that the other becomes convinced that his outcomes will be improved if he behaves in the manner suggested or desired.
>
> Thus, leadership is defined in an organizational context in terms of techniques that will produce compliance on the part of subordinates without producing resistance. Note that in the definition, the influence recipient has the option of deciding whether or not to comply without incurring coercive penalties. It depends on the leader's competence at the particular task, and his ability to understand his subordinates in order to provide convincing evidence of the desirability of the task he seeks to accomplish.[5]

To even further complicate the defining of leadership, Barnard says that leadership is often confused with preeminence or extraordinary usefulness. After attending a conference where the subject of educational leadership was being discussed, he observed:

> Leadership was confused with preeminence or extraordinary usefulness both by speakers and by audience. In their view a leading writer, artist, pianist, mathematician, or scientist exemplifies leadership substantially as does an executive or leader of an organization. No one appeared to be aware of the double meaning of "leadership" and its implications for the discussion of the subject of preparing "leaders." Among the meanings of the verb "to lead" we may say that one is: "to excel, to be in advance, to be preeminent"; and another is "to guide others, to govern their activities, to be head of an organization or some part of it, to hold command."[6]

Thus, in attempting to define leadership, we have seen that, as Barnard states, there can be two meanings to the verb *to lead;* that effective leadership is dependent on the leader's ability to convince his subordinates that they

[4]James Gibson, John Ivancevich, and James Donnelly, Jr., *Organizations, Structures, Processes and Behavior* (Dallas: Business Publications, Inc., 1973), p. 285.
[5]Ibid., p. 290.
[6]Chester Barnard, *Organization and Management* (Cambridge, Mass.: Harvard University Press, 1956), p. 81.

should follow and that leadership is not synonymous with a formal title like manager; that there are various kinds of leaders—formal and informal, responsible and psychological; and finally, that the struggle for leadership in the hierarchy is dynamic and can be observed in both the animal kingdom and human interactions.

THEORIES AND TYPES OF LEADERSHIP

Basil summarizes the three most prevalent ways of defining leadership: the *great-man* theory, the *traitist* theory, and the *situational* theory:

> Three clearly definable schools of leadership theory have been in vogue at one time or another. In its simplest form, the great-man theory of history says that a man with great leadership ability arrives on the scene of action and does great deeds. This theory was used to explain the advent of Charlemagne in the Dark Ages. Before he gained power, there had been no great organization of states in Europe, and after his death the Dark Ages closed in again.
>
> The traitist theory of leadership is somewhat akin to the great-man theory. It holds that the possession of certain traits permits certain men to gain positions of leadership. The traitist approach is common in business today, and many articles are written which attest to the traits required for leadership.
>
> The third generally accepted leadership theory might be termed situational. This theory is an outgrowth of the behavioral scientists' change in thought about environmental or behavioral theories. In its simplest form, the situational theory holds that the situation calls forth the appropriate leader. This theory accepts the findings of the group dynamics experts, who contend that any number of leaders exist in a group, and that the group will choose a particular type of leader to fit the situation.[7]

Great-Man Theory

Bellows is even more specific in his discussion of the great-man theory of leadership. He says there are three distinct ways to measure the import of the "great man": (1) the person's ability to influence the completion of tasks, (2) the number of acts that can be accomplished in a designated period of time, and (3) the amount of support he gets from his followers.[8]

All three theories of leadership have been criticized. The great-man theory is considered by many to be an oversimplification of the leadership process, in that leaders are not born and then suddenly, by providence, arrive on the scene and "save" the group they end up leading. There continues to

[7]Douglas Basil, *Leadership Skills for Executive Action* (New York: American Management Association, 1971), pp. 54–55.
[8]Bellows, *Creative Leadership*, p. 295.

be support for the great-man theory, however, and many believe that a person cannot be trained or educated to be a leader if he does not have the basic ingredients for leadership in the first place.

> This idea implies that the emerging human personality can be molded and shaped according to any psychological specifications. Genetic research and experimental psychology dispute this. Certain fundamental personality factors are built in. Also, by the time a man is ready for management responsibility, experience has already forged his basic attitudes, habits, and values. While further development is always possible, major psychological changes will not take place. A young manager may become wiser, but his intelligence pattern is already set. He can be taught certain skills that leaders possess but no one can teach him to integrate and apply those skills to achieve leadership performance.[9]

Traitist Theory

Those who ascribe to the traitist approach list the following kinds of traits as necessary for the effective assertion of leadership:

> Capacity (intelligence, alertness, verbal facility, originality, judgment). Achievement (scholarship, knowledge, athletic accomplishments). Responsibility (activity, sociability, cooperation, adaptability, humor). Status (socio-economic position, popularity).[10]

The traitist approach, which is similar to the great-man theory, has been attacked because although certain traits, like intelligence and aggressiveness, may be helpful in one group, they can be overwhelming in another, and the person may be rejected for those very characteristics that are supposed to be positive leadership traits.

> The traitist theory makes no clear-cut distinction between innate and acquired traits; both intelligence and aggressiveness are listed as desirable. However, aggressiveness certainly can be acquired, but intelligence is generally considered to be innate.
>
> Furthermore, the traitist theory holds implicitly that the leader, because he possesses certain traits, will automatically be able to exercise leadership. This belief assumes an essentially static situation, but human relations are dynamic, with constantly changing group relationships and group demands. One situa-

---

[9]Tom Comella, "Call to Leadership," *Automation,* (Cleveland: Penton Publishing Co., 1967). [Found in Paul Preston and Thomas W. Zimmerer, *Management for Supervisors,* (Englewood Cliffs, N.J.: Prentice-Hall, 1978, p. 158–170).]

[10]Ralph M. Stogdill, "Personal Factors Associated with Leadership: A Survey of the Literature," *The Journal of Psychology,* XXV (1948), 35–71; reprinted in Bellows, *Creative Leadership,* p. 293.

tion may demand aggressiveness in the leader, while another situation with the same group may require him to be reticent and unassuming.[11]

Situational Theory

Stogdill and others, however, have added the additional variable of *situation* when discussing the necessary traits of an effective leader. Even though there are certain people who have the traits to lead under almost any kind of conditions and others "who could not lead a troop of hungry Girl Scouts to a hamburger stand,"[12] situation plays a critical factor in the leadership process:

> A wide variety of causes may propel a man into a leadership position, and many of these causes are totally unrelated to personality attributes. One of the surest ways of becoming company president is to come from a family which owns the company. Another is to have unusual technical skills and to be available at the right time. Furthermore, men tend to rise to leadership positions as they gain in age and experience. This means that younger or less experienced men with leadership potential may remain non-leaders until they have gained the necessary technical qualifications or experience necessary to assume leadership positions. Leadership traits, if they exist, would, therefore, be masked by many effects, and hence difficult to identify.[13]

A realistic way of viewing leadership, then, is that even though certain personality traits like intelligence, judgment, and alertness may be essential, the situation also plays an important part most of the time. When the person is not in the "right situation, traits like height, weight, appearance, self-control, dominance, surgency (alertness, cheerfulness, generosity) and intelligence have little relationship to leadership."[14]

Behaviorist Theory

Behaviorists take an all-inclusive approach; included in their definition of leadership are the traits and attitudes of the leader, the situation, the tasks to be performed, and the expectations of the group. Smith and Wakeley have developed an illustration, shown in Table 4-1, to show leadership assumptions that range from the great-man theory to the behaviorist approach.

[11]Basil, *Leadership Skills,* p. 55.
[12]Fred E. Fiedler, "Leadership and Leadership Effectiveness Traits," in Luigi Petrullo and Bernard M. Bass, *Leadership and Interpersonal Behavior* (New York: Holt, Rinehart & Winston, 1961), p. 180.
[13]Ibid., p. 180.
[14]Phillip B. Applewhite, *Organizational Behavior* (Englewood Cliffs, N.J.: Prentice-Hall, Inc., 1965), p. 114.

TABLE 4-1

Theories of Leadership

The Great-Man Theory

Leadership ability depends on a leadership trait or the specific combination of a few traits. In the extreme view, people either have leadership or they do not. The more moderate view would be that there is a continuum of leadership ability.

Low leadership ⊢————————————————⊣ High leadership
ability .... ability

Behavioral Theory

Leadership depends on the attitudes a person has about his job and how these attitudes fit the expectations of the group of followers. The two most important areas of attitudes are attitudes toward the people in the work group and attitudes toward the tasks the work group is supposed to accomplish.

Initiating Structure

High concern with tasks

Consideration
Low concern ————————|———————— High concern
with people .... with people

Low concern with tasks

Source: Henry Clay Smith and John H. Wakeley, *Psychology of Industrial Behavior*, 3rd ed. (New York: McGraw-Hill, 1972), p. 134.

Besides the factors listed above, the behaviorist approach also views performance and the results obtained as a necessary ingredient of leadership. Comella says that leadership

> . . . is an exceptional quality of personality characterized by specific attitudes, talents, and abilities which combine to produce extraordinary performance in a given endeavor. The performance is measured by results. The results are interpreted in terms of goals. It is this performance—not status or position—which will identify leaders of the future.[15]

[15]Comella, "Call to Leadership," p. 168.

In too many organizations, police departments included, the people promoted to leadership positions are those who are thought to have the traits to lead because of their presence, physical stature, or verbosity. But once in the leadership position, such people often do not have the attitudes or capabilities to influence and motivate their subordinates. As a result, their mode of operation begins to include extreme manipulation, threats, deals, patronage, and even outright lying.

The problem can be compounded in a police department where high-ranking commanders assume that the macho image is the most important characteristic of first-line supervisors. "Don't show emotion or weakness, or your men will take advantage of you," one chief was overheard saying to a new group of sergeants. (This same chief, who himself was 6'4" tall, would not promote anyone to a supervisory position who was less than 6 feet tall or did not have a physique like Mr. America.) Supervisors in this type of organization erroneously assume that they are exhibiting leadership qualities by constantly making the point to subordinates that they are in charge. The mere fact that the organization has given them the formal designation of supervisor makes them feel they will be influential in all their interactions with their subordinates.

However, leadership involves many factors, some relating to the traits of the leader and some to the situation, but mainly, as behaviorists emphasize, the quality depends on a combination of interacting variables ranging from the attitude of the leader toward his subordinates to the attitude of the group toward the tasks it is expected to perform.

As mentioned earlier, managing and supervising are not synonymous with leadership, and the formal title does not always produce results. (For the present purposes, *manager, administrator,* and *supervisor* are here used interchangeably.) Jennings distinguished between an administrator and a leader by saying that "the administrator is one who fits into the organization and is commanded by it, and the leader is, of course, one who gives direction and character to that organization and represents a focal point of it."[16]

Applewhite differentiates betweeen leadership and supervision:

> Supervision is concerned with acts issued from a formal or appointed position in the organization by someone with authority, the "legal" right to act. "Legal" here means issued officially by the organization. Leadership, on the other hand, concerns acts issued from a formal or informal position in the organization by someone with power, the ability to act, which implies nothing about the legal right.
>
> A revolutionary in a country does not have authority, a "legal" right to take

[16]Eugene E. Jennings, *An Anatomy of Leadership: Princes, Heroes, and Supermen* (New York: Harper & Row, 1960), p. 186.

up arms against the government, but he can have the power or ability to do so. Of course, both supervision and leadership, as concepts, may occur together and, in fact, it would be desirable for a supervisor to have "leadership"—that is, to have the ability to initiate group goals within the organizational structure.[17]

Rice, while identifying the difference between the manager and the leader, sees overlap:

> A leader has to be able to carry his followers with him, inspire them, make decisions on their behalf, with or without their collaboration, and communicate the decisions to others; he has to be able to act in ways that will not only further task performance but enlist the cooperation of his followers by mobilizing the appropriate basic assumption. A manager has to get the best results out of the resources he has available or can make available—money, time, materials, and people. Both leaders and managers have to deal with different numbers of followers and subordinates, extending all the way from the small, intimate face-to-face group of immediate colleagues to extended commands and even crowds.
>
> To be successful, a manager has to display qualities of leadership and use techniques of management appropriate to the tasks of the group he is managing. Nevertheless, some leaders are clearly better at inspiring their followers and at leading institutions than they are at managing them; some managers are better managers, in the sense that they apply management techniques effectively, than they are inspirational leaders.[18]

Rice seems to be saying that leadership is related to the traits of the person leading. The most effective leader would be the one who combines his leadership skills with proper managerial techniques. Management techniques can be taught, and through experience, the manager will become astute at selecting the appropriate technique for the situation, thus performing adequately even though he does not have inspirational qualities that produce "blind obedience."

Aside from his qualities and training, the leader-manager is constantly grappling with the conflict between what he is actually doing and what he should be doing. This relates to his "middleman" role.

> Since organizations are usually hierarchically structured, with members situated at various levels of responsibility and authority, the leader is placed in a position, at whatever level he occupies, where he is confronted with several sets of demands and expectations. These come from both superiors and subordinates and from persons who are on the same organization level as himself. In

[17] Applewhite, *Organizational Behavior*, p. 111.
[18] A. K. Rice, *Learning for Leadership* (London: Tavistock Publications, 1965), p. 20.

addition, he holds his own expectations concerning appropriate behavior for the position which he occupies. To the extent that these expectations are contradictory, which they often are, the leader's behavior cannot possibly satisfy the expectations of all. Nevertheless, the responsibilities of his position require him to make decisions. Because of the pressures of the demands made upon him, what the leader does may not correspond to what he believes he "ought to do." Individuals in leadership positions thus frequently recognize the discrepancy between what they are doing and what they believe they should do.[19]

In the final analysis, there is no one definition of leadership that is applicable in all situations and under all conditions and circumstances. Although personality traits do play a part, situational factors determine whether the leader will be allowed by the group to lead; the formally designated person is not always the leader; and leadership is dynamic and can change in accordance with the task to be performed. Behaviorists recognize the many factors involved in the leadership process and the importance of their interactive effect in different situations.

ASPECTS OF EFFECTIVE LEADERSHIP

Sergeants as leaders, although they have many different personality traits, must all accomplish certain common tasks, and therefore they must have in common certain aspects of leadership.

The effective sergeant may not have been born with genes that produce a 6'4" physical frame or a voice that can be heard six blocks away, but still has qualities that will contribute to motivating officers and accomplishing goals. This section of the chapter will discuss some of these qualities. It is not expected that a sergeant would possess all the qualities mentioned, or that even if he did, the supervisory job would be automatically accomplished. As pointed out earlier, situational factors and interacting variables—such as the personalities of his supervisees, the orientation of his superiors, and the task to be done—play an important part.

The effective sergeant-leader is first of all a person who has his head "screwed on straight"—knows his strengths and weaknesses and uses his attributes to the best advantage in the supervisory process. He has a positive feeling about himself and, although not an egotist, projects an air of *self-confidence.* Moment and Zalesnik found in their studies of successful middle- and upper-management leaders that they had obvious high self-esteem. They were also "found to be spontaneous, integrated and varied in their communi-

[19]Ralph M. Stogdill, Ellis L. Scott, and William E. Jaynes, *Leadership and Role Expectations* (Columbus: Bureau of Research, Ohio State University, 1956), p. 7.

cation with others; they had confidence in themselves, could defend a position while remaining flexible in attitude, and could relate well in general to others. They were viewed by their associates as leaders."[20]

Wilson feels that the effective leader-supervisor not only needs self-confidence but has to act in a responsible fashion to instill confidence in his subordinates. In order to do this, he has to deal successfully with any situation that may develop and must have "(1) an ability to display his self-confidence in a natural and acceptable manner; (2) knowledge and skill in his own job and in the work of his subordinates; (3) an ability and willingness to make decisions promptly but not hastily; (4) an insistence on having all the facts before taking action; (5) soundness of judgment; (6) a willingness and ability to accept responsibility and especially to accept liability for failures without passing the blame on to subordinates; (7) an ability to maintain poise (mentally, physically, and emotionally) under criticism and attack; (8) the initiative to investigate unsatisfactory conditions and the courage to take corrective action; (9) absence of prejudice, especially in reference to race, politics, religion and labor; (10) unquestioned personal integrity and insistence that the department be free of graft, including petty handouts; (11) uncompromising attitude toward crime and corruption, but recognizing the necessity for correct timing in dealing with outside forces over which he exercises no direct control; (12) energy and a willingness and ability to work hard; (13) physical and emotional strength to withstand the strain of demands on his time, energy and patience."[21]

The effective leader is also a good *communicator*. (Later sections of this chapter will be devoted to the communication process.) Almost every facet of the supervisor-leader role involves communication—guiding, directing, coordinating, giving feedback on performance, interpreting, translating and transmitting policies, and counseling. Much communication by the leader extends beyond merely telling people what to do:

> The first error lies in assuming that communication is, essentially, telling others what we mean, think, or feel. Communication certainly does involve self-expression, but it also involves being able to understand what others mean, what they think or feel. . . .
>
> A leader learns how his audience ("audience" is used in the broad sense here, meaning any person or group to whom one attempts to communicate) reacts and feels by watching the expressions on their faces, by noting what they do (or don't do) as they listen to him or read his communication, and by listening to their tones of expression and gestures while they talk. He tries to spend as much time as possible in listening, for it is through listening to people with as

[20]John V. Gilmore, *The Productive Personality* (San Francisco: Albion Publishing Co., 1974), pp. 37–39.

[21]O. W. Wilson, *Police Administration,* 2nd ed. (New York: McGraw-Hill, 1972), p. 10.

much sensitivity and perception as one can muster that one gains an understanding of the ways in which they see things, the frames of reference into which they fit all that they hear and see.[22]

The ability of the leader to articulate clearly and concisely is directly related to the amount of power, status, and influence he will have with his supervisees:

> Perceptions of leadership, status, and power depend heavily upon communication. People will rate a position in a scale of leadership, status, or power at least partly in accordance with information they have about that position. The control of information, therefore, and the management of impressions, become important techniques in the struggle for authority, status, and power.[23]

Regardless of the leader's personality traits or his formal title in the organization, he will have little effect if he is not perceived to have at least some power. The sergeant whose department does not allow him input into departmental policy formulation or who is merely perceived as a "super patrol officer" will have little power, a fact that can directly affect his job as a supervisor:

> If the supervisor has *little* power or influence, then neither his helpful behavior nor his restraining behavior will have much concrete effect on the employees. He cannot help them to get what they are after or restrain them substantially. Neither behavior will have any marked effect on their satisfaction. In fact, the more helpful he tries to be, the more we might expect to find some increase in dissatisfaction, because employees' hopes will have been aroused, only to be disappointed.[24]

The effective leader is also *considerate* of his supervisees, able to *empathize* with them, support them when appropriate, and correct their behavior when need be. Numerous studies have shown that the considerate leader who takes a personal interest in his supervisees will have the best results:

> The subordinates of considerate supervisors strongly agree with statements like the following about their superiors:
> He sees that a person is rewarded for a job well done.
> He makes those in the group feel at ease when talking to him.

[22]Henry Clay Lindgren, *Effective Leadership in Human Relations* (New York: Hermitage House, 1954), pp. 153, 163.
[23]Victor A. Thompson, "The Reality of Appearance," in James David Barber, *Political Leadership in American Government* (Boston: Little, Brown, 1964), p. 349.
[24]C. G. Browne and Thomas S. Cohn, *The Study of Leadership* (Danville, Ill.: The Interstate, 1958), p. 191.

He backs up his men in their actions.

The workmen under an inconsiderate leader strongly agree with statements like the following:
He refuses to give in when people disagree with him.
He changes the duties of people without first talking to them.
He doesn't give credit when credit is due.[25]

As mentioned in Chapter 3, a police department that does not have a clear conception of how an effective semimilitary organization operates will often be "supermacho" in its orientation, projecting this not only in its attitudes in the community, but also in the attitudes of the first-line supervisors toward their subordinates. The statements above about inconsiderate leaders will be common in such a department, because, as one sergeant stated, "We know what's best for our people, and many of them are like little kids that need to be taken care of and told what to do." When the supervisor takes an interest in his supervisees and is willing to listen to them, the work environment will be more conducive to effective dialogue and communication. The supervisor's leadership qualities will be felt by the supervisees; they will not have to be constantly reinforced by bragging, degrading subordinates, and strutting around like a banty rooster.

A sergeant who has adequate ego strength, feels good about himself and is competent, will not have to be aloof, withdrawn, and inconsiderate. His effectiveness as a leader will be the result of his ability to empathize with his people. The leader, whether formal or informal, should be a reflection and representative of both the organization he is a part of and the group that he is supervising:

> In general, groups choose as leaders those persons who represent their own superegos, or ideal selves; the leader is selected as a model with whom they wish to identify.
>
> These observations are supported by a neatly designed experiment by Chowdhry and Newcomb (1952), which showed that the person chosen as a leader is one whom the group perceives as having the ability to judge their own opinions on the particular issues which are relevant to them. In other words, leaders are chosen partly because of their recognized quality of empathy, or sensitivity to the feelings of the others in the group. The findings also indicated that, in addition to a sense of fairness and good judgment, the leader must demonstrate a specific ability to deal with the problems of that particular group; thus his knowledge or competence must be in the area that is central to its concerns. The leader, if he is to lead effectively, must be able to communicate his ideas clearly and easily to others. Jennings (1943) observed that leaders

[25]Henry Clay Smith and John H. Wakeley, *Psychology of Industrial Behavior,* 3rd ed. (New York: McGraw-Hill, 1977), p. 121.

seem able to establish rapport quickly and effectively with a wide range of other personalities. Another characteristic of leaders, then, is friendliness, which is also an expression of empathy.[26]

Usually, the leader will attempt via the communication process to *persuade* his supervisees to perform the tasks required for goal achievement:

> Ability permits the leader to serve as an indirect or secondary reinforcer of the behavior of others. He cues the other members concerning how they may obtain their goals. This is persuasion. If B is persuaded by A's suggestion or secondary reinforcement of the responses leading to goal attainment, B will accept A's suggestions both publicly and privately. If B is coerced by the direct reinforcement power of A, he is likely to accept publicly A's suggestions, although not necessarily be committed privately to them.[27]

In the process of persuasion, the leader usually has a specific goal in mind and directs the energies of the group so the problem can be solved. Even though he is ego-involved, he will maintain objectivity.[28] In fact, it has been hypothesized that one of the goal-directed leader's main functions is to maintain the group as a unit[29] and use whatever imaginative means are available to *motivate* it. Motivation is not a simple process; a conscious effort must be made by the supervisor-leader to influence and motivate his people. He cannot merely rely upon the power and status of his formal position, or even expect that all the workers will be motivated by the same factors:

> The manager cannot shrug off his motivational responsibilities by demanding that the subordinate be a self-starter or self-motivator. Rather, he must recognize realistically that the individual's goals are not necessarily related to those of the organization. It is the responsibility of the manager to provide mutual goals or to coordinate the personal and institutional goals through the process of motivating his subordinates.[30]

An important element in the process of motivating is allowing members of the group to *participate,* so that they feel a part of the problem-solving process. *Delegating* responsibility is closely akin to participation; it induces not only a feeling of being a part of the group, but the realization that the leader has confidence in them and their ability to produce. Allowing participation

[26]Gilmore, *The Productive Personality,* p. 34.

[27]Bernard M. Bass, *Leadership, Psychology and Organizational Behavior* (New York: Harper & Row, 1960), p. 163.

[28]Louis Cheskin, *Problem-Directed Men* (Indianapolis: Bobbs-Merrill, 1964), p. 75.

[29]John K. Hemphill, *Situational Factors in Leadership* (Columbus: Bureau of Educational Research, Ohio State University, 1949), p. 58.

[30]Basil, *Leadership Skills,* p. 53.

by the line officers and delegating responsibility will help coalesce individual and group goals so that they are directed at common departmental ends, thus making the sergeant's job easier:

> The need for close supervision may be reduced, and less disciplinary action may be called for. Subordinates who have participated in the process leading toward a determination of matters directly affecting them may have a greater sense of responsibility with respect to the performance of their assigned tasks and may be more willing to accept the authority of their superiors. All managers possess a given amount of formal authority delegated to them by their superiors. But formal authority is not necessarily the equivalent of effective authority. The real source of the authority possessed by an individual lies in the acceptance of its exercise by those who are subject to it. It is the subordinates of an individual who determine the authority which he may wield. Formal authority is, in effect, nominal authority. It becomes real only when it is accepted. Thus, to be effective, formal authority must coincide with authority determined by its acceptance. The latter defines the useful limits of the former. The use of participation as a managerial device may result in a widening of these limits, reducing the amount of resistance to the exercise of formal authority and increasing the positive responses of subordinates to managerial directives.[31]

By knowing the strengths and weaknesses of his supervisees, the sergeant can work with their individual skills and help correct their weaknesses. In this way he is doing more than contributing to the department's goals; he is helping to *develop* his supervisees.[32]

But goal achievement requires more than merely knowing the individual strength and weaknesses of one's supervisees. The sergeant has to meld the individuals into a working, coordinated group. This requires the *resolving of role conflicts:*

> Resolving role conflicts, both his own and those of others, appears to be one of the major challenges of leadership. The leader's own accomplishments are dependent upon the role expectations and the role behavior of others. Some members may be limited in capacity to discharge their responsibilities, while others who are highly skilled in the techniques of their responsibilities are limited in capacity to interact with others. Each member carries into the organization his past experience, his needs, ideals, personal goals, and commitments to other organizations which may modify and determine his capacity for participation. Within the constellation of conflicting expectations presented by the members, the leader is confronted with the

[31]Robert Tannenbaum, Irving R. Wechsler, and Fred Massarik, *Leadership and Organization: A Behavioral Science Approach* (New York: McGraw-Hill, 1961), p. 94.
[32]Basil, *Leadership Skills,* p. 51.

problem of coordinating the efforts of all toward the attainment of the goals of the organization.[33]

This section has briefly described some of the aspects of effective leadership that should be a part of the behavior of the police sergeant. Not all sergeants will necessarily have these attributes, nor will they be manifested in the same way in all situations. They are, however, important guidelines to be aware of if the sergeant is going to be effective and able to get the job done.

THE INEFFECTIVE LEADER AND HIS REACTIONS

Even though groups look for leaders, both formal and informal, the person who has assumed the leadership role can very quickly become involved in conflict with his "followers." He cannot satisfy all members of the group—not to mention his superiors. As Shortle has astutely pointed out, "We want persons in leadership roles, and yet we do not want to place limitations upon ourselves to submit to leadership."[34]

Not only does the group comprise many different kinds of people, often with differing orientations, but the dynamics of groups are always changing, so the group leader, even if he has the majority's support, will still have problems trying to lead and supervise their activities. Some officers, when promoted to sergeant, feel that the new role will automatically be translated into action, but this is not the case; the sergeant has to work at being successful.

Compounding the supervision-leadership problem of never being able to satisfy all supervisees is the fact that the sergeant has to be mentally healthy, because "the most important instrument with which the leader has to work is himself—his own personality and the impression which he makes on other people."[35]

Overriding anxiety and internal conflicts will deplete the sergeant of much of the energy he needs to be an effective supervisor-leader. Thus, the sergeant's conflicts will be both external and internal.[36] The sergeant who has extensive inner conflicts will usually try to overcompensate for his real or imagined inadequacies by placing "greater emphasis on the use of rationality, direction, control, rewards, and penalties. In practice this tends to mean that they begin to check on other people's work not only to see if it's done, but

---

[33]Stogdill, Scott, and Jaynes, *Leadership and Role Expectations*, p. 8.

[34]Ibid., p. 5.

[35]Lewis A. Dexter, "Some Strategic Considerations in Innovating Leadership," in *Studies in Leadership*, ed. Alvin W. Gouldner (New York: Harper & Row, 1950), p. 592.

[36]Abraham Zalesnik, *Human Dilemmas in Leadership* (New York: Harper & Row, 1966), p. 40.

also how it was accomplished."[37] This constitutes oversupervision. Obviously, a sergeant who oversupervises is not very effective in fulfilling the necessary aspects of leadership discussed in the last section (delegating, motivating, participating, and so on).

One of the characteristics of many leaders is *manipulation.* Manipulation, although realistically acknowledged as a part of the leadership process, can be counterproductive if it becomes the primary means by which the sergeant motivates his officers, and it is a very negative reaction of the ineffective leader.

Dyer has developed typologies of the manipulative leader. He calls them the illusionary democratic leader, the benevolent autocrat, the pseudofamily, the managerial facade, the phony proposer, the public praiser, and the impotent committee.[38] Here are his definitions of these types, with pertinent examples relating to the manipulative sergeant.

The *Illusionary Democratic Leader* pretends to be including input from the group in his decisions, but he has already made up his mind what he is going to do. This approach is typified by the sergeant who, wanting his officers to believe he is democratic, encourages participation—but accepts only those comments and suggestions that coincide with his own orientation and rejects those that don't fit his predetermined decision.

The *Benevolent Autocrat* uses his supposed vast experience and fatherly role to tell his supervisee what to do. This is the sergeant who has "been around" and "knows what is best" for his officers. "You may not agree with what I am doing at the moment, but ultimately you will realize that it is for your own good," was a comment heard often from a stoic, classically oriented sergeant who resented his younger officers' acting independently.

The *Pseudofamily*-oriented leader tells individual group members that if they work hard and produce, they will be accepted by the group. The manipulative sergeant who uses this approach will often tell outright lies to his officers in individual face-to-face contacts. For example, on separate occasions and in private, he will tell the officer, "If you keep your nose clean and do what you are told, I will push you for promotion, and someday you will be running the unit." What the officer doesn't know is that this same story has been told to most of the others in order to get their compliance. Obviously, this form of manipulation, like the others, usually works for only a short period of time. When the sergeant's cover is broken, officers transfer out of the unit, new officers transfer in, and the manipulative game starts all over again.

---

[37]Chris Argyris and Roger Harrison, *Interpersonal Competence and Organizational Effectiveness* (Homewood, Ill.: Dorsey, 1962), p. 47.

[38]William Dyer, *The Sensitive Manipulator* (Provo, Utah: Brigham Young University Press, 1972), pp. 104–8.

The *Managerial Facade* leadership approach has the leader gathering his supervisee "friends" together informally prior to the group pseudo-decision-making meeting. A sergeant who was in charge of an intelligence unit used the technique of first having an informal, social get-together with his "trusted" supervisees to tell them his strategies. Then he would call his formal unit meeting and have those strategies suggested by the planted officers, so that the group would feel that the ideas had come from their peers rather than the administration, represented by their sergeant.

Dyer describes the *Phony Proposer* leadership style as similar to the style above, in that the strategies for problem solving have been worked out prior to the formal meeting; thus, when the sergeant does make a proposal, it has already been cleared through his cronies, so support is expected and predictable at the formal meeting.

The *Public Praiser* is an autocrat in disguise. He constantly praises his people in public but uses and abuses them in private. He is the type of sergeant who uses force and threats to get compliance, but, because his public posture is so much different, anything critical his intimidated supervisees say in public is not believed. In addition, they like the public praise, and this neutralizes some of their hostility toward the sergeant and reduces the chances that they will band together to "blow the whistle" on their deceitful, coercive leader.

In the *Impotent Committee* leadership approach, the sergeant would attempt to "divide and conquer" his supervisees—say, by putting them on separate committees to discuss various aspects of team policing. The members of each committee would then discuss their particular aspect of it with their sergeant. They are instructed, however, not to discuss their findings with officers on other committees because of the "sensitive nature" of the topic. The sergeant and his superiors then use what fits their purposes and eliminate what does not. When members of a committee complain that they wasted their time because their recommendations were not included in the final report, the sergeant says, "Even though yours were not used, we did use the recommendations of the other committees, and hence the participatory process of which you were a part was useful and successful."

These approaches of the manipulative leader may not be used in their purest form, says Dyer, and a combination of them may be used by one leader. The manipulative sergeant may use them for a variety of reasons: He may be incompetent and incapable of motivating his people and achieving results in more acceptable ways, or he may be getting so much pressure from his superiors to get things done their way that he uses manipulation for his own survival in the organization. In other cases, the sergeant may be in collusion with his superiors to manipulate his officers as a means of pleasing his supervisors so that he will be promoted or receive other organizational rewards.

Although manipulation of supervisees by supervisors is a realistic fact of life and not usually harmful in small doses, the sergeant for whom it is the sole method of relating to his supervisees will gain no more than short-term results; in the long run, he will usually be "pegged" and his techniques will be neutralized and rejected, because *trust* is the basis of a productive and meaningful supervisor–subordinate relationship.

> Regardless of one's personal needs or desires, if a leader cannot trust his subordinates with open participation in administrative decisions, he should at least spare them from the hypocrisy of illusionary democracy. Perhaps the autocratic executive must ease into a freer managerial style by allowing decisions of lesser import to be made by subordinates and then gradually delegating more and more authority to them. Upon evaluating the quality of their decisions, and after observing the valuable error-detection mechanism of group discussion, the executive may become aware of the tremendous potential creativity which he has unlocked in his underlings and himself as well.[39]

There are several ways to evaluate the effectiveness of the leader. Some of the most popular are ratings by superiors, ratings by external observers, "critical situations," and self-appraisal.[40] Olmsted, in interpreting the work of Simon, points out that leadership adequacy is ultimately related to "the degree to which organizational goals have been reached," and how efficiently "the goals have been reached relative to available resources."[41]

In the process of reaching organizational goals as efficiently as possible, the leader needs to be both a realist and an idealist, rather than a manipulator:

> It is the nature of the leader's work that he should be a realist and should recognize the need for action, even when the outcome cannot be foreseen, but also that he should be an idealist and in the broadest sense pursue goals some of which can only be attained in a succeeding generation of leaders. Many leaders when they reach the apex of their powers have not long to go and they press onward by paths the ends of which they will not themselves reach . . . yet old men plant trees.[42]

Summary

In the words of Theodore N. Vail, "you can never tell what a man will do by what he has done; but it is the best guide you have."[43]

This section of the chapter and the preceding section have discussed the

---

[39]Dyer, *The Sensitive Manipulator,* pp. 109–10.
[40]Donald W. Olmsted, *Social Groups, Roles and Leadership: An Introduction to the Concepts* (East Lansing: Board of Trustees, Michigan State University, 1961), pp. 44–45.
[41]Ibid., p. 44.
[42]Barnard, *Organization and Management,* p. 110.
[43]Ibid., p. 108.

interrelated aspects of leadership, pointing out that leaders are neither completely *born* nor *made*. One of the most important aspects of effective leadership is the leader's own motivation, and as Gardner points out:

> We must understand that high motivation is as precious a commodity as talent and that if we do not have a system which selects for this attribute as well as for talent we shall have to resign ourselves to a good deal of flabbiness in our leadership ranks. And we must recognize that one way of bringing highly motivated people to the top is to impose barriers which must be hurdled on the way to the top.[44]

Schultz has developed what he calls the FIRO theory—Fundamental, Interpersonal Relations Orientation—which appears to include the basic elements, in a summary form, of the aspects of effective leadership required to motivate supervisees. Schultz says there are "three fundamental interpersonal needs—*inclusion, control,* and *affection*—and in order for an individual (or group) to function optimally he must establish and maintain a satisfactory relation in all three areas."[45] The leader's job is to facilitate the process.

This relates to every employee's need to feel a part of the organization. As was mentioned earlier, it is some people's conception of a semimilitary organization that input should not be solicited and that communication should be only from the top down. To feel included and a meaningful part of an organization means more than mere physical presence. The effective supervisory leader will see as a part of his job the tapping of his most important resource—his supervisees—for their ideas and suggestions.

At the same time, the subordinates will also want to feel that they have some control over their work environment. The employee who is indiscriminately moved from shift to shift, assignment to assignment, without having input into the decision or given the reasons for it, will feel a total lack of control. This feeling of helplessness in the work environment can cause interpersonal problems both on the job and in his family life.

Many contemporary workers feel that they have little control in anything that goes on around them—taxes are increasing, inflation continues to rise, politicians do what they want to do—and if the work supervisor as leader fails to include them in important decisions that affect their lives, thus giving them no control over any part of their work destiny, then they will not be contented and productive employees. Without *inclusion* and *control,* they will surely not feel that their department has much *affection* for them. Even though the first-line supervisor may not himself have much of an impact on his department because of his own lack of input, he can still, as the leader,

[44]John W. Gardner, *Excellence: Can We Be Equal and Excellent Too?* (New York: Harper & Row, 1961), p. 100.
[45]William C. Schultz, "The Ego, FIRO Theory and the Leader as Completer," in Petrullo and Bass, *Leadership and Interpersonal Behavior,* p. 57.

project an attitude of concern and a willingness to transmit problems to the administration to the best of his ability.

In formal organizations, and particularly large ones, supervisors are reluctant to empathize and show affection for their supervisees for fear that by getting too close, they will not be able to perform such necessary supervisory functions as monitoring, disciplining, and making undesirable assignments.

Research does support the belief that psychological distance between supervisor and supervisee is appropriate. Fiedler says that psychological distance between the leader and the group is "a consistent, reliable, measurable personality attribute which differentiates effective from ineffective leaders."[46] Other research studies also support this idea. These studies are often cited by police administrators, who frequently criticize their first-line supervisors for being too close to their subordinates and unable to discipline and take corrective action with their friends. The first-line police sergeant, as mentioned in Chapter 1, differs from his business and industry counterparts in being a sworn officer expected to uphold the law, and because he will perform line functions when necessary, a natural camaraderie arises between him and most of his subordinates. Thus, police sergeants are usually closer psychologically to their supervisees than are supervisors in other organizations.

The department should realize that it is doubly difficult in these circumstances for the first-line police supervisor to maintain psychological distance. Departmental training programs should address the inevitable; the astute police administrator will give the sergeant tools like adequate general orders, clear role definition, and backing. Then psychological distance will not be as important, because the sergeant will have the means to deal effectively with the small percentage of subordinates who may take advantage of the interpersonal closeness. In addition, the supervised group will use peer pressure to control such "con men." Without department support, the sergeant will have difficulty being an effective leader.

THE SERGEANT AS COMMUNICATOR

A sergeant can have all the traits and training necessary to be a supervisor but still be an ineffective leader because he cannot communicate well.[47] Communication is the basis for all human interactions, and since over 90 percent of the sergeant's time may be spent dealing with personnel problems, or problems his personnel have, he will have to understand the communica-

[46]Fiedler, "Leadership and Leadership Effectiveness Traits," pp. 32–33.

[47]Most of this section was written by Samuel L. Dixon, and taken from Robert C. Trojanowicz and Samuel L. Dixon, *Criminal Justice and the Community* (Englewood Cliffs, N.J.: Prentice-Hall, 1974).

tion process, his own particular ways of communicating, and the characteristics of his supervisees' communication patterns, so that he will know "where they are coming from."

Whisenand believes that:

> Communication is the vehicle for supervisory control. In other words, the police supervisor is a key person in building and maintaining effective organizational communications as he interacts with subordinates, peers, supervisors, and the citizenry. . . . A communication, or in terms of organizational setting a communication system, provides the means by which information, statements, views, and instructions are transmitted through an organization. . . . A police supervisor decides issues based on information received in conjunction with previously developed strategies, procedures, or rules. . . . In fact, if supervision were thought of primarily as decision making and if the decision were considered essentially a communication process including a network of communication systems, then supervision could be viewed as a communication process.[48]

Communication does not take place only in the formal department operation via the chain of command. Much work-related communication originates in social gatherings, after work, or over a cup of coffee at break time. A sergeant may golf with one of his supervisees or play cards with the chief. Influence and interaction with communication as the vehicle for transmission is such an integral part of our everyday behavior that it is taken for granted. The effective first-line supervisor needs to be an astute communicator and listener.

There are many different ways of communicating:

> A manager forgets how many ways he has of communicating with his employees and how few ways they have of communicating with him. To begin with, numerous written channels are open to the manager and largely closed to the employee. Practically all managers, for example, use bulletin boards, and most of them send bulletins to employees, insert notices in pay envelopes, distribute employee magazines and handbooks, and write letters to individual employees. They call meetings, use the public-address system, or ask individual employees to come to see them. Of course, most managers have an "open-door policy" for receiving communications from employees—but few employees go through the door.[49]

In one police department, the commander in charge of investigative operations used to communicate by means of an overabundance of written memos, to the point where nobody bothered reading them. He became known as "Captain Memo." The communicator should not take the communication

[48]Paul M. Whisenand, *Police Supervision: Theory and Practice,* 2nd ed. (Englewood Cliffs, N.J.: Prentice-Hall, 1976).
[49]Smith and Wakeley, *Psychology of Industrial Behavior,* p. 146.

process for granted and assume that everyone accepts and appreciates his particular method of communication.

The sergeant, as the "man in the middle," is sandwiched between the department's administration and his supervisees. Roethlisberger explains the dilemma of the man in the middle by using the foreman as an example:

> The crux of the foreman's problem is that he is constantly faced with the dilemma of (1) having to keep his superior informed of what is happening at the work level (in many cases so that his superior may prepare in turn for the unfavorable reaction of his superior, and so on up the line) and (2) needing to communicate this information in such a way that it does not bring unfavorable criticism on himself for not doing his job correctly or adequately. Discrepancies between the way things are at the work level and the way they are represented to be by management cannot be overlooked; and yet the foreman feels obliged to overlook them when talking to his boss. This makes the foreman's job particularly "tough" and encourages him to talk out of both sides of his mouth at the same time—to become the master of double talk.[50]

As the quotation above illustrates, the first-line supervisor is critical in the communication process. He can freely transmit information, delay it, garble it, confuse it, or withhold it. Sometimes his organizational survival depends on how he transmits information to his boss.

Furthermore, if the supervisor and his subordinates are not on the same wave length, communications can be misunderstood, affecting a common orientation to problem solving. George reports a study in which foremen were asked to rank ten job-related expectations in the order that they thought their supervisees would rank them, and then the supervisees were asked to rank the same items. The study showed (see Table 4-2) that supervisees have different priorities from their supervisors.

This finding can have implications for the way the supervisor relates to the needs of his people in daily interaction. What the supervisor brushes off as unimportant may be extremely meaningful for the employee, to the point of affecting the supervisor–supervisee relationship. Effective communication can help eliminate many of the pitfalls of misperceptions between the sergeant and his officers.

What is Communication?

Communication is essentially interaction. It is defined as the methods used by one person to affect or change the behavior, attitude, or mental state of another. This definition implies that a *communicator* is one who wants to influence another by sending or transmitting some stimuli designed for that

[50]Roethlisberger, 1945. (Found in Smith and Wakeley, p. 146.)

TABLE 4-2

Priorities of Employees and Supervisors

Employee Ranking	Item Being Rated	Supervisor Ranking
1	Appreciation of work well done	8
2	Feeling of being "in on things"	10
3	Sympathetic help on personal problems	9
4	Job security	2
5	Good wages	1
6	Interesting work	5
7	Promotion and growth in company	3
8	Personal loyalty to employees	6
9	Good working conditions	4
10	Tactful disciplining	7

Source: Claude S. George, Jr., *Supervision in Action: The Art of Managing Others* (Reston, Va.: Reston, 1977), p 107.

purpose; a sergeant, for example, transmits a new policy to his supervisees. A *communicatee* is one whom the communicator wants to influence. The communicatee receives, digests, translates, and interprets the meaning of the communicator's stimuli, and thereby responds. The responses of the communicatee, in turn, evoke counterresponses in the communicator, and cumulative interactions result. This means that each person in the communication process affects the other and is in turn affected by him.

It also implies that communication is interactional and transactional, and goes beyond messages transmitted by the casual awareness of another person. While the sergeant is transmitting the messages, all his actions are being observed. For example, a sergeant was reading to his officers a general order about the wearing of the service cap at all times when talking to citizens. The chief felt that this was a very important policy and that transgressors should be reprimanded. The officers were aware that the sergeant transmitting the order did not like to wear his service cap, and he read the order with little emotion, slouched over on a chair and pursing his lips. He was doing his job by relaying the chief's concern, but it was obvious by his nonverbal communication that he did not agree with the order.

Successful communication is determined by the accuracy of the receiver's interpretation of the sender's message. The communicator intends by his stimuli to set up some specific response in the communicatee—to change his behavior, attitude, or mental state. The communicatee responds according to his understanding of the communicator's intentions. The meaning of the stimuli to the sender and to the receiver is distinguishable by their differences in interpretation. A sender may be motivated to deceive the receiver, whose specific responses will be determined by whether he realizes the sender's intention to deceive.

The essence of communication is the relationship established as a result of the discriminative responses of the receiver to the stimuli of the sender. Again, this will be determined by the accuracy of the receiver's interpretation of the meaning of the sender's messages. A willingness to communicate is predicted on the hope that the action will result in some benefit to each person involved. When this is no longer believed to be possible, efforts to communicate stop. Such is the case when either the police union or management walks out of the negotiating conference.

Understanding Communication

Communication is the interaction of two or more people in a specific context, be it social or business. In this situation, a communicator, the sergeant, consciously or unconsciously seeks to affect the behavior of his supervisees by transmitting signals or messages. Therefore, the communication starts with an idea, feelings, an impulse, or a message from within the sergeant. But events or experiences cannot be communicated as they actually occurred; they have to be translated into words, gestures, or some other form of behavior. So the sergeant must encode; that is, he must translate his ideas or feelings into symbols or some behavior that expresses the desired message. These translations become the symbolic representation of the actual feelings and experiences. Complicating the issue is the fact that the sergeant is not the originator of the policy, procedure, or order. He has received the message from someone above him, who has himself translated ideas into symbols.

The method chosen to express the message depends on many factors. First and foremost is the *social context* in which all communication takes place. Generally, a police officer will communicate differently when in uniform on official duty from the way he will as John Q. Public on his day off. A suspect may react one way to questioning when it takes place in his neighborhood or on a noisy and busy street, and another way in the police station. Life *experiences* are a second factor determining the choice of a method of communication. Man's life is a continuity of experiences, and the method of communication reflects those experiences. Hence, people from different communities, cultures, and subcultures have different frames of reference, and therefore, different communication patterns. Other factors determining the method of communication or encoding are *self-concept, educational attainment, image of the receiver, status relationship,* and *previous experience* in communicating with the receiver.

What is being communicated by the motorist who shouts, "Why are you stopping me?" before the officer has a chance to say anything? There can be many meanings to the message; for example:

1. The motorist could feel "picked on" as a result of previous experience with police officers.
2. He could be angry about the delay.
3. He could be feeling guilty about his violation, and therefore be defending himself against his guilt feelings by projecting the blame on the officer.

In any event, it is most important to recognize that the consequence of the communication process is determined by how the officer interprets the motorist's message, since that is what will determine his own reaction. This becomes clear when it is recalled that communication is a process of cumulative social interaction.

The stimuli or message from the communicator travels by various channels to the communicatee. Each person has a receiving system, a processing system, and a transmitting system. The receiving system consists of the sense organs; most noticeably used are the eyes and ears. Once a stimulus has been received by one of these receptors, the decoding process is initiated. This process involves interpreting the message, making it consistent with the receiver's frame of reference. How the message is received and interpreted is determined by the characteristics of both the sender and the receiver. In addition, however, the receiver may recall previous experiences or previously stored information, and compare it to the current situation. Thus, he instantly thinks about the message, evaluates it, and translates it into his own meaning. In doing this, he will retain some items from the incoming message, omit others, and change some into acceptable or justifiable patterns. The receiver then formulates a response, called "feedback," which consists of the signals sent back to the original sender by the receiver in response to the original message. These signals are the primary means by which the original sender may gauge the effect of his message on the receiver.

Some sergeants are very effective in communicating departmental directives, and others are not as articulate. Thus the importance of immediate feedback from the officers, to make sure they understand the communication and its ramifications. A sergeant in one department would become very defensive when he was asked questions about policies he had just transmitted. His defenseiveness was manifested by sarcasm, and his officers learned not to ask questions for fear of being berated. As a result of the faulty communication process, the officers on his shift made many more mistakes than those on other shifts, and the ineffective sergeant took this personally, thinking his officers were being deliberately contrary. Once it was pointed out to him that the problem originated with the communication process, the situation began to improve.

The transmission by the communicator of stimuli designed to affect the attitude, behavior, or mental state of the receiver would be a simple transaction if the message were clear and forthright. However, a person's life experiences and particular psychic system—his own unique characteristics—affect how and what he chooses to communicate. A very important additional consideration is the fact that the true meaning of the message communicated may be unknown even to the communicator. Here we are referring to the unconscious motivation inherent in communication. Sometimes the message accomplishes the opposite of what the sender says he wants. In the example of the sergeant transmitting the service-cap code, his manner of presentation and the officers' previous knowledge of his attitude probably did more harm than good; it may have encouraged the officers to disregard the policy.

We must keep to the forefront the real goal of communication—that is, to change or affect another person. How one goes about this relates to his internal processes and habitual patterns of communicating. Even before a thought or feeling is transmitted, it passes through a series of internal screens and is generally modified. A great deal of anticipatory thought is involved in most communication. The sender will attempt to anticipate the response of the receiver by trying to shape his message in such a way that the desired response is elicited. If he believes that an idea expressed in its original form will work to his disadvantage or be rejected by the receiver, he will not express it clearly, but will either disguise it in such a way that rejection is avoided or refrain from transmitting it entirely. In other words, stimuli that would tend to work against us will generally be encoded.

These internal screens prevent the transmission upward of emotionally unacceptable thoughts and ideas from the sergeant who does not want to make his boss mad. Many words, thoughts, ideas, and feelings are never encoded because of anticipated consequences—for example, curse words and hostile or derogatory remarks. It should be clear that a great deal goes on within the communicator prior to his encoding a stimulus, to increase the possibility of getting what he wants or needs and, at the same time, to prevent negative consequences.

Once a decision is made that a stimulus is appropriate for expression, the channel or method of transmission can be selected. Since we are talking primarily about verbal symbols, the choice of words must be made. We have already indicated that these choices will be predicted on the social context, life experiences, educational level, and linguistic ability. Since communication is instantaneous, it may not seem possible that so many forces can be brought to bear on one's mind prior to the actual communication interchange. But the human brain has an enormous capacity to serve as a communication center.

What determines the way a person responds to the communication stimuli? What is his capacity? How does his predisposition influence the way he reacts to the stimuli presented? To answer these questions, we need to call on as much knowledge as possible about individual psychology.

Reception is no less complicated a process than transmission. The communicatee has his own set of mental barriers and screens that control the reception of messages or stimuli. An officer, for example, may dislike a particular sergeant and therefore disregard or misinterpret everything he says. People screen the stimuli presented to them in all situations, either consciously or unconsciously selecting certain stimuli to which they will respond while omitting others. Through this selection process, the whole meaning of the message may be changed. The officer is on guard against messages that make him feel anxious or uncomfortable, or that disturb his perception of himself or his psychic equilibrium. Personal criticism in front of a group will cause him much anxiety. Many internal needs and concerns resulting from the development of his unique psychic system render him particularly sensitive to certain stimuli, or make him avoid others.

People in general will notice most things that interest them and affect their own welfare, whereas they will ignore or omit those that have little reference to their own needs and interests. Just as the transmitter has a motive for the communication, the receiver has premessage motives and attitudes that facilitate his reception of certain stimuli and the avoidance of others.

It should be pointed out here that hearing is not receiving. The process of selective perception enables us to hear only what we want to hear and the way we want to hear it. Adaptive maneuvers play a tremendously important part in the reception and selection of stimuli. For example, in *projection,* we hear the message in terms of what we would have said in that position rather than what was said; consider the officer who thought he heard his sergeant say, "You must be a nut," when he actually said, "You must be in a rut." Sometimes we hear the opposite of what was said; in the use of *repression,* we do not hear the message at all. These adaptive maneuvers, so inherent in mental processes, affect the degree of accuracy in the reception of messages transmitted. They help to protect us from hearing what would be inconvenient, harmful, or anxiety-producing by distorting the communication received.

Because man attempts to preserve his self-image, he will usually hear favorable communications more accurately than unfavorable ones and distort or avoid information destructive to that image. Also, a person's own position on a subject largely determines whether he will receive a message on that subject accurately, distort it, or ignore it. In order to maintain internal consistency, people tend to perceive information in accordance with their predispositions and self-images.

Our expectations also greatly affect the accuracy with which we receive messages. We sometimes hear what we expect to hear, whether it is said or not. Stereotyping is a good example. If a man is identified as a policeman, we expect him to behave like our idea of a policeman. If a person wears a beard, we may expect him to talk like a hippie. There is a general tendency to attribute to people the characteristics of the group they are associated with; and often what is heard is what they are expected to say rather than what is said. Since effective communication is sharing, a police officer must under-stand all the different groups with which he works, just as the sergeant must understand all his supervisees.

Reception of stimuli takes place when the message has been psychologi-cally received and the process of decoding is initiated. Decoding consists of the digestion and interpretation of the communicator's stimuli, according to the *personal meaning* it has for the receiver. That is, each individual has a communication system determined by his own unique life experiences. Just because all the sergeant's officers are standing at attention and look alike in their uniforms does not mean that their internal receptive devices are the same. It is a common mistake in military and semimilitary organizations to think that wearing a uniform makes people think the same and have the same personal qualities and abilities.

Cultural, ethnic, educational, and socioeconomic differences must also be taken into consideration in the communication process. Just as the police officer is regarded differently by different groups—respected by one group and perceived by another as an enemy—the sergeant as communicator will also be viewed differently by his supervisees from different backgrounds and with varied experiences. Transmission of the policy regarding the handling of drunks will mean one thing to most officers but something much different to an officer who has an alcoholic parent. Thus, the social context in which the communication takes place also affects how the communicatee will re-ceive, interpret, and respond to stimuli.

We can see that the full meaning of the form and content of communi-cation requires consideration of both the receiver and sender. It must be emphasized that reception, interpretation, and response are highly subjec-tive. Just as the communicator has some goal or purpose for his communica-tion, the receiver, having interpreted the sender's message, has some purpose for his response, which sets up the cumulative social interaction. That pur-pose is generally to benefit himself in some way, even if it is only to assure the sender that he has got his point across.

The Meaning of Language

Successful communication results when both the communicator and communicatee feel that they have benefited by the exchange. They under-stand each other. Successful communication, however, is not easy to achieve, not only because of the factors just discussed, but because of the nature of language.

It may sound paradoxical, but the greatest obstacle to communication is language itself, owing to its symbolic nature. Language is not the actual feeling, idea, thought, or experience; it is a symbolic representation of it. Thus, it is a reference to, or substitute for, the reality that it attempts to represent. And reality is much more complex than the meaning language can convey; for example, the word *dog* is very simple, but the animal it symbolizes is extremely complex. However, as long as everyone shares the understanding that certain words stand for certain things, communication can take place.

But a language is a collection of words that have common meanings to a specific social group, whose members agree that each word in the language will have a common meaning for all. The meaning of a specific word is arbitrarily assigned by the social group. The person we call a police officer in the United States is known as an *agent de police* in France. The critical point is not only that the assignment of meaning to a specific word is somewhat arbitrary, but that its meaning must be understood by everyone in the social context. To communicate, people must share the same language and use it in relatively the same way. Those who do not understand the common meaning cannot communicate.

However, the process of communication is not made simple by the sharing of a common language; there are not enough words in any language to give an exact representation of all shades of ideas, feelings, and experiences. Consequently, one word, or a combination of words, has to serve more than a single function. In addition, since words are a human creation, each with its own history, they are more than arbitrary signs; they include associations as well. Words not only express feelings but call into play other feelings, and memories associated with previous experiences. Because language is symbolic, whatever meaning it evokes for the receiver is based on his experience with the symbol. The "dictionary definition" of a word, its objective meaning, is called its *denotation;* the meaning it has for the individual, based on his unique experience, is its *connotation.* Connotation is entirely subjective and differs from person to person. Consequently, only those symbols with which there has been some experience facilitate communication. In other words, simply speaking the same language is only half the communication process. Experience is what gives language meaning.

Therefore, communication, even with a common language, is best facilitated through common experiences. People in the middle and upper socioeconomic classes may have difficulty understanding each other because, owing to their different life experiences, words take on different meanings for them. To this extent, both the sender and the receiver must recognize that words may have different meanings to each of them. What one officer considers just a drunk, the officer with an alcoholic parent thinks of as a person who needs help.

In most communication situations, the sergeant assumes that the officers are on the same frequency as he and that the words used are of common meaning. This is often a fallacious assumption, and communication fails. Since words take on meaning associated with personal experiences, they may not be used and understood identically by the sergeant and his people, especially if they have different backgrounds and experiences.

Functionally, language has a broader purpose than social interaction; it is also a way in which man can control his environment and extend it beyond his physical capacities. Words in the natural sciences are much less confusing because they generally represent empirical objects whose meanings are understood by all scientists. But used as a communication medium, words are emotion-laden, have multiple meanings, and represent fictional concepts.

In our everyday speech, we tend to rely on a relatively limited vocabulary, whose content we take for granted because of its familiarity. Consequently, we unconsciously think that the words we use are real things rather than representative of some aspect of reality. It is on this basis that words have such a great capacity to evoke strong feelings of love, hate, fear, happiness, and so forth. For example, words such as *democracy, equality,* and *independence* have different meanings to different people, and even more so under certain conditions. The word *independence,* to an adolescent attempting to emancipate himself from his parents, can be a powerful emotional stimulus. Some words are so emotive that responses often exceed rationality or logic. The words *pig, nigger, bitch,* and *Polock,* for example, can arouse strong emotions, especially when used by a person in authority. A prejudiced sergeant who has difficulty concealing his animosity toward certain groups can have a great deal of influence on how his officers behave on the street. Key trigger words at roll call or over a cup of coffee can give license to discriminatory behavior, especially by impressionable young recruits.

Words can make rational and logical people behave and think illogically. They can be used for deliberate deceit, or for creating prejudice. Words can evoke emotions of enormous proportions because of the tendency to confuse the word with what it represents. It should be remembered that words are imprecise methods of communication because they are references for reality and not reality itself. Furthermore, the degree of imprecision is related to the choice of words used. Words with double meanings or very emotive words increase subjective interpretation, which decreases acceptance and understanding.

It is important to reiterate that the meaning of many words is determined by the individual's life experiences, education level, and social context. Certain words may have a different meaning to a black man than to a white man. For example, a sergeant's referring to "you people" may be interpreted as derogatory by a black officer when the intended meaning was line officers in general.

Emotions stick to words because they are inseparably associated with previous emotional experiences, even though those experiences are generally irrelevant to current situations. The sergeant who has an extreme dislike for "drunks" may not be aware that he has a problem drinker as a supervisee, and his reference to a "no-good drunk" may have a special significance for that officer.

Even the simplest word has different connotations to different people. The word *man* brings different images to the minds of John Wayne and Germaine Greer, the word *house* to those of a millionaire and a sharecropper. The connotative meaning of a word is all the meanings, ideas, and feelings it suggests to the individual. The word *class* is defined as "a group of individuals ranked together as possessing common characteristics or as having the same status," but it can be used to imply nearly the opposite—that is, nobility, sophistication, or refinement that is out of the ordinary, as in, "Man, that's class!" or, "He's in a class by himself."

Nonverbal Communication

Nonverbal communications are those messages transmitted by behavior other than speech. They include gestures, facial expressions, postures, various movements of the body, and, quite frequently, dress, i.e., the example of the sergeant transmitting the service-cap policy, little emotion in his voice, slouched over a chair, pursed lips, unenthusiastic attitude. They can occur in conjunction with verbal communication, often to reinforce it—a greeting and a handshake, for example—or independently of verbal communication, such as a clenched fist, a smile, a frown, or a grimace. Generally, the meanings of nonverbal communications are determined by social context.

Head and hand movements are probably the most frequently used methods of nonverbal communication, they are often used in conjunction with speech, for emphasis—for example, pointing gestures, or tracing of an object with the hands. Hand gestures and facial expressions are used to convey emotions such as happiness, anger, surprise, fear, sadness, or frustration, especially if one has difficulty expressing feelings verbally. Movements transmitting a message of anger are easily interpreted. The police officer directing traffic communicates his feelings by the intensity with which he lets motorists through, especially when one motorist is slowing traffic down or makes a wrong turn. The important point is that gesturing reflects feelings. Body posture and movement indicate interest and enthusiasm or the lack of them.

Nonverbal behavior is an important part of communication, largely because people are influenced by what they see. It reactivates in the mind an image of a previous, similar experience or situation, thereby affecting communication. The sender transmits nonverbal clues advising the receiver of how he ought to respond; and the sender's perception of the nonverbal clues sent by the receiver tell him about the success of his message.

The clearest communication occurs when verbal and nonverbal messages are both simultaneous and congruent. A grimace by an officer after the sergeant has relayed a new general order may bring a response by the sergeant, "What's the matter, Smith, you got a problem?" Smith may respond by telling the sergeant why he doesn't like the order; but he may say nothing because his grimace had nothing to do with the order. It may have been caused by a sudden jab from a painful backache, which happened to occur at the same moment the order was transmitted. The point is that even though nonverbal responses may be directly related to verbal communication, they may also be totally unrelated.

Barriers to Communication

The first barrier to communication, the nature of language, has already been discussed in detail. This occurs because there is a tendency to connect the symbols of language with reality. Consequently, rather than recognize that words are referrents with personal, emotional meanings, we give them the effect and power of the objects they represent. This situation often prevents a comparison of words with reality. For example, when the sergeant can not explain the rationale for some procedure, it is often explained by saying that it has always been done like that. There is no comparison of what is done with reality. A second, barrier to communication, the fact that thinking processes, beliefs, and attitudes are developed by life experiences, has also been mentioned, but a few more points should be made.

Because words are symbols, the meaning they convey corresponds only to one's experiences with those particular symbols. This implies that successful communication occurs when experiences are shared or held in common and mean the same for all in the communication situation. In other words, language must be related to experiences. The police training academy is intended as a vehicle for teaching techniques to recruits so that they will have a common orientation to handling problems. The department's general orders are an attempt to create a uniform code to give each officer common experience with the document. However, the general orders and the training academy do not negate an officer's background and past experiences. Personal interpretation and discretion become an important part of how the officer acts. The sergeant who understands this fact can be more effective in his individualized supervision.

A third barrier to communication is stereotyping, which is a kind of predetermined communication process based, as we have seen, on anticipated behavior not founded in fact, or on previously held beliefs about or attitudes toward people who have been labeled in some fashion. For example, policemen may be stereotyped as flatfooted, or Polish people as dumb. Stereotyping can also relate to occupations, such as thinking all Puerto Ricans are busboys, or all stenographers must be women. Stereotypical beliefs limit open communications, since they are invested with emotionalism that deters the sharing of common experiences. Again, the sergeant can have a great influence on reducing or perpetuating stereotypes by his verbal and nonverbal behavior.

The Basis of Effective Communication

Good communication occurs when the sergeant's message is encoded and transmitted freely and clearly, and decoded in such a way that the officer receives the intended meaning of the original message accurately. Since, as we have said, experiences with its symbols facilitate communication, efforts should be made to identify areas of common understanding and to translate problems into a common language.

Communication not only is the result of life experiences but is affected by experiences during the process itself. These experiences, in turn, facilitate future communication. If an officer perceives his sergeant as merely getting his "kicks" out of telling people what to do, he will not listen intently to his sergeant's instructions and this may affect his work performance. A sergeant who, in a nonauthoritarian manner, projects his willingness to help, listen, and give advice when necessary, can counteract and neutralize negative past experiences and help the officer interpret future communications more positively.

To ensure good reception, the officer must also consider the sergeant's frame of reference. The sergeant may not personally agree with a particular order, but it is his job to enforce and monitor it until it is changed. Word selection is important; the message is apt to be perceived more accurately if care is taken in the transmission. Once it is transmitted, it cannot be taken back; and how it is received is difficult to modify. Since the motives and previous experiences of the receiver greatly affect how a message is received, regardless of how it is sent, serious consideration should be given to the officer's background. Talking down to someone, using a patronizing or condescending tone and belittling words, should be avoided.

In addition, the sergeant should realize that just as his officers have had differing experiences, they also have varying degrees of police experience; what older officers might understand with minimal explanation, younger supervisees may need extended individualized explanations about. Again, the fact that a police department is semimilitary in orientation doesn't mean that everything is uniform.

Communication is a cumulative social interactional process. This means that the people in the process affect each other. Consequently, in addition to all the other things that are involved in communication, interpersonal relationships are very important. The emotions between those involved, whether positive or negative, greatly affect their communication. The most successful communication will occur in the context of a positive relationship. The essence of successful, effective communication is ultimately based on whether the sergeant and his supervisees respect each other's human dignity, regarding each other as nothing less than equal, regardless of organizational rank or status in life.

SUMMARY

Communication is a process of social interaction in which people attempt to influence each other for the purpose of achieving some more-or-less specific goal.

Although communication occurs on all levels, true communication takes place when there is interaction and transaction between the people involved. In this regard, the process consists of the transmission and reception of stimuli consisting of signals and symbols having predetermined meanings. Communication is based on feedback, and its success is determined by the accuracy of the receiver's interpretation of the sender's message. Messages are encoded and decoded according to the backgrounds of the communicators, including their culture, education, socioeconomic status, training, and life experiences. Good communication occurs when an idea is encoded and transmitted freely and clearly and the message is decoded accurately. Although it may be easier to communicate with those who share similar experiences, areas of common understanding should be a primary focus in all communication. A willingness to communicate is based on the hope that to do so will result in some benefit to all involved.

The sergeant who is an effective communicator will have a much easier time performing his duties and being an astute leader.

CHAPTER FIVE

The Operational Role
of the Sergeant

by Richard A. Gleason*

Formal job descriptions or role definitions for the police line sergeant seldom adequately or accurately characterize this vital function as it is actually practiced. This is not meant as a condemnation of either organizations or individuals, but is rather a long overdue recognition of what in fact exists— a reality that should be accepted by administrators if they are to understand what is (or is not) happening within their organizations.

There are in general three types of assignments for sergeants: patrol, investigations, and the specialized unit or function. Whether or not the basic responsibilities are the same for each of the three types depends upon the organizational structure and assignment policies of the department. As an example, some agencies routinely assign the ranks of detective sergeant, and sometimes lieutenant, to field investigation, in which case the sergeant would not have the same responsibilities as those of a sergeant who is in charge of a squad of investigators.

For the purpose of this analysis, then, the assumption will be made that the sergeant is assigned to a position involving the supervision of subordinates whose work efforts are his direct responsibility. The success or failure of a sergeant in these circumstances is based upon the performance of his subordinates and not on his own work effort.

There are a number of written descriptions of the duties, responsibili-

*Mr. Gleason, a holder of a Masters Degree from Michigan State University, is presently Chief of Police in Lansing, Michigan.

ties, and roles of sergeants, but most describe those of the outstanding person operating under near-perfect conditions in an ideal agency. Some attempt to categorically list each and every task the sergeant might be called upon to perform, results in a seemingly endless number of them. It is fortunate that most of those listed, if accomplished at all, are done in an offhand manner in keeping with a conditioned reflex or response to the situation at hand; otherwise, the sergeant would not have the time to function in this all-important position. I do not say that these descriptions are useless in the study of law enforcement, but it must be recognized that they resemble computer programming more than they do actual human actions and reactions.

What, then, is the role of the law-enforcement sergeant? What are his responsibilities and duties in fulfilling that role, and approximately how much time is spent at each of the tasks involved? First, let us examine the sergeant's main duties; then we shall discuss a survey that was made to determine the percentage of his time taken up by each of them.

COMMUNICATION

Probably one of the most time-consuming and important roles of the line sergeant is that of communicator (also see chapter 4). Law-enforcement administrators depend heavily on the sergeant rank to transmit to those who actually do the work all the directions, controls, policies, procedures, and general information deemed necessary for the good of the organization. Just as important, but often overlooked, are the communication channels between the sergeant and the top administration positions. Knowledge of the field officers' attitudes, needs, and problems is important to top administration officials if their goal is a well-functioning agency.

Within the small agencies—20 to 40 sworn officers—two-way communications are relatively simple, but as agencies become larger in size, formal communications originating at the administrative level tend to increase as informal communication between administrators and first-line supervisors decreases. It is not that the sergeants have less to say; to the contrary, they have much to say, but the channels of communication upward have become clogged with lieutenants and captains, making it difficult, if not impossible, for the sergeant's voice to be heard by the top administrator. Of course, administration may hear the sergeants' thoughts and ideas via the lieutenants and captains if the chain of command is functioning properly at all times. But it is just as possible that ideas that cannot be implemented at the lieutenant or captain level will die for lack of action at that level, or will be incorporated into some lieutenant's or captain's own presentation to the administration.

In reality, then, a major aspect of communications from the sergeant's point of view is translation of the numerous procedures, orders, directives, and so on, originating at the upper levels of the administration, into actions by those under the sergeant's immediate supervision. Whether or not the sergeant's interpretation of the communication to his subordinates is correct depends on his perception of it. Other factors influencing the sergeant's response to a problem-solving directive are whether or not the sergeant agrees with the solution expressed in the directive, and whether there was a problem to begin with that justifies the solution he is now charged with transmitting to his subordinates.

Middle management and administrators alike would be well advised to consider carefully, first, whether there is really a need for yet another order or directive, and then, if so, its wording. It is advisable to briefly explain the need for the directive by outlining the problem early in it. This will show the sergeant at the outset that a problem exists for which a solution is being presented. It may come as a surprise to administrators that all too often, directives baffle line sergeants because they were written to solve problems the sergeants did not know existed. In addition, the solution offered may not remedy the perceived problem; but if the sergeant understands and supports the need for the directive, he might modify the solution offered in such a way that it will work to remedy the problem. It also may come as a surprise to the administrator that many times directives written to resolve a problem as defined by the administration may address a symptom of the problem rather than the cause.

Another aspect of communications in which the sergeant has responsibility is that of being the source of all information required by the field officer. If the sergeant does not have the required information, he must know where to get it, if it in fact exists.

Field officers are usually very perceptive in identifying sergeants who fulfill their job responsibilities inadequately by failing to respond satisfactorily to the subordinate's need for guidance or by exhibiting reluctance to make hard decisions when the need arises. The latter instance is perhaps the true test of a good supervisor. The complexities of law enforcement are such that it is impossible to formulate a set of guidelines that will cover each and every incident. Good supervising sergeants must exercise common sense and good judgement in guiding their subordinates through situations for which guidelines do not exist. All too often, a supervisor gets into more trouble by not making a decision when the need arises than by making a decision that later proves faulty. Repeated failures by a sergeant to communicate and direct subordinates responsibly in these instances can lead to their isolating and ignoring him, in which case he can hardly be called a leader.

There are, of course, many other duties and responsibilities of the sergeant that require communication to some extent. In the pages that follow, the question of which is more important, the responsibility itself or the communication involved in that particular responsibility, will not be addressed. The emphasis will be on the responsibility, with the assumption that required communications will be adequately achieved.

Attempting to establish the amount of time involved in communications is difficult. In a survey to be discussed later, sergeants did not identify communication as a separate responsibility, even though the ability to communicate was an important component of the survey.

INSPECTION

Another major time-consuming activity of the sergeant is inspections. Beginning with self-inspection prior to going on duty, through the first contacts with subordinates, until going off duty, conscious and unconscious inspections are continually being made by supervisory personnel.

Inspections may be defined and practiced in several ways, ranging from a line-up inspection conducted by a sergeant to the activities of fully operational inspectional service units or divisions employed by larger agencies. Although the inspection function may be developed into a very formal and sophisticated program, the justification for inspection remains simple: It is a tool used by administrators to determine to what degree the agency's procedures and policies are being followed, whether activities are being done as the administration believes they should be, and if not, why not. Whatever the method of inspection, the administration expects and depends on the sergeants to perform inspectional responsibilities on a continuing basis.

> The goal of inspection and control is operational efficiency and effectiveness. Although infractions uncovered during the process of inspection should be handled according to agency policy and the particular circumstances, inspection and control should not be viewed as a disciplinary process. It should be a fair, impartial, and honest appraisal of employee efforts. The inspection procedure should help those who inspect to do their job better. The inspector or inspection party should have a positive, constructive attitude; they should not instill fear and distrust in the inspection process.
>
> Because the purpose of staff inspection is to provide information to improve police service, it must include inspection of material resources, personnel, and procedures. The objectives of staff inspection are well stated in the Staff Inspection Procedural Manual of the Dade County, Fla., Public Safety Department:
>
> Inspections will be conducted with the following objectives:
>
> 1. To obtain a complete evaluation of operations and administration;
> 2. To learn of new techniques used in one segment of the Department which can be applied in other areas;
> 3. To secure uniformity of operations;

4. To discover existing weaknesses and provide the necessary correctional measures;

5. To assist in solving problems and to anticipate future needs;

6. To achieve economy and efficiency in operations; and

7. To promote good teamwork and morale.

The Staff Inspection Division Manual of the Kansas City, Mo., Police Department lists the following broad objectives of staff inspection:

1. To learn whether the task is being performed as outlined. Are regulations and procedures being complied with? Has the operation developed as planned?'

2. To learn whether the anticipated results are being realized. Does the operation accomplish what was expected of it?

3. To discover whether the resources of the Department are being utilized to the best advantage.

4. To reveal the existence of need.[1]

The manner in which sergeants actually respond to this obviously important function depends on several factors, the most important being their perception and understanding of their role as inspectors and whether or not the agency's resources are being utilized properly. As previously mentioned, large agencies normally have an inspections division or bureau whose responsibility it is to determine if rules, regulations, policies, procedures, and the like are being followed by the agency as a whole. But in general, formal inspection units are concerned more with things and the overall management of the agency than with the individual members of the agency. Under these circumstances, sergeants and other command ranks that work closely with the field operations are responsible for the productivity, compliance with rules, and so on of those members.

One might make the observation that inspection units are a duplication of the sergeants' responsibilities, and the observation is essentially correct. But sergeants seldom carry out all their responsibilities in an even-handed manner; some just do not qualify for the position of sergeant, and others do not know the responsibilities involved when they take the position. Therefore, the inspectional role must be carried out by higher-ranking command or a unit specifically charged with the responsibility. An example of the unqualified sergeant would be the older sergeant, promoted years ago, who cannot adapt to the currently changing role of law enforcement or management. The problem is compounded by the fact that this type is not promotable to a higher rank, and as a result has become embittered and is usually in conflict with the administration. Additionally, he has an adverse effect on the younger sergeants and on those under his supervision. Thus, in the inspection role, this sergeant is more apt to criticize the regulation, policy, or

[1]The National Advisory Commission on Criminal Justice Standards and Goals, *The Police* (Washington, D.C.: U.S. Government Printing Office, 1973), pp. 58–59.

procedure than the person found to be in violation of it. It is difficult for administration to resolve this problem, because the rank and file, while critical of the old timer's competence, are quick to defend him out of respect for his long years of service.

The average sergeants—younger perhaps, better educated, more in tune with the changing times—accept to a larger degree the responsibilities of the more rudimentary aspects of inspections, such as personal appearance, condition of equipment, and in some instances quality and quantity of output. Usually, the average sergeants' activity regarding inspections is in direct relationship to the amount of pressure applied by the administration. Indeed, all too often this applies to all their activities. Occasionally a sergeant will emerge possessing qualities of dedication and determination to be the best supervisor in every respect, and if peer pressure does not defeat his ambitions, he will probably reach whatever goal he has set for himself. This may seem a harsh judgment, but the fact remains that sergeants too often seek the path of least resistance, especially in the matter of inspections.

Administration is not entirely blameless, however, for the failure of sergeants to fulfill the expectations held for them at the time they are selected for promotion. Most law-enforcement agencies do not have the time or resources to properly prepare the newly promoted sergeant for the position. The sergeant is suddenly transformed from the inspected to the inspector, and the shock can be significant—one day a part of the rank and file, the next day a supervisor. There is an immediate change of attitude on the part of both the promoted and the subordinate.

As the subordinate begins to assess the strengths and weaknesses of the new sergeant, trying to determine which leadership style he will develop—the authoritarian, democratic, or laissez-faire—the sergeant begins to test the waters of supervision. In all probability, he has at least some college education, giving him some formal knowledge of the requirements of supervision; however, he will more than likely rely most heavily on his image of what a sergeant should be, formulated after having observed the traits of many supervisors, noting their good and bad points until he has established in his own mind the role he will fulfill if and when he is promoted.

With the sergeant's perception of his role regarding inspections developed in the foregoing manner, administrators must accept the elementary level of inspections that will be conducted instinctively by first-line supervisors. These inspections generally concentrate on the appearance of the individual officers, their personal equipment to some extent, and occasionally the agency equipment. In some agencies, supervisors are also required to inspect the officers' investigative reports before they are submitted to the records section, initialing the report after reviewing it for content and mistakes. And yet, every so often a report thus initialed but that should not have been approved comes to the attention of administration, resulting in a reprimand for the sergeant.

Why do these things happen? Why do sergeants take the easier path? Why do they apparently need constant motivation and pressure from administration? Probably the most significant reason for much of this behavior is that the craft of law enforcement deals almost entirely with the interaction between people. The supervisor, by the very nature of his additional responsibilities, is even more people-oriented, and few sergeants are psychologically suited to cope with constantly directing and controlling the actions of subordinates, constantly inspecting numerous facets of their behavior, and constantly being critical of the way they fulfill their responsibilities. The only rewards for being a good sergeant are self-satisfaction, an occasional word of praise—and in turn, the passing on of a word of praise to a subordinate —and, if all goes well, promotion.

Particularly in patrol supervision, and to a lesser degree in any assignment to supervision, the indispensability of inspectional activities works to the detriment of a supervisor's feeling of well-being. It is much easier on the nervous system to occasionally overlook a transgression than to take corrective action on every one observed. The rationale used to justify overlooking "minor" problems may be acceptable in some circumstances; however, to ignore even small problems with any great frequency will seriously weaken a supervisor's effectiveness.

In addition to the avoidance of corrective action, another weakness of supervisors is resistance to enforcing a regulation because the supervisor does not personally support it. If the sergeant's reluctance to enforce a regulation results in no enforcement over a long period of time and administrators fail to react, then the regulation may become void by default. A common example is a restrictive hair regulation. Despite the trend toward longer hair, many administrators prefer short hair, particularly on those officers working in uniform. Younger sergeants tend to be more modern in their attitude toward hair style and, unless pressured by the administration, will allow their subordinates to wear their hair longer than the written regulations permit. When no action is taken by some supervisors, others will follow suit. If this trend is allowed to go unchecked over a long period of time, too many officers become involved, making it perhaps more of a problem than it is worth to reestablish the old hair style.

A recent sequence of events in a large city shows how administration had to deal with this problem. The commissioner of police had noticed the sloppy appearance of the uniformed officers and brought it to the attention of his staff. (Note that the commissioner of police had taken notice. What had happened to all the command rank between the commissioner and the police officer in this multi-thousand-member agency?) But even though the top administrator had raised the issue, nothing happened, so an inspectional unit issued more than 1,000 disciplinary citations to officers for violation of the hair code. This action still did not bring the desired results. Then, someone decided to issue written disciplinary notices to the sergeants whose subordinates were not in compliance with the hair regulations. Compliance followed almost overnight.

Experience indicates, however, that such an incident is the exception rather than the rule. Sergeants are not often criticized verbally by middle management, and written reprimands would be most unusual. One aspect of the incident is worth closer examination: The disciplinary action that worked was initiated by staff personnel rather than line personnel.

DIRECTION

Inspection and communication responsibilities join with directing the work of subordinates in making up a major portion of the sergeant's daily duties. One would expect that directing subordinates would require nearly all the sergeant's time, but in most agencies this is not true. Although directing is an essential duty, the many activities and responsibilities that have been added to the sergeant's workload have greatly reduced the time available for it.

Directing subordinates covers a multitude of activities. Provision of on-the-job training is of considerable concern to patrol sergeants, because it means they will have not only the most subordinates, but also the most who are still inexperienced and need assistance. In addition, some will be officers who have been passed up in the promotional process because of various weaknesses, and a good sergeant will try to correct their deficiencies if he can.

In many instances—such as homicides, armed robberies, accidents causing serious injury, and other cases requiring the efforts of several officers, the sergeant will probably take command and direct the activities of his subordinates. But on many other types of calls, the sergeant will act as an observer and source of information and guidance for the officer. In these situations, the sergeant should not assume command unless he determines that the officer is having problems that require the sergeant's direct command involvement to resolve.

Assuming command of a situation when it is not required is a fault of many otherwise good supervisors. Sergeants must develop a sense of when to assume command early in their careers, because taking over when the subordinate is doing a satisfactory job not only will impede the sergeant's ability to develop into a good administrative officer, but will be a detriment to the subordinate's development of self-confidence.

The policies and procedures of all law-enforcement agencies require that sergeants respond to or be responsible for some types of incidents, among which are the discharge of firearms, accidents involving departmental vehicles, and incidents in which officers sustain injuries. Nearly all law-enforcement agencies today require investigations of all discharges of firearms, accidental or otherwise, and if someone is wounded, the summoning of a board of inquiry or similar action. The justification for the use of deadly force is becoming more limited as our society becomes more liberalized. In addition, many citizens are taking offense at an officer's unholstering his weapon for reasons other than readily identifiable self-defense, and accidents that result from such actions are frequently followed by public protests and lawsuits. For these reasons, law-enforcement administrators are tightening restrictions on the use of firearms, and it is the supervising sergeant's responsibility to thoroughly investigate incidents involving his subordinates' use of them.

Society's propensity for civil suits is also a great influence on the requirement that accidents involving law-enforcement vehicles be completely investigated by supervisors in addition to the standard accident investigation. Aside from the civil responsibility, the sergeant must determine whether or not departmental requirements regarding safe driving have been met.

DISCIPLINE AND GRIEVANCE HANDLING

Human nature being what it is, most sergeants find it difficult to dispense formal discipline. Like anyone else, they try to avoid conflict when they can, and their close working relationship with subordinates makes the task even harder. However, the effective sergeant understands the department's general orders, policies, and procedures, has trained and guided his supervisees, and is fair and impartial in dispensing discipline when it is deemed necessary. It is the sergeant's role in the disciplinary process that will be emphasized here, rather than those of the department's chief executive or the internal investigations officer.

There can be many reasons for behavior that necessitates the use of discipline, and the sergeant should be aware of them. Bittel lists them as:

Boredom
Discontent
Idleness
Lack of interest in the job
Lack of work and assignments resulting from inadequate supervision
Misunderstanding of policies and their need and purpose
Lack of uniform enforcement of regulations
Resentment

Poor communications

Emotional strain

The above can be manifested in the form of a sudden change of behavior, preoccupation, irritability, increased accidents, more absences, increased fatigue, and too much drinking.[2]

A workable discipline procedure is mandatory to protect the integrity of the department and provide reference points for the officers, to affect morale and performance positively.

> Whatever discipline system evolves within a policy agency, it should not be preoccupied with the few at the expense of the many: the agency and its many dedicated employees. Peter Drucker, a noted management consultant, believes that today's organizations are much too concerned with identifying employee defects and guarding against employee errors, generally at the expense of productive employees and the ultimate goals of the organization. While this is partially true of the police profession, a police organization cannot afford to overlook the possibility of employee misconduct and must be prepared to deal with it positively and fairly. A balance must be found and maintained.[3]

Care should be taken to ensure both thoroughness in investigating the complaint and fairness to the employee. The procedure at many agencies is to refer all complaints to an internal affairs unit, which makes a record of the complaint and then refers it to the supervisor of the officer named in it. This assignment is designed to personally involve the supervisor in the investigation of the complaint, thus enabling him to learn firsthand the extent of his subordinate's involvement in the incident. Because of his personal knowledge of the subordinate's character and past behavior, the sergeant's judgment should carry a good deal of weight in reaching a conclusion; however, internal affairs officers must be alert for any indication of overprotectiveness by the sergeant.

About the only satisfaction a sergeant can derive from investigations of complaints comes when a complete investigation justifies the actions of his subordinate. Most complaints prove to be unfounded, but in any case, the sergeant must learn to accept and investigate them objectively and thoroughly, because the most effective means to prevent abuse of the public is through vigilance and prompt disciplinary action when abuse is found.

Participation by the officers in the establishment of procedures can be helpful in reducing their defensiveness and hostility. To be sure, first-line

---

[2]Lester R. Bittel, *What Every Supervisor Should Know*, 3rd ed. (New York: McGraw-Hill, 1974). Reprinted in *Supervisors Handbook*, International Association of Chiefs of Police, Gaithersburg, Md., 1976, p. 4.

[3]Ibid.

supervisors should have a say in the development and administration of discipline. It is often at their level that the complaint originates or that the initial information is gathered.

Some departments have effectively incorporated their policies, procedures, and rules into ongoing training programs and use questions about them in promotional examinations. This helps reinforce awareness of the rules and regulations.

Even though most departments have a specific person assigned to investigate complaints, the accused officer's immediate supervisor will have a part to play in the investigation, even if it is only initial fact-finding and verification of events. In cases involving minor infractions, such as improper uniform or tardiness, the immediate first-line supervisor should verify the facts, talk to the employee, and even do the disciplining. Training programs can incorporate the most appropriate procedures and techniques to ensure that the sergeant is doing the best job possible.

The National Advisory Commission says:

> During the adjudication phase of internal discipline proceedings, a police agency must insure that the accused employee's immediate supervisor is consulted in developing the recommendation for the complaint's adjudication. More than anyone else, the immediate supervisor should be able to evaluate the overall conduct and performance level of his subordinate and, if a penalty is indicated, to determine how severe it should be.
>
> The supervisor's recommendation must be subject to administrative review for objectivity and consistency. The police chief executive can use this recommendation as one factor in determining his final decision on the complaint's adjudication and penalty. Consistency is needed to insure, among other things, that patrol officers are not disciplined more harshly than detectives who commit similar acts of misconduct.
>
> Civil service regulations, or others that limit penalty determination, may hamper the entire process. A choice between a 30-day suspension or termination does not provide enough flexibility for penalizing an employee who is guilty of serious misconduct but who nevertheless can become a valuable member of the agency.
>
> When an internal discipline complaint is sustained, a determination must be made as to the course of corrective action. In a few cases, the misconduct can be attributed to the police agency's failure to provide the employee with adequate equipment or training. In some cases it may be a result of a faulty procedure or policy. Such findings may provide a basis for the police chief executive to effect changes in procedures. Incidents such as these may not require any action against the employee.
>
> Usually, however, it is the employee's behavior that must be changed. Corrective measures include retraining, psychological assistance, or reassignment from a particular job classification. Most frequently, disciplinary actions are

called for, such as reprimand, relinquishment of time, suspension without pay, or, as a last resort, removal. The first question to ask in determining a penalty should be: What will make the employee reliable and productive in the future? Of equal importance is: What effect will this determination have on other employees and on the public? Police chief executives also should consider the effect the penalty will have on the employee's family, a factor that can seriously affect his future performance.

A few agencies announce in advance the specific penalty for a specific act of misconduct with provision for more severe penalties if the act is repeated. The greatest pressure for this system comes from labor unions, who desire consistency and prior knowledge of potential penalties.

This system severely restricts the chief executive's flexibility to fit the penalty to the needs of the employee. The set schedule does not allow for consideration of mitigation, motive, and intent. A set penalty system is inadequate to correct the employee who never commits the same act twice but seems to commit all of them once. If an employee knows the penalty he is risking, he may decide to commit the act anyway and take a chance on not being discovered. Although there is a need for some degree of consistency in imposing penalties, the set schedule of disciplinary penalties carries overweighing disadvantages.

A form of plea bargaining in assigning penalties is favored by a few police agencies on the grounds that it saves the time and expense of an administration trial board and satisfies the employees. Under this system, the employee acknowledges his misconduct but is allowed to challenge the recommended penalty. The penalty is resolved either through discussion between the chief executive and the employee, or through a hearing by a board of review empowered to judge only the degree of penalty.

Such a system departs from sound disciplinary philosophy. Although the accused should be allowed to enter a plea regarding the penalty during the process of adjudication, the chief executive should not waiver once he has exercised his responsibility of setting a penalty. If the employee disagrees with the decision, he should appeal it through the regular channels of review available.

Some police agencies publish an internal statistical report of complaint disposition and a brief description of sustained investigations. Such reports provide a vehicle by which the police chief executive can communicate the philosophy and policies of the administration of internal discipline to the police employees. If the administration of internal discipline remains confidential, even internally, it can create rumors.

A statistical report, however, should not name the involved employees. Some persons feel that because a disciplinary penalty is so personal, individuals' names should not be reported to the entire police agency. Knowledge of the penalty could linger in the minds of other employees and cause the sanctioned employee unnecessary work problems such as continued alienation, job discrimination, and limited personal advancement. Employees claim that such a document cannot convey the facts of the incident accurately or completely, and thus creates rumors and misimpressions.

Currently some police agencies are experimenting with conciliation, a form of adjudication. Conciliation allows for the complainant and accused officer to meet in a controlled, supervised discussion of the allegation. The initial requirement of conciliation is that both parties agree to it. Normally the meeting is productive, resulting in a conclusion satisfactory to all parties. Conciliation can speed up the complaint process and reduce the necessity for investigating the incident.

However, the Hartford, Conn., Police Department, which uses this technique, acknowledges that conciliation is potentially volatile as an adjudication device. The conclusion may be satisfactory to all parties, but it may not be satisfactorily supported by documentation or fact; this can be a serious disadvantage for the police chief executive if the incident is later challenged by the complainant or employee. Conciliation without investigation and documentation should be discouraged because it allows a police agency to dispense with complaints without investigation, and, therefore, without future review and audit.[4]

The International Association of Chiefs of Police emphasizes that in the disciplinary process, the supervisor's actions must be *legal, reasonable, consistent,* and *timely.* Inconsistency and favoritism in the application of discipline will have devastating effects on employee morale and ultimately on productivity. If disciplinary action is necessary, the following should be considered:

The employee's past work and disciplinary history, including the nature and recency of other offenses;
The nature and extent of the employee's contributions to the agency (awards, commendations, special projects);
The opportunity for constructive rehabilitation;
The nature of the position to which the employee is assigned (the more responsible the position, the more rigorous the standard of performance or conduct);
The type and consequences of the offense;
The possibility of misunderstanding, misinterpretation, enticement or provocation;
The existence of contributory inefficiency or misconduct on the part of others;
The degree to which the employee could control timing, location or events;
The types and severity of corrective action available.[5]

Of course, the most effective means of avoiding disciplinary action is prevention of misconduct. But when disciplinary action does become neces-

[4]The National Advisory Commission on Criminal Justice Standards and Goals, *The Police,* pp. 60–63.
[5]U.S. Air Force, "Discipline and Adverse Action for Civilian Personnel," AF Regulation 40–750, p. 6. Reprinted in *Supervisors Handbook,* p. 19.

sary, a grievance may be filed by the disciplined officer, and this often involves dealing with the union. The use of common sense, fairness, and the following checklist, developed by Leggat and McNamara, will be helpful in reducing conflict with the union, seeing that the officer gets a "fair shake," and ensuring that proper procedures are followed.

A Checklist for Grievance Handling

1. Receive the grievance well:
   ( ) Give the man a good hearing.
   ( ) Listen—don't interrupt.
   ( ) When he has finished, ask questions, but take no position.
   ( ) Take notes. KEEP RECORDS.
   ( ) Ask the man to repeat his story.
   ( ) Then repeat the essentials in your own words.
2. Get the facts—all the facts available:
   ( ) Learn the section of the contract allegedly breached.
   ( ) Check the union contract.
   ( ) Ask questions requiring more than a "yes" or "no" answer.
   ( ) Ask advice if necessary.
   ( ) Check department policy and practices.
   ( ) Check previous grievance settlements for precedent.
   ( ) Check the experience of others in similar cases.
   ( ) Reach a preliminary decision in the case—but temporarily keep it to yourself.
3. Take the necessary action:
   ( ) Avoid confusion.
   ( ) Settle the grievance at the earliest moment that a proper settlement can be reached.
   ( ) Explain your position.
   ( ) Once it is made, stick to your decision.
   ( ) Make the corrections required by your decision if possible.
   ( ) If necessary, pass all the facts to the next step or level.
4. Follow up:
   ( ) Make sure the action was carried out.
   ( ) Be alert to situations which might bring grievances.
   ( ) Correct such situations before a grievance is filed.[6]

Preventing misconduct is better than dealing with it once it occurs. The sergeant who is on top of the situation can do a great deal toward prevention.

[6]Al Leggat and Joseph P. McNamara, "Day to Day Dealings with the Union," *Campus Law Enforcement Journal*, Vol. 6, No. 5 (September–October 1976), 36.

As the National Advisory Commission on Standards and Goals mentions, most police agencies do a good job of investigating such incidents once they have occurred, but they do little to prevent them in the first place. The police sergeant should not be crisis-oriented, waiting until the misconduct occurs; he should be prevention-oriented, trying to determine the reasons for misconduct, so that future incidents can be prevented. The sergeant has a key leadership role.

DISCIPLINING THE SERGEANT

In view of the fact that officers will protect each other in many more than just in life-threatening situations, it is reasonable to assume that command officers in positions of direct supervision over field personnel will probably go to great lengths to protect fellow supervisors. In short, it would seem that lieutenants are reluctant to take official action against sergeants for supervision transgressions unless officers of a higher rank bring them to the lieutenants' attention and demand action. This would appear to be a survival reaction, based on a belief that finding fault with sergeants will cause the sergeants to look for reportable areas of criticism involving the lieutenants. Administrators are often critical of police officers for not readily reporting a fellow officer for improper conduct, and not reporting the violation is a violation itself. Perhaps administrators should seek improved methods of holding supervisors and middle management more accountable for their own actions and inactions; many problems now attributed to the police-officer rank might be eliminated if supervisors could be motivated to fulfill their responsibilities.

Usually included in a sergeant's job description is wording to the effect that although he may delegate authority to a subordinate, the sergeant is held responsible for the actions of the subordinate. Along with his responsibility for these actions from the negative standpoint—that is, for things done wrong—there is also responsibility for the quality and quantity of a subordinate's production. In reality, the foregoing is seldom practiced, and why sergeants are not held more accountable for subordinates' actions or inactions in law enforcement is not easily explained.

One possible reason is the legal orientation of the law-enforcement occupation. Seldom can a person be charged with a crime committed by a subordinate just on the basis that, as the supervisor, he is responsible for the subordinate's actions. He must have shared in the fruits of the crime, had foreknowledge that a crime was to be committed, shared in the commission of the crime, or planned the criminal act. This concept provides the near-perfect crutch on which middle management can lean, either intentionally or unintentionally, when faced with the prospect of disciplining a sergeant for the misdeeds of a subordinate.

Middle management, and even administration, would probably want to be certain the sergeant was at least aware of a subordinate's misdeeds before taking some disciplinary action against the sergeant. As an example, a middle-sized agency is known to discipline sergeants who approve subordinates' field reports that are later determined to be improper, to the extent that it should have been obvious to the sergeant if he had, in fact, read the report before giving his approval. In this instance, superior officers can be at least reasonably certain that the sergeant failed to carry out his responsibilities, especially since he initialed the report.

Although disciplinary action against a sergeant might be justified in the minds of superiors in some instances, far more often superiors are simply not certain enough of a sergeant's action or inaction to formally institute a complaint. This is particularly true when assignments are made by a radio dispatch system from a center that is not directly responsible to the sergeant involved. Policy may dictate that a sergeant is responsible for day-to-day direction of his subordinates in such a manner that he would challenge questionable assignments from a dispatch center. The problem arises when the question is asked, "Did the supervisor hear or otherwise have knowledge of the questionable assignment?"

Disciplining members of a labor organization would be another aspect of holding sergeants responsible for the actions of subordinates. In the event of a grievance and possible arbitration hearing, the proofs needed to uphold a disciplinary action sometimes exceed those required to sustain a criminal conviction.

Accountability

The foregoing would indicate that in many instances, sergeants are not or cannot be held accountable for the actions of their subordinates. This is not to say that the philosophy of responsibility as discussed here does not have merit; but the reality of the circumstances establishes the fact that sergeants can be held accountable only under certain limited conditions.

One such situation in which a sergeant might be held accountable could relate to traffic-law enforcement. For example, the administration finds that a traffic accident problem has developed and notifies patrol and traffic commanders of the fact, anticipating an increase in enforcement action. If enforcement does not increase and the accident rate continues to climb, it is reasonable to assume that administrators will hold someone accountable. Generally, that someone will be a sergeant or sergeants, depending on the size of the organization, because the sergeants are held directly responsible for the effectiveness with which the work assignments are carried out. Whether or not the administration would initiate disciplinary action that would touch the sergeants is another question. The justification for taking action is sound, since responsibility must be maintained from patrolman to chief administrator. The means, however, must be approached cautiously. It would be violating organizational principles for a chief administrator to discipline a sergeant directly if the organization had a chain of command and the chief administrator circumvented that chain of command. To accomplish his goals, the chief administrator must motivate those closest to him in the chain of command and then observe the results.

INVESTIGATIVE SERGEANTS

Agencies that utilize sergeants as squad leaders in investigations usually require that the sergeants do not investigate criminal complaints themselves, but direct and coordinate the activities of their subordinates by assigning the case, discussing its merits with the investigator before and after the investigation process is completed, and reviewing the investigative report. At times, the investigations sergeant will go into the field with his subordinates to observe their investigative techniques. At other times, he may contact a complainant to ask whether he is satisfied with the subordinate's efforts to resolve the complaint.

Most squad sergeants, however, run their operations from a desk in the investigations division. With six to eight persons to a squad, each with a caseload, the sergeant must remain at a centralized location to be available to them. The notable exception to this procedure is the method of operation of the sergeant in charge of the homicide squad. During the initial investigation of a homicide, the squad sergeant is quite apt to be on the scene, directing the investigation, because normally all his available subordinates will be assigned to the same investigation. And in addition to those regularly assigned to his squad, the sergeant may have need of additional investigators or patrol officers assigned under his direction, depending on the nature and scope of the incident at hand.

Agencies that assign initial investigations to patrol must take steps to ensure that the investigation report is complete and accurate. The intent of this procedure is to assign to the investigations division personnel for follow-up only those cases that indicate a reasonable probability of closure. In the years before the present major crime wave started, it was the general practice to assign all investigations of criminal acts directly to an investigator when reported. But as the tempo of crime increased, the investigative caseload became impossible to manage. In addition, when an emergency call turned out to involve a crime, the patrol officers answering it were expected to secure the scene and wait for the investigative team to arrive and take charge, and the officers resented being thought incompetent to investigate criminal cases.

Clearly, a change in procedure was called for. Agencies that changed the procedure and shifted responsibility for initial criminal investigations to patrol elevated the prestige of patrol officers and relieved the investigators' workload. But the change did place additional responsibility on the sergeants, because the key to the success of this procedure depends on the accuracy of investigative reports.

SPECIAL SERGEANTS

As agencies increase in size, sergeants are assigned to command units that have specific areas of responsibility and carry out these responsibilities with little or no direction from higher authority. The school safety unit, for example, is found in most city police agencies. Administrators generally review the school safety program annually and, if they are satisfied with its content, objectives, and so on, delegate authority and responsibility to the sergeant to carry it out. Monthly reports keep the administration informed of the activities of the unit, and barring and unforeseen event or the need to readjust the program, the sergeant will need no further direction to carry out his assignment.

To conform with organization principles, units such as school safety, helicopter, and crime prevention are assigned to the patrol division. This establishes the chain of command that provides direction if the need arises during emergency conditions. It also establishes a means for review of the activities of semidetached units, by having all reports pass through the chain to the divisional commander, who is responsible for notifying the chief administrator when a change of direction is indicated.

A growing number of law-enforcement agencies have recognized a need for concentrated efforts in both criminal intelligence information and internal affairs activities. Each of these areas of concern is extremely sensitive, demanding the chief administrator's personal attention and responsibility. Supervisors assigned to command intelligence and internal affairs units must be among the most dependable in the agency. They must also be psychologically suited for this assignment; many supervisors with outstanding qualifications shun assignments to internal affairs or intelligence because they do not want to associate with the clientele involved.

Supervisors in charge of intelligence units must be able to judge the character and abilities of subordinates exceptionally well. Much of the time, members of these units work undercover and alone to gain needed information on criminal activities. The possibilities of injury or corruption are great, and precautionary methods must be uppermost in the thoughts of the supervisors. Supervisors and subordinates must be noted for both ingenuity and common sense. Through the supervisor, all members of an intelligence unit must be constantly aware of the legal and moral limitations on their activities.

Control of intelligence units is maintained through a reporting system that goes directly from supervisor to chief administrator, with no stops in between. Supervisors of these units also have direct access to the chief administrator without regard to the chain of command. It is the chief administrator's responsibility to determine who shall receive the information developed by the intelligence unit.

Internal affairs units are also the direct responsibility of the chief administrator, so the supervisors of these units also must have direct access to the chief administrator. He must not only be fully aware of all investigations being conducted by the internal affairs unit, but also be certain that these investigations are being conducted in an acceptable manner. The objective should be to learn the truth of a matter as far as it can possibly be ascertained. An internal investigation is not to be used for a hatchet job, or started with the premise that the officer is guilty and used to seek out only evidence that proves his guilt. At present, the most effective means of controlling the behavior of law-enforcement officers is the chief administrator's ability to demand the truth from an officer even though it may be self-incriminating. Although such a response could not be demanded in a criminal proceeding, it can be used in an administrative proceeding that may result in disciplinary action.

ALLOCATION OF THE SERGEANT'S TIME

As part of the preliminary planning for a supervisors' school, an agency that has 18 sergeants assigned to the patrol division formulated a survey to gather data on a sergeant's activities. Using the agency's job description, the sergeants were requested to note the time in tenths of an hour that they spent on each of the duties listed. Some duties required of a sergeant, such as assigning leave days, are performed only about once a month; others may be required only once a year. The respondents were to list all duties, whether daily, monthly, quarterly, annually, or on demand. (Of course, an exact accounting of the time spent in each activity would be impossible, because in many instances several activities are being performed almost simultaneously, or the sergeant may be shifting rapidly from one activity to another in response to the circumstances at hand.)

The results of this survey indicate that the direction of subordinates, even though considered to be the primary function of a sergeant, accounts for only about one-third of a sergeant's normal working day.

It would seem that comparatively little time is spent on the function that justifies the existence of sergeants. Administrators with a growing concern for the quality of supervision in their organizations would do well to examine the sergeant's duties and responsibilities that have been increasing steadily in recent years. In many instances, the increases are identified with administrative paperwork, which reduces the available time for supervision of subordinates. It is interesting to note the change in the amount of this paperwork over the last 15 years. Until the early 1960s, sergeants were seldom required to spend any significant amount of time in either the production of or response to paperwork. In those days, the sergeant started his shift, transmitted a limited amount of information during it, and then accounted for personnel at the end of the shift. He spent most of his time checking, advising, and supervising his subordinates.

Incorporating the information learned from the study in this chapter requires clarification of some points. The first is that of the sergeant's involvement as a communicator. This analysis essentially started with the observation that a considerable amount of the sergeant's time was spent in communication. But although the survey requested responses to a number of duties that could be associated with those of a communicator, the data were not specific in establishing a definite percentage of time; however, it will be noted that each of the activities involves communication to some degree.

The sergeant's workday usually begins at least one-half hour before the shift is scheduled to go on duty. This *half hour* is used to put in order the *paperwork* that will be given to the officers, including information on criminal activity, training bulletins, complaints, subpoenas, and so on.

Ten to twelve minutes are spent at *line-up,* where pertinent information, duty assignments, and special assignments are given to the officers, and personnel and equipment inspections are conducted. Notice that in just this brief span of time, the activities of communication and inspection are taking place simultaneously.

The survey indicates that during the tour of duty, a sergeant will spend about *one-half hour checking at random with victims and complainants* to determine how an officer handled the service. This activity can be identified as quality control or an inspection activity, and if carried out properly, it is an excellent method of determining training, counseling, or disciplinary needs. It is imperative that this activity be accepted by the personnel as a means of improving service that is applied evenhandedly and objectively, and not as a witch hunt with application based on subjective prejudice.

A number of *administrative duties* account for about *one-half hour* each day, such as making out the assignments for the next day. Recording leave days, sick time, vacations, and other absences in the time book is an extremely important task, even though boring. With all the sophisticated bookkeeping systems utilized by the various levels of city government, there are still a significant number of instances when reference to the old-fashioned time book resolves a major problem in determining the amount of vacation or sick time that an officer has used in years past.

Next to the direction of subordinates, *checking subordinates' paperwork* is the most time-consuming activity of sergeants. For the sergeants surveyed, it took a little over *two hours* a day; but in this department, nearly all initial investigations are assigned to patrol, so criminal investigation reports are part of this paperwork. In addition, sergeants must check traffic tickets, accident reports, and other administrative reports.

Two hours a day may seem a great deal of time to spend on checking material that should be relatively free of mistakes in the first place, but mistakes will happen, especially when people are working under pressure. The sergeant is responsible for subordinates that are still at the recruit level and learning, as well as for older, indifferent officers who try to get by on the least amount of effort. In between these two extremes are good officers, trying to do their best but subject to human error. It is the responsibility of supervising sergeants to reduce these mistakes as much as reasonably possible.

The sergeant closes out his working day by *checking in his subordinates.* It takes about *one-half hour* to check them in and sort out the paperwork they have generated during their tour of duty. Because they are often late coming into the station at the end of their tour, the sergeant is also delayed, because all personnel must be accounted for, and it is the sergeant's responsibility to account for his subordinates.

In addition to the sergeant's daily responsibilities, he has a number that occur monthly, quarterly, annually, or at random. The assigning of leave days is a lengthy chore, but one that can have a very decided effect on morale. In agencies where assigned leave days seldom change, each officer should receive a fair assignment of weekends, holidays, and other days that have special meaning to him. To balance out a leave-day schedule for 30 to 40 officers, accommodating requests, maintaining an adequate work force each day, and making certain each officer gets his allotted number of days spread fairly evenly over the month, requires considerable time and effort. It is difficult to estimate the time given to this duty, because the sergeants and lieutenants often take turns so that one person does not get stuck with it every month.

Reviewing subordinates' monthly activity and *counseling* those who are low requires about *two hours* per month. Close attention to self-generated activity, such as traffic violations and street interviews, will often disclose symptoms of a dubious attitude, low morale, or a personal problem that the sergeant may be able to assist in resolving before it reaches a magnitude that defies simple solution.

Sergeants sometimes ride with subordinates through part of a tour of duty. The reasons for this are many—getting better acquainted with the subordinate, observing his reactions under stress or his driving habits, assessing his knowledge of his patrol area and the people within it, learning his attitude toward traffic-law enforcement, determining the state of his morale, hearing his suggestions on resolving crime problems, and so on. Riding with subordinates occurs at random, and assignment of a time value is impractical.

About *one and one-half hours* are spent each month preparing *performance evaluations* that are used at the division level to determine the progress of recruit officers, education and training needs, and the like, and are also used to inform officers of their strong and weak points that affect their progress in the department.

At one time, performance evaluations were considered in the promotion process, but owing to two problems that came to light several years ago, they now only form a basis for recommendations by the divisional commander to the administration. One problem was the failure of sergeants and lieutenants to be objective when rating their subordinates. Supervisors seemed to be displaying competition by means of these ratings: "My people are as good as yours, so if you rate yours on an average at 90 points, I will rate mine at 91." The other problem had to do with the differing value systems of the investigation and patrol divisions. The investigators were generally rated by supervisors who were very conservative, and patrol officers by those who were very liberal, so that investigators were being rated lower on the average than were patrol officers. This was obviously unfair, and the system was discontinued.

The formal training sessions conducted by sergeants for their subordinates, usually in the form of *roll call training* sessions utilizing videotaped programs, are conducted at least once a month and take up to *one-half hour* for each session. It will take at least two sessions for any one group of patrol officers to view one tape, because of time off, court time, and the like. In some months, of course, there will be several roll call training sessions, placing greater demands on the sergeant's time.

In addition, most sergeants will themselves attend some form of training session each year. It would be difficult to determine how much time is spent in these sessions, since they vary in length from part of a day to several weeks, and although some occasional subject matter might dictate the attendance of all sergeants, it is more likely that only a few sergeants will attend any one session.

An average of nearly *two hours* each month is spent on *special assignments* —such duties as parades, annual events such as festivals, the escorting and protection of visitors who require the service, or sporting events. This amount of time was calculated by making an annual computation and then dividing by twelve. In some months, there would be little or no activity that would be classified as a special event, and then perhaps a three- or four-day festival sponsored by the city, or a visit by some high political figure, would require an all-out effort for several days.

Of course, any active field supervisor will become involved in incidents that subsequently end up in court. The survey indicates that nearly *three and one-half hours* are spent each month *appearing in court*. In most instances, this is a waste of time, but the courts of today operate under the concept that all *res gestae* witnesses must be available to the defense even if there are dozens and each has exactly the same thing to say. Only rarely is a supervisor able to testify to something that is not covered in a subordinate's testimony, but court rulings require the presence of the supervisor with little regard to the time involved or the cost to the taxpayer.

Citizen complaints that are referred to supervising sergeants for investigation require an average of somewhat over *four hours* per month. With 18 sergeants involved in the survey, the average of over four hours per sergeant multiplies into a considerable amount of time; however, if the time is not expended by the supervising sergeants, it will be required of some other unit, such as internal affairs, because of the importance of quickly resolving a citizen complaint.

To most sergeants, the *recognition of subordinates for a job well done* or a written commendation for an outstanding achievement is one of the more rewarding experiences of being a supervisor. Of course, there are always a few who find it difficult to commend subordinates for doing a good job, feeling perhaps that the subordinate is just doing the job for which he is being paid. For the most part, however, sergeants recognize the human need for a pat on the back and will average about *two hours* a month in this activity.

There are numerous duties and responsibilities that have not been discussed in this analysis, some because, while they are important, they do not occur more than once or twice a year, such as the *inventory of the officers' equipment and uniforms*. Others, like *updating the callback sheet*, are seldom done. But this task takes only a few minutes each month to change addresses and telephone numbers, and when they are needed in an emergency, administrators become extremely upset on learning that a significant number of personnel cannot be contacted because the callback lists are out of date. *Proficiency in firearms*, required of all sworn personnel, must be demonstrated monthly. Although he is only required to meet minimum qualifications, the sergeant should be concerned with setting an example for his subordinates and be well qualified. These last two responsibilities take *less than an hour* of time each month but nevertheless are extremely important.

The survey indicated that disciplinary actions require the involvement of sergeants only on occasion. Whether this is a true evaluation or not is difficult to determine, but it is reasonable to assume that for the purpose of this survey, only formal disciplinary actions were considered, those involving a written document, not the verbal corrective actions that are frequently taken but seldom reduced to writing.

The sergeant has many other duties that cannot be measured by an analysis such as this. For instance, he spends countless hours *communicating with and counseling subordinates* on a great many matters—marital problems, conflict with fellow workers, money troubles, and so on.

Although the duties and responsibilities addressed here have been expressed primarily as they relate to the patrol sergeant, with few exceptions they can be applied to all sergeants assigned to positions of supervision; however, emphasis may be altered to fit the circumstances or assignment. A simple example would be the inspection of personnel and their equipment. Patrol sergeants will base inspections on the principles of a military appearance. Investigative sergeants will inspect for neatness and cleanliness, but they expect their subordinates to be inconspicuous in their surroundings—casual dress and hair style, and the like.

SUMMARY

It should be obvious by now that the activities of sergeants do not necessarily conform to their job descriptions. This says nothing about their fitness to supervise; it says, rather, that sergeants are human beings, usually doing the best they can under trying circumstances. Job descriptions are highly idealistic documents, setting goals and objectives of which only a few can possibly be attained at any one time. They are probably written in this manner with the hope that if some of the goals are achieved some of the time, the system is better than one with no formalized goals or objectives.

It has often been truly stated that the patrol division is the backbone of any law-enforcement agency; it is also true that sergeants are the nervous system for that backbone, as well as for the remainder of the body.

CHAPTER SIX

Supervisory Promotional Practices

by Kenneth E. Christian
Steven M. Edwards*

INTRODUCTION

Peter Drucker, more than a quarter of a century ago, warned the business community, "The prosperity if not the survival of any [organization] depends on the performance of its managers of tomorrow."[1]

For the most part, this statement has gone unnoticed and certainly unheeded by most police departments. Their predominant personnel practice has been simply to hire sufficient personnel to ensure an adequate number available for promotion when vacancies occur. This orientation is based on the belief that the only times the department has suffered in the past were not when people were not capable, but when the department was numerically under strength. It is assumed that the cream of the organization will rise to the top—that on-the-job training and experience will provide the skills and qualities necessary for successful performance not only for the present but for the future.

In part, much of the neglect of police personnel processes has been a

*Dr. Kenneth E. Christian, a member of the faculty of the School of Criminal Justice, Michigan State University, has served with the Bloomington, Minnesota Police Department, and the Minnesota Crime Bureau, and as a personnel consultant for law enforcement agencies.

Dr. Steven M. Edwards, a member of the faculty of the School of Criminal Justice at Michigan State Unversity, has served as a personnel consultant for several police departments in recruitment, selection, promotion, and employee turnover.
[1]Peter Drucker, *The Practice of Management* (New York: Harper & Row, 1954), p. 182.

result of the reliance on technological developments for improving policing. Historically, the advent of the patrol car, two-way radio, and telephone have made major changes in the police function. More recently, policing has grasped such technological innovations as vehicle locator systems, helicopters, computer information systems, hardware, and software. There is no question but that these developments have streamlined police operations.

However, the fact remains that, regardless of the technological advancements to improve the work conditions of the police officer, policing is a labor-intensive occupation and will continue so. It has been estimated that as much as 85 percent of police department expenditures are for personnel, but in the rush for professionalism and technological sophistication, personnel development—the issues of recruitment, selection, training, and utilization—have been ignored. One explanation may be that the outcomes of technological developments are easier to comprehend than the outcomes of the personnel process. In any case, this orientation circumvents the issue of labor. Police departments can no longer afford to pride themselves on having a progressive manpower policy by offering a competitive wage, attracting a reasonable number of college graduates, conforming to EEOC guidelines, and keeping an accurate record of impending retirements. With police agency budgets drawing tighter, largely owing to the fiscal crises in the cities, it is past time for administrators to make a serious examination of their most precious resource—personnel.

Over the years, police departments have grown in size, in the belief that more of the same is better. What were once one-man departments have burgeoned into major agencies. But they have given little attention to the efficient use of police officer talents. Now, however, several factors are operating that will require the successful department to make sophisticated use of its personnel. And the most important factor is precisely the increased size of departments.

Growth in size rapidly multiplies the complexities of organizational operation. The tasks of supervising, managing, and guiding large departments call for people with greater skill in coordination and communication. It is doubtful that any department is so well supplied with such talent that it has no need to improve its methods of identifying, developing, promoting, utilizing, and evaluating the talent as soon as possible.

Another factor, the rapid pace of technological advancement, has thrust on supervisors a new set of problems, requiring different skills from those needed to maintain a relatively stable operation. No longer can a supervisor just call on experience to solve a new problem. Difficult decisions must be made in the supervision of personnel of whom many are doing technical work.

Police departments have also been insensitive to the problems of identifying supervisory talent. Administrators have preferred to rely on an officer's knowledge of police work and his performance as indicators of promotability. While thinking they were capable of recognizing and effectively utilizing talented officers, administrators have bemoaned the lack of them. The "shortage of talent" was not perceived as related to a problem of identification, but rather to the failure to recruit the right types of people, the failure of society to instill appropriate values in the young people of today, or the failure of the educational system to develop the appropriate skills.

Much of this thinking is a result of reliance on the "good man" theory, which permeates police departments. What this "theory" says is that a "good man" can do anything and everything, and will rise to the top of the department no matter where the officer is assigned. The theory has been perpetuated by observation of a few exceptional officers who have done a good job in several assignments; it overlooks the fact that those officers had extraordinary personal qualities and should have been placed whenever possible in assignments that made the best use of them.

A more serious implication of the "good man" theory is that in order to contribute effectively as a supervisor, an officer should prove his capability in all, or nearly all, of a set of skills thought to be characteristic of all good supervisors. Proponents of the theory are apt to feel that all supervisors should be highly intelligent, incisive, analytical, decisive, articulate, aggressive, emotionally restrained, sensitive to the needs of others, consistently motivated, inspirational in personal contacts, and efficiently organized. Actually, no one of those qualities is critical to supervisory success unless the organizational climate and operating situations specifically require it.

Eligibility qualifications requiring all candidates for promotion to supervisor to meet minimum common standards in all ability and skill areas severely limit the degree to which exceptional talents and strengths can be identified and utilized. The department that sets idealistic minimums for promotion will be hard pressed to find its "good men." The department, therefore, should concentrate on identifying, analyzing, and documenting the talents of its personnel and their potential performance as supervisors.

REVIEW OF PROMOTIONAL TECHNIQUES

The personnel process in police departments, specifically in regard to promotions, has been largely unaffected by the innovations of progressive businesses and industries. Evidence of this was found in two studies of police personnel practices, one by the Educational Testing Service (ETS) and the other a joint project of the Police Foundation and the International Association of Chiefs of Police (PF/IACP).[2] The ETS survey was limited to 15 large

[2]Richard G. Kohlan, "Police Promotional Procedures in Fifteen Jurisdictions," *Public Personnel Management* (May–June 1973), pp. 167–70; and Terry Eisenberg, Deborah Ann Kent, and Charles R. Wall, *Police Personnel Practices in State and Local Governments* (Washington, D.C.: Police Foundation, 1973).

cities; the PF/IACP survey included 493 large and small police departments, with the small departments predominating.

Both studies reported that the departments surveyed used only a limited number of promotional techniques. The studies found variations in the techniques used in the different departments, but the variations were essentially in different numbers and combinations of techniques, rather than new ones. The studies provide a framework for examining the techniques of current promotional programs.

Written Examinations

The dominant factor in the promotional process in both the ETS and the PF/IACP studies was the written examination. In all 15 of the departments surveyed in the ETS study, written examinations were used as a part of the promotional process, whereas only 55 percent of the departments in the PF/IACP survey used them. In the ETS survey, the 15 departments relied on the multiple-choice test format, averaging about 150 test items. For the most part, the questions ranged from general intelligence and reading comprehension to traditional police content (law, investigation, patrol and department procedures) and principles of supervision and administration. Most jurisdictions used a general test plan or outline, usually based on an official job description, to identify the important content areas to be covered. However, neither the outlines nor the job descriptions were very detailed. Likewise, most departments had never conducted a formal job analysis of the police supervisor position.[3]

The major criticisms of this technique are, first, that in most cases where the written examination is used, no job analysis has been conducted prior to its formulation. As a result, the contents do not meet the criteria for selecting the best people, nor are they in line with the Equal Employment Opportunity Commission (EEOC) guidelines. Additionally, the examinations generally consist of a series of multiple-choice questions drawn directly from a group of selected textbooks, and the same questions are often used in examinations for various promotional levels despite a gross disparity in the functions and responsibility of those being tested. These practices bring into question both the validity and the reliability of the examinations.

The last major criticism is that many times examination writers lack in-depth knowledge of the subject matter. The test designer, attempting to simplify a rather complex process, relies on the work of others by reviewing a few standard police personnel texts or examinations from which he formulates questions. The problem is that some texts are sim-

[3]Kohlan, "Police Promotional Procedures," pp. 168–69.

plistic in regard to the police function, while others are either narrowly defined or outdated.

> This approach precludes the use of many texts that, while not particularly police-oriented, contain much useful information in such areas as personnel administration, organizational design, management, and organizational development, to name a few. The obvious results are tests that do not meet the needs of the organization, do not adequately assess the test taker, and are not validly job-related. They are obviously easy to score, very objective, and inexpensive to prepare and administer. However, viewed in terms of unfilled organizational needs and inefficiencies in the use of human resources, their cost makes them far too expensive to accept.[4]

Oral Examination/Interview

The ETS and PF/IACP surveys found that 30 and 35 percent respectively of the police departments surveyed made use of the oral examination/interview in their promotional process. The only variance was in the weighting assigned to it. In one agency, it was assigned as much as 50 percent of the total promotional score.

Oral examination/interviews have been endemic to most police department promotional processes, but the great variance in weighting is evidence of the broad gaps that exist in this technique's ability to serve in the selection process. Interviews tend to be subjective and to appeal to the most skilled interviewers' prejudices. Further, there are wide inconsistencies in the quality of the interviewing by various managers from various divisions in the department. The interviewer tends to narrow the selection criteria to one or two specific skills—probably those he himself has or most admires in others —plus a number of other traits, including appearance, demeanor, experience, and perceived weaknesses. Such myopic views serve only to exclude many who might make significant contributions to the agency.

Before oral examinations/interviews can be recommended as part of the promotional process, precautions must be taken to ensure that they function impartially and effectively, with limited subjectivity. These recommendations can improve the validity and reliability of oral interviews:

1. The most appropriate dimensions for rating in an oral interview must be identified, based on a thorough job analysis.
2. These dimensions must be used to judge each candidate's performance.
3. The rating scales interviewers use must be "behaviorally anchored." (This will be discussed later.)

[4]John Sturner, "Personnel Selection and Promotional Processes: Some Considerations," *FBI Law Enforcement Bulletin* (June 1977), p. 8.

Seniority/Service Requirements

Promoting strictly by seniority means that when a vacancy is to be filled, it goes to the person with the most time served at the next lower level who meets the minimum qualifications for it. A service requirement as a promotional criterion means that the person must have served a required amount of time in the department to be eligible for promotion. Although few police departments today promote strictly by seniority, a large number have a minimum service requirement for promotion.

The ETS survey found that in all the departments examined, seniority in rank was taken into account in the promotional process. Most departments gave little weight to it, but three allowed up to 29 percent and two assigned more than 30 percent of the total promotional score to it. In the PF/IACP survey, approximately one-third of the departments reported that seniority within rank was an eligibility requirement for promotion.

The significance of seniority as a requirement for promotion lies in the arguments for it, which tend to incorporate terms such as "loyalty" and "reward for a job well done." The position that a person is entitled to special consideration because of long years of service becomes tenuous if the purpose of the selection process is to promote the most qualified person. Length of service beyond that necessary to learn the specific job skills has never been shown to be a valid criterion of supervisory ability.[5]

Additionally, a heavily weighted seniority system conflicts with the professional model of career development for the police. It hinders the recruitment of college-educated, ambitious young people who are career-oriented. Those who do join up frequently become restless, develop morale problems, and leave the department in their most productive years. Agency administrators must remember that, given the recruitment, selection, and training, they have a nonrefundable investment in those who leave early.

Education

Even though the National Advisory Commission on Criminal Justice Standards and Goals has recommended that a bachelor's degree be required for employment as a police officer by 1982,[6] there does not seem to be a nationwide move to require additional education for promotion to the supervisory level. Only 18 percent of the departments in the PF/IACP survey reported having an educational requirement for promotional eligibility. An-

[5]William B. Melnicoe and Jan Mennig, *Elements of Police Supervision* (Beverly Hills, Cal.: Glencoe Press, 1969), p. 29.
[6]National Advisory Commission on Criminal Justice Standards and Goals, *Police* (Washington, D.C.: U.S. Government Printing Office, 1973), p. 369.

other 10 percent gave extra credit for education, and 12 percent considered education in their ranking of candidates. Only three of the 15 large departments surveyed by ETS gave credit for advanced education, and in no case was the amount of credit more than 10 percent of the total promotional score.

There have been many studies exploring the differences between college and noncollege police officers; their points of reference have generally been behavior styles, personality development, values, intelligence, cynicism, authoritarianism, dogmatism, role perception, misconduct, and citizen complaints.[7] The results of these studies are generally similar to those expressed by the Cohen and Chaiken study[8] and the Guller study.[9] Cohen and Chaiken concluded that officers who obtained their degrees either prior to or after joining the force were good performers and that the department should attempt to attract and retain similar personnel. However, they believed that non-college-educated people with average intelligence were needed for assignments such as traffic duty, where they appear to perform well and become stable, satisfied employees.[10]

Similarly, Guller stated that because the college-educated senior police officers in his study were on the average older and more firmly rooted in their jobs than the college freshmen who were not police officers, one might expect greater rigidity from them—but the opposite was true. He concluded that barring unknown variables, greater exposure to college education is what seems to make the difference.[11]

It appears that if higher education is job-related, it has a place in the promotional process. However, since this has only been alleged, police departments should concentrate on developing a job-related promotional program rather than giving credit for college education per se.

Promotional Potential

A promotional-potential rating attempts to predict the candidate's performance at the next level while only 16 percent of the departments in the PF/IACP survey required promotional-potential ratings as a condition of eligibility for promotion, 26 percent used them in ranking candidates. Only two of the 15 large cities in the ETS survey reported using these ratings; one

[7]Kenneth E. Christian, "A Comparison of the Behavior Styles of College-Educated and Non-College Police Officers" (Ph.D. dissertation, Michigan State University, 1976), p. 19.

[8]Bernard Cohen and Jan M. Chaiken, *Police Background Characteristics and Performance: Summary Report* (Washington, D.C.: U.S. Government Printing Office, 1972), p. 31.

[9]Irving Guller, "Higher Education and Policemen: Attitudinal Differences between Freshman and Senior Police College Students," *The Journal of Criminal Law, Criminology and Police Science,* Vol. 63, No. 3 (1972), 396.

[10]Cohen and Chaiken, *Police Background Characteristics,* p. 31.

[11]Guller, "Higher Education and Policemen," p. 401.

department gave them 25 percent and the other up to 10 percent of the total promotional score.

There are distinct advantages to using neutral raters who are unfamiliar with the candidates and will rate them according to their demonstrated performance. However, some police administrators advocate that supervisors maintain information logs on each of their subordinates so they will be able to support recommendations for or against promotion.[12] The problems with this approach are the potential abuses in such an emotional situation as promotion. Candidates have a right to be confronted with any information that will be used in the promotional process. Past performance should be reflected in performance-evaluation scores that have been periodically reviewed with the employee by the supervisor. If performance-evaluation scores have been made a part of the total promotional score, they can stand on their own, just like written-examination scores and any other objective test scores. All the scores taken together, with their respective weights, result in a total promotional-potential score.

Performance-Evaluation/Service Ratings

It is difficult to find support in the literature for the use of supervisory ratings in the promotional process.[13] However, about 30 percent of the jurisdictions responding to the PF/IACP survey reported making use of performance evaluations in determining eligibility for promotion. In the ETS study, 15 percent allowed extra points on the basis of evaluation reports, and 32 percent used the evaluations in their ranking of candidates. Eight of the 15 large jurisdictions used performance evaluations in their promotional process, with weights ranging from less than 10 percent to more than 30 percent of the total promotional score.

A performance evaluation could be a valuable aspect of a promotional process, but typically it contributes little. Almost everyone is rated "above average," so in practice it is nearly the same as adding a constant to each candidate's score.[14] The reliability and validity of performance ratings depends on the basis from which the rating criteria are developed and the manner in which the supervisors of the program approach the job of rating. If the criteria have been developed through a job analysis, and if the supervisors approach the rating objectively, use a painstaking, clinical approach,

[12]Benjamin Shimberg and Robert J. di Grazia, "Promotion," in *Police Personnel Administration,* O. Glen Stahl and Richard A. Stanfenberger, eds. (Washington, D.C.: Police Foundation, 1974), p. 111.

[13]Shimberg and di Grazia, "Promotion," p. 110; Melnicoe and Mennig, *Elements of Police Supervision,* p. 28; Sturner, "Personnel Selection," p. 9; and Kohlan, "Police Promotional Procedures," p. 168.

[14]Kohlan, "Police Promotional Procedures," p. 170.

allow adequate time for it, and incorporate it into their training programs, then it could serve as a part of the promotional process.[15]

Other Promotional Criteria

One of the ETS survey respondents reported that marksmanship was considered in the promotional process. Awards and commendations, evaluations by fellow employees, and in-service training were eligibility requirements for promotion reported by some departments in the PF/IACP survey. Each of these may have some validity as a criterion for eligibility for promotion. That is, in order to be eligible, the candidate must have performed adequately as a police officer. However, of these criteria, only evaluation by fellow employees can be rationally considered a potential predictor of successful performance as a supervisor.

The last promotional criterion reported by departments responding to the PF/IACP survey was veteran's preference. It was reported as an eligibility requirement by 4 percent of the departments, as a criterion for extra points by 18 percent, and for ranking purposes by 7 percent. Veteran's preference may have a place in the initial employment of police officers by the allotment of extra points after the veteran has met all the minimum employment standards. It may even be necessary to allow the veteran "absolute preference" (placement at the top of the employment list) if the state law so dictates. However, veteran's preference does not serve a rational purpose in the promotional process. If the purpose is to select the most qualified person for the position, then political, emotional, and other non-job-related criteria should not be considered.

Conservative Personnel Practices

Most police departments have been reluctant to initiate progressive personnel practices; their watchword has been *compromise.* They have made decisions on promotions, but only when they felt the decisions would be judged as fair, automatic, and justified. Promotions may be based almost entirely on length of service, time in grade, or veteran's preference, the idea being that if two people have been performing equally well as police officers, the promotion should go to the one with seniority or preference—and that is probably a good choice.

One of the clearly conservative promotional practices of agencies is the use of provisional, probationary, or "acting" appointments. This is a "safe" decision from the police administrator's point of view, since it moves a person into a supervisory position whose level of responsibility

---

[15]Melnicoe and Mennig, *Elements of Police Supervision,* p. 28.

is only slightly greater. A heavily weighted factor for the administrator in making this decision is experience, even to the extent that a person who has not done an entirely satisfactory job as a patrol officer is still moved into an "acting" position because he has had a good number of years of general experience. Because there is a feeling that the person with experience has earned the right to be promoted, the tendency is to perceive that person as having demonstrated some skills as a patrol officer, despite his shortcomings, that will transfer to the higher level. This reliance on experience is considered as valid as some of the paper-and-pencil tests and also solves the problem of what to do with the marginal performance of some senior police officers.

Such a promotion is followed by the best correcting device for the possibility of having promoted the wrong person, close supervision. Audits, daily inspections, close examination of his reasons for recommendations before granting approval of them—in effect, train closely, supervise closely, but delegate very little. Almost any cooperative individual can succeed with the supervisor controlling most of the critical situations.

A third compromise practice in police promotions is to fix very strict eligibility requirements in easily defined areas, such as seniority, experience, special assignments, training, and education. These "objective" requirements are easily quantified and rationalized by police administrators even if they are not rational or job-related.

If we agree that police personnel practices are conservative, what, if any, are their negative effects on a police department? For one thing, their restriction in range seems to offer little likelihood of much difference in the abilities of those at the top of the department and the newly promoted at the supervisory level. Because of the lack of effective selection criteria, many of the truly qualified people may not be promoted, or may be promoted too late to contribute as they should have over their careers. Unfortunately, some of these will either become dissatisfied and leave the department or "semiretire" on the job and contribute far less than they could.

When special training, advanced education, conceptual thinking, analytical skills, originality, and drive are not recognized in the promotional process, new ideas and enthusiasm are not apt to be generated at any level in the department. What we find is an organizational climate characterized by staying out of trouble—"Don't rock the boat"; giving a steady performance—"A ticket a day keeps the sergeant away"; conventional thinking—"When you think, it hurts the team," or, "Stick by the book and you won't get in trouble," or "That's the way we've always done it"; and patiently waiting one's turn on the promotional merry-go-round.

Summary

From this brief review of current promotional practices in American police departments, it is evident that leadership and supervisory skills are not prevalent criteria in the supervisor-selection processes. The overwhelming majority of departments use selection criteria that are dimensions of the patrol-officer position rather than of the supervisor position. Those responsible for supervisor selection may be more concerned with avoiding failures than with selecting successes, a procedure that results in emphasizing functional knowledge and police experience at the expense of supervisory abilities.

In many respects, it is not only the efficiency of a particular department but the effectiveness of our total complex system of local law enforcement that rests on its personnel practices. Unless we implement promotional practices that will discriminate among personnel and use relevant, reliable, job-related criteria, our service, prevention, and enforcement activities will be unavoidably inefficient. The area of police personnel development has been studied by national commissions since the 1930s, but it is still characterized more by platitudes than by constructive practices.

ASSESSMENT CENTERS

The main defect of the traditional police promotional processes is that they have evolved without the benefit of adequate job analysis. No effective promotional system can be developed without specific and comprehensive information on what the supervisor does and is expected to do. And this requirement cannot be satisfied by only casual attention, or by utilizing job descriptions alone.

Police supervisory performance is unquestionably multidimensional and must be considered as such in the development of promotional systems. The need seems to be for identification and management of several functionally unique but administratively related areas (patrol, traffic, investigation, and so on) to allow for the development of a number of dimensions for the role of the police supervisor.[16]

In order to select the best supervisors, then, the promotion process must consider all the duties of the supervisor; it must be job-related. The assessment-center concept meets the criterion of a job-related promotional process.

[16]Deborah Ann Kent and Terry Eisenberg, "The Selection and Promotion of Police Officers," *The Police Chief* (February 1972), pp. 29–30.

Historical Development

The ancient Chinese developed formal assessment procedures for screening civil-service candidates.[17] Their system was adopted and modified by the East India Company for the selection of colonial administrators around 1830.[18] Multiple-assessment procedures were used on a large scale by German military psychologists prior to World War II. They believed that paper-and-pencil tests took too "atomistic" a view of human nature, so they substituted what they called a "holistic" outlook, observing a candidate's behavior in a complex situation to arrive at a "holistic" appraisal of his reactions.[19]

During World War II, the British (in 1942) and the Americans (in 1943) adopted the multiple-assessment approach using "real-life" or situational exercises in their selection of military officers and intelligence agents.[20] Peacetime applications of group assessment were pioneered by American Telephone & Telegraph.[21]

Current Use

The assessment-center method of personnel selection and promotion is in use in city, state, and federal agencies in Canada, Great Britain, and the United States. The Federal Bureau of Investigation, the Michigan State Police, and the New York City Police Department are only three of the major law-enforcement agencies that are using the assessment-center method in selection, promotion, and career-development programs.[22]

An assessment center is not a place. Byham describes it:

> Basically, an assessment center is a formal procedure incorporating group and individual exercises for the identification of dimensions of managerial . . . success identified as important for a particular person or level of management. It differs from other techniques in that a number of individuals are processed at the same time, trained managers who are usually not in a direct supervisory capacity conduct and evaluate the assessment, and multiple exercises are used to evaluate behavior.[23]

[17]C. Northcote Parkinson, *Parkinson's Law* (New York: Ballantine, 1957).

[18]D.W. Bray and J.L. Moses, "Personnel Selection," *Annual Review of Psychology,* 23 (1972), 545–76.

[19]H.J. Eysenck, *Uses and Abuses of Psychology* (Baltimore: Penguin, 1962).

[20]OSS Assessment Staff, *Assessment of Men* (New York: Holt, Rinehart & Winston, 1948).

[21]Bray and Moses, "Personnel Selection."

[22]Muir Adair and Peter Moon, "Managers for Tomorrow—Identifying the Future Police Executives," *RCMP Gazette,* 38, 9 (1978), 1–5.

[23]William C. Byham, "The Assessment Center as an Aid in Management Development," *Training and Development Journal,* Vol. 25, No. 12 (December 1971), 10.

An assessment center can also be defined as a method of selection, in which:

> ... several different types of assessment techniques are applied to the subjects and the final assessments are made by the combined judgments of several assessors concerning the subjects' predicted behavior outside of the assessment situation. These procedures are "multiple" in two senses: with respect to the techniques and with respect to the assessors.[24]

Job Analysis

What is unique about the assessment concept is that it requires a thorough look at the requirements for the particular job, starting with a comprehensive job analysis. Only after a department has conducted a thorough job analysis can it begin to develop procedures to select the best-qualified candidates.

There is no perfect model to follow in conducting a job analysis. The goal of the analysis is to ascertain what supervisors do on the job, the types of emergency situations they must face, and the criticalness of their tasks.

The first step is to determine the requirements of the position. Again, there is no one approach. Incumbents and their supervisors can be surveyed with a questionnaire such as the Supervisory Position Evaluation,[25] which, when analyzed, can measure the critical skills necessary to perform as a police supervisor and will identify environmental factors related to the position. Other techniques to ascertain the requirements of the position are a review of the literature and an analysis of critical incidents for a particular position.

The next step in a job analysis is analyzing and defining the characteristics a person must have in order to function effectively on the job. It is important to differentiate between characteristics a person must possess before becoming a supervisor and those acquired through training and on-the-job experience. However, it is imperative that assessment strategies be devised to identify as reliably as possible those who come closest to meeting the requirements derived from the job analysis.[26]

Simulation Exercises

Only after the relevant dimensions of supervisory performance are clearly identified and defined can simulations of the position be developed. The objective is to select criterion-referenced job samples that produce activ-

---

[24]R. Taft, "Multiple Methods of Personality Assessment," *Psychological Bulletin,* 56 (1959), 333.
[25]Ed Yager, "Assessment Centers: The Latest Fad," *Training and Development Journal* (January 1976), pp. 41–44.
[26]Shimberg and di Grazia, "Promotion."

ity that can be reliably judged by observers or assessors. A critical aspect of the simulation is the realism (in regard to police problems) in the eyes of the candidates as well as of the assessors. Accordingly, the exercise should bring the candidate as close as possible to realistic problem solving, with as little "role playing" as possible.

The assessment-center approach consists of putting each candidate through a series of these simulation/situational exercises, which are designed to bring out ability and personality characteristics directly related to successful performance in supervisory responsibilities. The exercises may consist of individual tasks such as writing recommendations on a number of letters, reports, schedules, requests, notices, and so on, typical contents of a supervisor's "In" basket; or they may require elaborate group activity, as of six or eight candidates serving on a task force.

To some degree, how well the situations are handled is informative— for example, the best recommendations on the "In"-basket items, or controlling the task force. Much more important is the picture obtained of the abilities, skills, styles, and personalities of the participants. Such characteristics are observed as degree of planning and organizing, willingness or reluctance to make decisions, initiative, clarity and impact of written and oral communications, awareness and sensitivity to the thoughts and feelings of others, problem analysis, management control of work activities, independence of judgment and action, delegation, energy level, leadership and motivation, work standards, risk taking, and stress tolerance.

The assessment center differs from traditional promotional procedures in that it does not measure past performance as a patrol officer, but rather records a candidate's current demonstrated aptitude for a supervisory position. Competition is secondary, since each candidate's behavior is rated on the degree to which each dimension is displayed during an exercise.

Assessment

The selection and training of assessors is critical for providing detailed and individualized evaluations of each candidate. Assessors may be selected from the department, usually one or two levels above the candidates, or from outside the department. For example, the Federal Bureau of Investigation uses its own personnel as assessors. The bureau conducts a five-day program to provide up-to-date training that will enhance the assessor's own supervisory techniques and perspective. Specific training is given in observing, eliciting, and recording supervisory behavior.[27]

In each exercise, the determination and explanation of exactly what the assessor is to observe and note is important. In individual exercises, the

[27]Robert C. Quigley, "Management Aptitude Program: The FBI Assessment Center," *FBI Law Enforcement Bulletin,* 45, 6 (January 1976), 5.

assessor may examine the results of an activity such as the "In"-basket, or may observe a formal presentation. For group exercises, observers may have specific assignments to concentrate on one or more of a group of candidates engaged in a work simulation. Here, the assessor may be given much or little structure, ranging from using a checklist to making observation notes.

The key element in successful assessor training is emphasis on the separation of observations and evaluations. It is essential that assessors record their observations immediately, postponing any evaluation until the conclusion of the exercise.

The ratio of assessors to candidates is ideally 2:1; however, 3:1 and even 4:1 ratios have been used by some departments. Likewise, the ideal number of candidates appears to be six, but some departments assess eight people at a time. A rotating schedule is generally used, so that each assessor observes and evaluates a different candidate or candidates on each simulation exercise, thus producing several different assessments. These assessments must then be combined through discussion into a consensus evaluation agreeable to all assessors.[28]

Summary

The effectiveness of a promotional program is best measured not so much by the number of highly qualified people on whom it bestows supervisory responsibility, but rather by the accuracy with which it excludes those who are performing in a superior fashion as patrol officers but who would become personifications of the "Peter Principle" if promoted to supervisors.[29]

A police department can develop an effective promotional program to fulfill the requirements considered basic to operating an assessment center, which include:

1. Establishing the dimensions assessed through analysis of relevant job behaviors
2. Using simulations as exercises
3. Using multiple-assessment exercises
4. Using multiple assessors
5. Distinguishing behavior observation from behavior evaluation
6. Pooling judgments as the final basis for evaluation[30]

Such an assessment center, with measurable and challenging job-related exercises and an opportunity for open and honest feedback, will meet the supervisory promotional assessment needs of police departments today.

[28]Deborah Ann Kent, Charles R. Wall, and Raymond L. Bailey, "Assessment Centers: A New Approach to Police Personnel Decisions," *The Police Chief*, 41, 6 (June 1974), 74.
[29]Quigley, "Management Aptitude Program," p. 11.
[30]Ibid., p. 8.

PERFORMANCE EVALUATION

Development of Performance Measures

Historically, police performance measurement is far from a novel idea. In a generic sense, it can be traced back to Sir Robert Peel.[31] In his analysis of police reform, Peel demonstrated to Parliament that the traditional patrol programs of London in the 1820s were seriously inadequate.[32] As a result, Peel was allowed to develop and establish a uniformed patrol force of "bobbies" that is now considered the model of modern police organization.

In the years since Peel, police performance measurement has continued, but in a less-than-organized manner. In the United States, the most prominent means of analyzing police performance has been the use of gross organizational summative statistics. In 1829, New York was the first state to systematically collect criminal statistics, with the dual purpose of using the information for administrative purposes and providing an index of the nature and extent of criminality.

In 1850, under a law that governed the censuses of 1860 and 1870, the gathering of federal statistics was attempted. Most of the information gathered concerned prisoner dispositions, which entailed examination of court records, and since court records were sporadic, the venture failed. Then in 1880, Fredrick H. Wines sought to enlarge the scope of the inquiry on crime for the 1890 census, through the use of court dockets, prison records, records of justices of the peace, and reports from police departments. But as before, the information that appeared in the census was of little or no value, owing to its incompleteness.

The period 1920–1930 produced a great deal of discussion concerning the best measures of assessing police activity.[33] Police chiefs of the early 1900s continuously judged programs or departmental performance in an informal, "seat-of-the-pants" manner. That is, methods or tactics were considered and appraised, but the process was not recorded or retained. Criteria underlying decisions of adequacy or deficiency were not clearly articulated and sometimes bore little relation to program objectives.

[31]T.A. Critchley, *A History of Police in England and Wales* (Montclair, N.J.: Patterson Smith, 1972), pp. 47–50.

[32]Lee Melville, *A History of Police in England* (Montclair, N.J.: Patterson Smith, 1971), pp. 227–30.

[33]For a comprehensive analysis of the development of criminal statistics, see Louis A. Robinson, "History of Criminal Statistics (1908–1933)," *Journal of Criminal Law and Criminology*, Vol. 24, 125–39; *Crimes of Violence*, A Staff Report to the National Commission on the Causes and Prevention of Violence, Vol. II (December 1969), 13–42; Sanford Bates, "Criminal Records and Statistics," *Journal of Criminal Law and Police Science*, Vol. 19 (1928), 8; Joseph A. Hill, "Cooperation between State and Municipal Bureaus and the Federal Census Bureau in the Compilation of Criminal Statistics," *Journal of Criminal Law and Police Science*, Vol. 12 (1922), 529; Fred A. Knoles, "The Statistical Bureau—A Police Necessity," *Journal of Criminal Law and Police Science*, Vol. 19 (1928), 383; John Koren, "Report of Committee on Statistics of Crime," *Journal of Criminal Law and Police Science*, Vol. 1 (1910), 417; and Thorsten Sellin, "The Basis of a Crime Index," *Journal of Criminal Law and Police Science*, Vol. 22 (1931), 335.

One of the best early examples of this "seat-of-the-pants" management was found by Raymond Fosdick in his analysis of detective bureaus. Fosdick noted that there was an "amazing lack of an ordinary business [sense] in the prosecution of work." He said:

> The head of a detective force deals with crimes which come to him generally in the shape of specific complaints. It would seem, therefore, that some knowledge of the relation between complaints and arrest—that is, between crimes known to the police and crimes "cleaned-up"—was absolutely indispensable to adequate supervision. In only a few departments, however, were records maintained upon which this knowledge can be based. . . . In most departments the records of complaints have no relation to the records of arrest, with the result that it is impossible for the head of the [detective bureau] department to establish any standard for measuring the effectiveness of his effort.[34]

Fosdick further reported:

> The annual report of most chiefs of police in the United States solemnly set forth the number of arrests during the preceding year as if this number, large or small as it may be, were something of a badge of distinction—a certificate that time had not been wasted.[35]

Because there was a trend toward improving police performance-measurement techniques, the Committee on Uniform Crime Records of the International Association of Chiefs of Police published the "Uniform Crime Reports," which established a systemized procedure to "consider all phases of police records and statistics in so far as [they] are related to national and state reporting."[36] As it developed, what the committee accomplished was the difficult task of establishing a foundation for the collection of police statistics of crimes and arrests.

Since this period had generated a great deal of interest in assessing the type and amount of crime by the establishment of a crime index, other formal measures were being developed, owing to the concern for increasing formality as well as administrative utility. One such attempt was made a few years after the establishment of the "Uniform Crime Reports," by Arthur Bellman in 1935. Bellman developed an extensive scale for systematic evaluation of a police organization's overall quality. In essence, the scale was a qualitative list of significant items designed to be completed by "experienced police analysts"; as Bellman put it:

> Inexpert persons or groups, looking for a chance to "stir up something," will come to grief if they attempt to use the score sheets, which are intended to be used by experts only. Many of the matters listed on the sheets are technical and

[34]Raymond B. Fosdick, *American Police Systems* (New York: Century, 1920), pp. 339–40.
[35]Ibid., p. 340.
[36]Bennett Mead, "Police Statistics," *The Annals* (November 1929).

require professional diagnosis. A rating by a layman would in all probability not present a true existing state of affairs at all.[37]

To refine his scale, Bellman developed broad functional areas, and then broke them down into 685 different questions that concerned departmental policies, procedures, and equipment. This process he based on the available literature concerning the topic, discussions with numerous police officials, and his personal investigation of police agencies in the United States. It was his belief that the development of such a method would "accomplish a two-fold purpose: the rating of a police organization according to certain standards, and the improvement of the service."[38]

In regard to the detective function, Bellman prepared a list of duties and then developed a rating process by assigning a maximum value of two points for each duty. Table 6-1 shows an example of how a detective involved in the investigation of a crime could achieve a "perfect score," 376 points.

TABLE 6-1

Detective Rating

	Number of Total Duties Performed per Function	*Total Possible Score*
1. General duties of detectives	11	22
2. Pawnshop	20	40
3. Fugitive	15	30
4. Forgery	17	34
5. Narcotics	19	38
6. Burglary	15	30
7. Homicide	15	30
8. Arson	13	26
9. Robbery	12	24
10. Auto theft	18	36
11. Bunco-pickpocket	13	26
12. Adult missing person	15	30
13. Post office	5	10
"Perfect Score"		376

Source: Arthur Bellman, "A Police Service Rating Scale," *The Journal of Criminal Law and Criminology,* XXVI (May–June 1935), 74–114.

[37] Arthur Bellman, "A Police Service Rating Scale," *The Journal of Criminal Law and Criminology,* XXVI (May–June 1935), 79.

[38] Ibid., p. 75.

Despite the fact that this massive effort by Bellman was a novel approach to examining a police organization to determine functional efficiency, it fell to attack in less than a year. Critiquing the Bellman Scale in the same journal was Spencer D. Parratt, who questioned the arbitrary weighting process that Bellman had assigned to the duties under each function. The basic question Parratt asked was, "To what extent is the Bellman instrument analogous to a yardstick, a balance, or a thermometer as a measuring device?"[39]

What Parratt was pointing out was that "quality" and "efficiency" in a police department did not necessarily mean a high score, since the Bellman Scale carried no instructions as to what was included or excluded in those terms. To illustrate his point, Parratt said that the "modern police department is at least as complicated as vegetable soup," and since the quality of soup can be evaluated only by listing every ingredient, the use of the "Bellman instrument as the formula for qualitatively describing a complete department is obviously deficient, since it is highly selective in its classification."[40] It is this rather selective classification process with regard to quality that makes police administration so complex. As Parratt said:

> Police administration is a composite of many continua, or variables, in behaviors, states of mind or attitudes and external conditioning factors. Quality is an abstract moral term which might be significantly applied in the balance of constituent elements in what the evaluator considers correct proportions of each. A police administering system is more or less of many things, but quality is a relationship between these many things in their operative conditioning. One cannot aspire to measure quality as a moral abstraction without first providing for evaluating the constituent elements contributing to its totality. The Bellman instrument has undertaken an insurmountable task in disregarding the fundamental and seeking to measure the composite. It seeks to erect superstructure where no foundation has been built.[41]

Contemporary Performance Measures

Since the Bellman and Parratt attempts, efforts have been undertaken to establish other police evaluation procedures. Many of them have been quantitative measures that have shifted from departmental activity to individual officer activity for the purpose of identifying job-related standards for police-officer selection. Through this sequence of events, the police role has

[39]Spencer D. Parratt, "A Critique of the Bellman Police Service Rating Scale," *The Journal of Criminal Law and Criminology*, XXXVII (March–April 1937), pp. 895–905.
[40]Ibid., pp. 897 and 898.
[41]Ibid., p. 898.

been defined by the activities of the officers, and personnel evaluation programs have evolved to measure these activities.

The National Advisory Commission on Criminal Justice Standards and Goals noted in its report that evaluation should be an integral part of the personnel development process, beginning with identification of personnel who appear to have the potential for intensive development, continuing with assessment of their progress, and culminating with their final evaluation for advancement or promotion. The report further stated:

> Evaluation of personnel should be related to the skills, abilities, and knowledge required for the target position. An employee should be measured by his grasp of these requirements and his performance of the tasks required in the advanced position. His progress should be documented.[42]

Despite the commission's recommendation that police departments make evaluation an integral part of the personnel development process, the tendency remains to associate measures of program performance (arrest rates, convictions, traffic citations, and so on) with employee performance.[43]

Marx, who has produced valuable materials on both program and personnel measures, noted in a 1973 paper, "Few measures are available with which to make comparative ratings between departments or men, or the same departments over a period of time. The few measures that are available are used too uncritically. . . . Many police departments make no effort to assess performance at all. The departments that do, tend to use measures which are inadequate on a number of grounds."[44]

Although the purpose of Marx's work and that of the National Project to Develop Police Program Performance Measures was to research measures of police programs, they found that individual-officer performance measures were interrelated and subject to the same shortcomings: They were too crime-control-oriented; tied to the reward system, which quantifies arrests, citations, and so on, focusing on how much rather than how well; used without regard to or knowledge of their relationship to police objectives; and defined by the police almost exclusively, not by the clientele.

It would appear that no one is willing to start with substantive role definition followed by a job analysis and then a comprehensive personnel performance-evaluation program. Instead, the state of the art is such that we

[42]National Advisory Commission, *Police.*

[43]National Project to Develop Police Program Performance Measures, "Police Program Performance Measurement—A Selective Review of Contemporary Literature" (unpublished draft American Justice Institute; Sacramento, 1976), p. 99.

[44]Gary T. Marx, "Alternative Measures of Police Performance" (paper delivered at the meeting of the American Sociological Association, 1973), pp. 1–2.

have the cart before the horse and now are trying, without reversing the procedure, to make a sulky out of the cart. In these circumstances, no matter how hard we try and how many scientific formulas we use, we will always be laboring under the handicap of the cart before the horse.

Most of the performance-evaluation systems currently in use in police departments are open to attack for two primary reasons—because of their subjectivity, and because of their focus on irrelevant criteria, criteria other than job performance. Subjectivity exists when two evaluators viewing the same job performance can come to different conclusions in evaluating it. The use of irrelevant criteria renders a performance evaluation invalid. Among the forms that have been subjected to attack are the following: general narrative or promotional-potential reports, paired comparison, rank order, behavior checklists, person-to-person evaluations, peer ratings, graphic trait scales, general ratings, and forced-choice ratings.[45]

Several police agencies across the country are now experimenting with various forms of management-by-objectives or goal-setting appraisal instruments. These types of appraisal tend to specify a job duty and then list observable job behaviors that identify whether and how well the job duty has been accomplished. It is hoped that further experimentation in this area will lead to validation studies and then to widespread use among police departments.[46]

The most promising developments dealing with performance evaluation in municipal police departments were begun in 1971.[47] Both projects involved the determination of critical components of patrol-officer behavior through job analyses, and the transformation of these dimensions into behaviorally anchored performance scales. The scales were developed with the goals of gaining acceptance by police officers, supervisors, and command officers, of being modified to fit the needs of any department, and of being technically sound.

As a component of their research, Dunnette and Motowildo developed eight different rating scales plus an overall performance scale for the position of sergeant, based on information provided by sergeants and their supervisors in a major metropolitan city.[48] The names of these scales are:

[45]David M. Hanley, "Forced-Choice Performance Evaluation in a Municipal Police Department," *Police Chief* (January 1975), pp. 34–35.

[46]Theodore H. Curry II and Gilbert H. Skinner, *Police Personnel Decisions and Equal Employment Opportunity* (East Lansing: Michigan State University, 1978), p. 65.

[47]Marvin D. Dunnette and Stephan J. Motowildo, *Police Selection and Career Assessment* (Washington, D.C.: U.S. Government Printing Office, 1976); and Frank J. Landy and J.F. Farr, *Police Performance Appraisal: Technical Report* (University Park, Pa.: Law Enforcement Assistance Administration, 1975).

[48]Dunnette and Motowildo, *Police Selection.*

A. Concern for Subordinates
B. Scheduling, Coordination, Deployment, and Manpower Allocation
C. Supervision
D. Performing Administrative and Inspection Functions
E. Decision Making and Initiative Where No Firm Guidelines Exist
F. Training and Planning
G. Integrity, Dedication, and Conscientiousness
H. Dealing Effectively with the Public and Superiors
I. Overall Job Performance

A review of Job Category A, "Concern for Subordinates," in Table 6-2 shows how these scales differ from the more traditional rating forms or scales. Each scale is a list of possible examples of behavior. The examples form an outline of what is involved in one aspect of the job of a sergeant, and they serve as guideposts or trail markers along the scale, marking off more and more effective performance. This type of scale has many positive properties: The dimension definition is adequate; the anchors are descriptive of levels of the performance dimension; and, since raters are requested to mark only at full or half-point intervals, the actual rating is made with a minimum of confusion.

In spite of their rather unusual appearance, behaviorally anchored scales differ from traditional scales primarily in development. They are based on the identification of critical incidents in the performance of people in a particular job—in this case, police supervisors. These incidents should clearly differentiate the good performer from the poor performer. Their identification and the cataloguing of the behavior they represent is the operation of job analysis, as described earlier. Further, the behaviorally anchored rating-scale procedure orders incidents describing a particular performance category according to the proportion of that category that they represent.[49]

THE USES OF PERFORMANCE MEASUREMENT

There are three primary uses for performance-appraisal information. Measurements of individual work performance may be used for administrative decisions, research purposes, or personnel counseling. Administrative decisions include such subjects as salary adjustments, special-duty assignments, layoffs, and promotions. Performance information could be used in

---

[49]The steps to be taken in developing a behaviorally anchored rating scale can be found in Frank J. Landy, *Performance Appraisal in Police Departments* (Washington, D.C.: Police Foundation, 1977); and Dunnette and Motowildo, *Police Selection.*

TABLE 6-2

Concern for Subordinates
Job Category A

Showing concern for subordinates; being considerate; taking personal interest in their problems; giving recognition when deserved; using human relations principles; filling in for subordinates who have special problems; being aware of subordinates' needs and feelings.

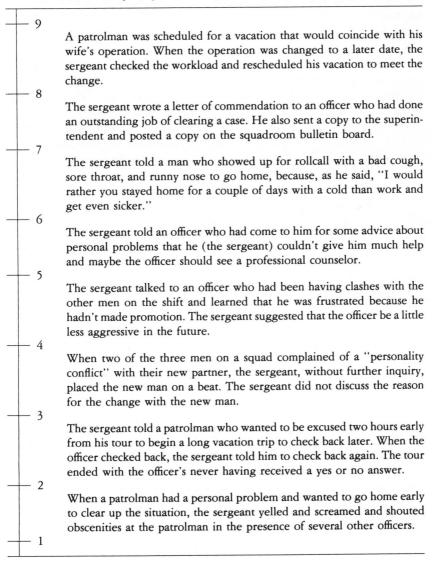

9

A patrolman was scheduled for a vacation that would coincide with his wife's operation. When the operation was changed to a later date, the sergeant checked the workload and rescheduled his vacation to meet the change.

8

The sergeant wrote a letter of commendation to an officer who had done an outstanding job of clearing a case. He also sent a copy to the superintendent and posted a copy on the squadroom bulletin board.

7

The sergeant told a man who showed up for rollcall with a bad cough, sore throat, and runny nose to go home, because, as he said, "I would rather you stayed home for a couple of days with a cold than work and get even sicker."

6

The sergeant told an officer who had come to him for some advice about personal problems that he (the sergeant) couldn't give him much help and maybe the officer should see a professional counselor.

5

The sergeant talked to an officer who had been having clashes with the other men on the shift and learned that he was frustrated because he hadn't made promotion. The sergeant suggested that the officer be a little less aggressive in the future.

4

When two of the three men on a squad complained of a "personality conflict" with their new partner, the sergeant, without further inquiry, placed the new man on a beat. The sergeant did not discuss the reason for the change with the new man.

3

The sergeant told a patrolman who wanted to be excused two hours early from his tour to begin a long vacation trip to check back later. When the officer checked back, the sergeant told him to check back again. The tour ended with the officer's never having received a yes or no answer.

2

When a patrolman had a personal problem and wanted to go home early to clear up the situation, the sergeant yelled and screamed and shouted obscenities at the patrolman in the presence of several other officers.

1

a personnel research program either to validate application tests or to determine whether a training program is effective. Finally, individual supervisors could use performance information to help subordinates achieve personal and organizational goals; that is, the information should be useful for counseling and personal development.

These three processes—administrative decisions, research programs, and personal counseling—go on in every department, regardless of its size or circumstances or the form of performance appraisal. Formal programs for the development and implementation of performance-measurement strategies simply try to improve the efficiency of the three procedures by providing more accurate and reliable data for making the necessary decisions.

Organizations and situations change, and a performance-appraisal system must change with them. Plans should be made to examine a system regularly to ensure that it continues to function as intended. Officers formed into groups to evaluate the adequacy of the system might suggest the addition of new dimensions, or the expansion of some old definitions, or the addition or deletion of some examples of levels of performance. All personnel should participate in the regular evaluation and modification of a basically good and well-developed system.

A performance-appraisal system should serve the needs of the department. It should not be so rigid and inflexible that the members of the department must change to fit the characteristics of the system.

Summary

Current individual-police-officer performance measures are tied to the quantitative measures of police department performance that were instituted by Sir Robert Peel in 1829. These organizational measures were formalized almost 100 years later by the International Association of Chiefs of Police as the "Uniform Crime Reports."

Various statisticians, researchers, and managers have attempted to refine organizational activities and to develop rating scales to measure and evaluate individual-officer performance. The most recent trend has been behaviorally anchored performance scales. Through job analysis, a range of possible behaviors in critical situations is identified and placed as guides along a scale marking off more and more effective performance.

It appears that behaviorally anchored performance scales meet the criticisms of most ratings or measures, subjectivity and irrelevant criteria. In addition, they are flexible and capable of being modified to fit the needs of any department.

A MODEL FOR CAREER DEVELOPMENT

Introduction

We have no doubt that many minor frustrations and grievances are traceable to lack of proper attention to enlightened attitudes towards management. Indeed, it is probable that failure to appraise men properly for promotion by putting too much weight on their qualities as policemen, and too little on their potential as leaders, has in the past had adverse effects on the service.[50]

For too long, police departments believed that the "cream would rise to the top," where it would easily be identified and skimmed off for the next available promotional vacancy. The result of relying on this organic process was that eventually, the "good man" was promoted to a position where he could no longer function effectively, and there he stayed.

Business and industry discarded the "good man" theory when a synthesis of "scientific" and "human relations" systems of management, called "career development," was put into use during World War II as a means of selecting, training, and placing thousands of new recruits in the war industries and the services. Its basic tools were task analysis, job specification, job-related training, and personnel data systems. This manufacturing approach looked at career development as essentially a production problem; programs were designed to produce the necessary supply of supervisory and managerial talent, à la "The Man in the Gray Flannel Suit."

Police departments, with their philosophy of management by command and control, soon became enamored of this scientific approach. Personnel units developed recruitment strategies, training programs, performance-rating systems, and promotional examinations. Police officers were recruited, oriented, trained, evaluated, and promoted by administrative fiat, leaving them with little alternative but to follow departmental policy.

The reliance on scientific-management development techniques, together with the hierarchical organizational structure of police departments, has produced an environment uncongenial to individual career development in law enforcement.

It is generally acknowledged that the police profession does not offer good career opportunities. For the most part, the system of career advancement is tied to the rank structure. The rank structure and accompanying reward

[50]Unpublished report on the Kansas City Police Department by Public Administration Service for the President's Commission on Law Enforcement and Administration of Justice, 1967.

mechanisms dictate that if you want to get ahead you must become a sergeant, then lieutenant, then captain, and so forth up the ladder. . . . There is no other way to go. A highly competent patrol officer must leave the street to get ahead. Too many times, the position of police officer is a dead end street.[51]

The scientific approach has served police departments' crisis-management orientation. In spite of its assumption that what is good for the department is good for the individual officer, some people do want some of the things such structured programs provide. However, experience has tended to support Douglas McGregor's observation:

There is almost no relationship between the amount of formal programming and machinery of management development and the actual achievement of the organization in this respect. I sometimes think the correlation may be negative! Programs and procedures do not *cause* management development, because it is not possible to "produce" managers the way we produce products. We can only hope to "grow" them, and growth depends less on the tools we use than on the environment which is created. If it is conducive to growth, the main job may be keeping the soil in good tilth and keeping the weeds down.[52]

Career development in industry is too narrowly confined and directed toward supervisory, middle-, and upper-management personnel. The need in the police service is for a system that emphasizes the career development of the total department; within this, supervisory and management abilities can be identified.

An alternative approach to career development is needed, one that focuses on the individual rather than the organization. Such an approach involves less emphasis on formal programming and techniques and more on controlling the organizational environment and the methods of development.

Organizational Environment for Career Development

There is no question but that career development within a police department is influenced by the organizational environment—which includes the organizational structure, the reward structure, the department's growth, managerial procedures, philosophy of job rotation, and the role of the immediate superior on the job. However, the case has been made that no organiza-

[51]Kansas City Police Department.
[52]Douglas McGregor, *The Human Side of Enterprise* (New York: McGraw-Hill, 1960), pp. 204–5.

tion has taken a systematic approach to developing a comprehensive promotional program. Police agencies can no longer afford to take a less-than-critical examination of their personnel practices, given the personnel costs in police departments.

Organizational structure. The traditional hierarchical structure of police departments, with rigid lines between units and hierarchical levels, reduces the occasions for individual supervisors to assume responsibilities, to innovate, and to exercise discretion, and this results in a structure that limits growth.

On the other hand, a less-centralized structure allows for an environment in which the supervisor must take responsibility for his behavior. By his actions, he can gain intrinsic rewards that in turn encourage him to take still more responsibility and to grow.

Reward structure. Career development in an organization is also influenced by the reward structure. In general, the centralized hierarchical structure and functional divisions in police departments restrict the opportunities of supervisors to assume responsibility, try new ideas, and exercise judgment. Instead, rewards are given for conformity and improving the unit's statistics.

Personal growth and career development involve learning, which in turn is a function of the reward structure. Individual development is influenced by the types of satisfactions on the one hand, or frustrations on the other, that are characteristic of the department. When supervisors are rewarded for unit loyalties and for their narrow efforts to improve their particular function, while behavior that contributes to the objectives of the organization as a whole goes unrecognized, the objectives of the unit will prevail at the expense of the department.

The department needs people who want to pursue line operations and staff careers as well as administration. But the salary and reward structure must be comparable at any given level. If some jobs are considered busy work or less glamorous than others, and do not offer comparable rewards even though they are essential, they will not attract people who will grow in specialized professional competence or who aspire to supervise and manage these units. The rewards, both formal and informal, must encourage aspiration to these essential positions as operatives and as supervisors.

Departmental growth. Obviously, an expanding metropolitan or suburban police department creates a different environment for managerial growth than does a static rural area or an urban area facing economic reversals. Regardless of the degree of control the department has over these characteristics, they do affect the nature and rate of managerial development. Within each environment, the managerial philosophy and practice can influence the nature and quality of the processes of growth.

Managerial procedures. The pressures to abide by managerial guidelines control the behavior of supervisors. Rigid systems of control cancel out the positive advantages of decentralization. When a supervisor is under constant surveillance by means of detailed reports on his behavior, he loses his freedom of action and his opportunity to grow.

Job rotation. Departments differ in the ways they give supervisors wide ranges of experience to try out their abilities, and the different ways yield different results. When the movement is rapid and the supervisor knows he will be there only a short time, he never really accepts responsibility. His concern is to not "rock the boat," to act as an assistant. Learning is minimal, probably no more than if he were an observer, never really getting involved.

The other extreme is to move people only at the higher levels. Rotation is usually confined to moves in the same unit until a person reaches the top, then to another unit that is completely unfamiliar to the employee. In this new environment, the pressures will be severe, his leadership will be inadequate, and the department will suffer, all in the name of job rotation.

Job rotation should be synonomous with growth, challenge, and career development. At the supervisory level, rotation into various positions in the same unit allows a person to learn supervisory techniques while deepening his substantive knowledge about the unit and his activities. Rotation into a new unit is less traumatic when the new supervisor is allowed time to acquaint himself with its functions and to observe the techniques of the predecessor.

The superior to whom the new supervisor reports can make the rotation a true learning experience. This takes time and consideration, and his efforts must be recognized and rewarded by the department for job rotation to be effective. Nurtured by the department, the nature and extent of the learning can be a source of growth for both the new supervisor and his superior. Whether it is, however, depends on the timing of the move, the type of position, the length of time in the position, the role of the superior, and the personal motivation of the new supervisor. To view job rotation in the abstract without careful consideration of the individuals and the organizational environment is comparable to setting out to sea in a boat without a rudder, hoping that the environment will guide the boat to its destination without serious problems.

The immediate superior. On-the-job training is a significant process in the career development of supervisors. Each contact between supervisor and superior involves some kind of learning. When the superior gives a command, assigns a task, delivers a reprimand, bestows praise, conducts an interview, calls a meeting, works with staff, or takes any other type of action, he is teaching. The style of the superior affects the attitudes, behavior, and expectations of the supervisor, either changing, modifying, or reinforcing them. Each on-the-job contact is so powerful that it tends to overcome the effects of unreinforced classroom supervisory training.

To say that each superior is responsible for the development of his subordinates is basic. Whether he will devote time, consideration, and energy to their development will depend on his style and on the environment of the organization. In policing, rewards and recognition generally go to those who excel in areas other than developing subordinates. In fact, one would be hard pressed to identify a police department that is recognized nationally for developing police talent. Unless superiors are held accountable, organizational climates are nurtured, and rewards and recognition are available, career development will continue to happen by chance rather than plan.

SUMMARY

If we reflect on it, we can see why the manufacturing approach to personnel placement is not desirable for career development in police departments. It focuses on formal programs without regard to the organizational environment. If police departments want to develop supervisory talent, they must give attention to the conditions that develop it. When they provide an organizational environment in which a supervisor participates in setting goals, is given responsibility for his own actions, and is allowed room for self-actualization, then he is personally and professionally encouraged to take on more responsibilities and to grow.

CHAPTER SEVEN

A Cross-Cultural Comparison of the Role of the Sergeant

by Stephen G. O'Brien*

INTRODUCTION

The study of comparative policing is becoming increasingly valuable, not only as an area of academic interest, but as one of practical value also. The international nature of crime and terrorism is one very cogent reason why the police of different nations should have a good understanding of one another's objectives and methods. Another practical reason, and one with which this chapter will be concerned, is to investigate whether there are any lessons to be learned from how and why policing styles have developed in another country—in this case, a country that has common roots with and many institutions similar to the United States of America.

This chapter looks at only one aspect of the comparison—that is, the role of the first-line supervisor—but attempts to place it in the context of policing as a whole. This involves, of course, some consideration of law, government, and social setting.

GOVERNMENT

The United Kingdom of England, Wales, Scotland, and Northern Ireland represents countries with different historical backgrounds, and there-

*Stephen G. O'Brien is currently Professor of Law Enforcement, Macomb County Community College, Warren, Michigan. He was formerly Chief Superintendent for In-Service Training, Metropolitan Police, New Scotland Yard, London, England.

fore a variety of social and economic needs and problems, along with the geographic differences.

However, the present discussion will be limited to the policing of England and Wales. That of Scotland and Northern Ireland is no less interesting, but for historical and administrative reasons it will be more suitable for the purposes of this chapter to concentrate on the former area. England and Wales together have a population of about 50 million, perhaps 8 million of whom live in the area of Metropolitan London. Note the high density of population this indicates, and think about it in a police context.

The observer, looking at the British system of government from a police perspective, will find more similarities than differences with that of the United States. For instance, despite the supremacy of Parliament, the small size of the country, and the bureaucracy of "Whitehall," the British equivalent of Washington, the Anglo-Saxon tradition of local government has not been extinguished. Over the years, however, a great deal of clutter of small units of local government, found to be financially and administratively impracticable, has been cleared away. The last reorganization produced, by 1974, a system of metropolitan counties, combined counties, and counties. There is rather more to it than that, but for the present purposes, this general description will suffice.

The picture is one of a central government consisting of a cabinet and democratically elected representatives. All legislation is made by Parliament, which delegates certain well-defined powers and duties to the local authorities outlined above. The counties in turn elect their representatives to carry out these duties. So there are chairpersons, mayors, councils, and chief executives, just as one would find them in the United States.

The main difference is that the unit of government is the county, and matters of policing and education, for example, do not devolve below this level, although there are county districts and parishes that have certain local responsibilities. The concept, good or bad, of the autonomous small city supplying all or most of its own services does not exist. Administrative and economic difficulties have placed unacceptable strains on small units of government, however deep-rooted the need and feeling for local self-determination.

HISTORY OF THE POLICE

Within the framework of government described above operates the police system of England and Wales. This section will explain how the police idea developed, and how it operates today.

The Anglo-Saxon origins of Anglo-American policing and law have been so thoroughly dealt with as to render superfluous any further treatment of the subject here. Rather, the eighteenth century presents itself as the most useful beginning point. Three aspects of England of that period will serve as a framework on which to erect the subsequent development of policing. These three aspects are (1) London, as city, capital, and metropolis; (2) rural England and Wales; and (3) emerging industrialization outside London.

In London during the eighteenth century, as elsewhere in the country, the ancient system of constable and watch prevailed in varying degrees of usefulness; as in the United States, it was only in the uncomplicated, closely knit rural society or small town that it was working with any degree of efficiency. Reform of the system was taking place in London, however, and for two broad reasons. First, this was, after all, the age of reform. Beccaria had published in Italy his essay "On Crime and Punishments," and Jeremy Bentham in England was advocating utilitarianism. These were not the sole reformers, of course; the most important from a police point of view were the Fielding brothers. Henry Fielding is best known as an author, but he and his blind brother John served as magistrates during the second half of the eighteenth century at the famous Bow Street Court in the center of London, where today there stands a museum of police history of considerable interest to historians of this era. The Fieldings performed an inestimable service by coupling rather efficient law enforcement with justice in the magistrate's court through the medium of the Bow Street Runners.

The second reason for reform was that London, functioning as both capital and financial center, was at the peak of a period of social disorder and street crime. This was despite the fact that improvements were taking place in the watch and court systems, and that a very effective river police had been established in 1800. This latter innovation was due to the vision and enterprise of Patrick Colquhoun, the author of *A Treatise on the Police of the Metropolis,* published in 1797. Critchley points out that Colquhoun was ahead of his time, particularly in his insistence that the first consideration of a well-regulated police was the prevention of crime.[1] (Note that although a kind of convenient legend has arisen linking the concept of crime prevention only with Sir Robert Peel, this is not the case.)

It was in this climate of events that Parliament eventually overcame its repugnance to a professional police force for London's streets, and Sir Robert Peel was able to get his Police Act passed in 1829. This act, it must be emphasized, applied only to Metropolitan London and not to the small but immensely rich area of the "City," which was left to make its own efficient policing arrangements that exist to this day.

Enough has been said on the subject of Peel and the Metropolitan Police so that I shall avoid repetition here. However, what is vitally impor-

---

[1]T.A. Critchley, *A History of Police in England and Wales,* 2nd ed. (Montclair, N.J.: Patterson Smith, 1972), p. 39.

tant for the reader to grasp is that the London Metropolitan Police, with headquarters at Scotland Yard, was answerable directly to the Home Secretary through the two (at that time) commissioners; and the Home Secretary in turn, as now, was answerable to Parliament. Further, the new police force was responsible for policing only the Metropolis, a radius of seven miles, and not the rest of the country. Incidentally, the Metropolitan Police District has grown with London over the years and now covers more than 800 square miles.

From 1829, it was only by a very gradual process that the cities, towns, and counties of England were persuaded to establish efficient professional police forces. The arguments that greeted successive parliamentary committees, and that all voiced fears of national police forces, would have a familiar ring in American ears attuned to the danger signals of central government control. T.A. Critchley tells us of some of the hostility that greeted the Police Bill of 1856, which sought to coordinate and centralize certain of the aspects of policing outside London toward greater efficiency.

> The House was warned against tampering lightly with those municipal institutions in which English liberty was cradled; the Bill was the most un-English measure ever introduced, and seemed more fitted for Naples than for England; it was an insult to the nation; no government, however tyrannical, could have constructed such a measure; the country would soon be overrun by 20,000 armed policemen—"perhaps Irishmen or foreigners"; the government betrayed an indecent lust for power; the boroughs should be subject to the degradation of inspectorship; the Home Secretary would become a second Fouché with spies all over the kingdom.[2]

However, events that were the obvious concomitants of a rapidly growing industrial society combined over the years to force the issue. In addition, two world wars and the police strikes of 1918 and 1919 were powerful motivators toward progress. All these ingredients have combined to produce the present organization of police forces in England and Wales.

THE POLICE TODAY

From a peak figure in England and Wales of 223 police forces in 1945, the number has now dropped to 43, with no force having fewer than 700 sworn personnel. Further amalgamations may take place, either voluntarily or on the orders of the Home Secretary in the interests of efficiency. (See Table 7-1.)

In the present system of local government, with its concept of powers and duties delegated by the national government in London, control of the

[2]Ibid., p. 117.

TABLE 7-1

Police Establishment and Strength in England and Wales, 1975

	Establishment	Total Strength	Women
Outside London	89,379	84,516	5,840
Metropolitan Police District	26,678	21,420	882

Individual Forces Some sample strengths and establishments				
	Establishment	Strength	Women	Population
Devon and Cornwall (combined County)	2,673	2,697	120	1,339,800
West Midland (Metropolitan County)	6,471	5,683	250	2,777,500
Dorset	1,018	1,099	72	572,900
Total number of forces in England and Wales = 43				

Source: Great Britain, Her Majesty's Stationery Office, *Report of Her Majesty's Chief Inspector of Constabulary, 1975,* Appendix 1, p. 90; and *Report of the Commissioner of Police of the Metropolis,* Appendix 1, p. 82.

police is a three-way partnership between the Home Secretary, the local authority, and the chief officer of the particular force. Thus, in accordance with the Police Act of 1964 and subsequent regulations made under the act, certain standards are laid down that are deemed necessary for the efficiency of the police on a national basis. These standards relate to selection, training, pay and pensions, discipline, and conditions of service generally.

Next, the police committees appointed by the duly elected representatives of the local government are, in turn, responsible for paying, housing, and equipping their police forces. The police regulations provide that a police committee shall be made up of two-thirds councillors appointed by the council, and one-third magistrates of the area of the police district. The magistrates, incidentally, although local and unpaid, are all appointed by the Lord Chancellor, not locally elected.

The reader may wish at this point to make a three-way comparison of local control and accountability between the United States, Britain, and Canada. Canada has police boards composed of both councillors and judges, and in Ontario, the Ontario Police Commission exercises a guiding and supervisory function.[3]

[3]William and Nora Kelly, *Policing in Canada* (Toronto: Macmillan, 1976).

Finally, the third member of the partnership, the chief officer (the chief constable), as a professional, is left free to recruit, promote, and discipline his subordinates below the rank of assistant chief constable, within the provisions of the police regulations. These matters and the operational control of his force are his responsibility, to be carried out without interference by the police authority. However, there must be accountability, and the chief constable reports both to the Home Secretary and to the police authority about how he has discharged his responsibility. Should he or his assistants be found wanting, they can be dismissed by the police authority, but only with the consent of the Home Secretary.

The only exception to this arrangement is the London Metropolitan Police, which is, as it started out to be, directly responsible to the Home Secretary, who is the police authority for that force.

Such an arrangement is heavily dependent on the quality of the senior officers of the particular force. When they are appointed by the police authority with the consent of the Home Secretary, they will conform to certain criteria. These criteria are in no sense political, but relate specifically to professional fitness for the appointment. Among them are adequate and varied experience in each rank, both operational and administrative; lateral movement between forces; and, of course, a full complement of all the professional training that the service provides at the national level.

In addition to the idea of quality control over the highest command positions, there is also financial control. Fifty percent of the total costs of policing have for many years been met by the central government, subject to the efficiency of the individual force. This efficiency is monitored by Her Majesty's Inspectors of Constabulary, appointed from the ranks of chief officers, who report to the Home Secretary concerning all aspects of policing.

The rationale of the foregoing is the feeling that certain matters must be standardized for the sake of both public and police; that in order to preserve the local character of policing, certain other matters must fall to local control; and finally, that the chief constable must, subject to public accountability, be left free to do his job as a professional.

POLICING ENGLAND AND WALES

Before going on to deal with the specific matters relating to sergeants in the police, it is essential to give some thought to what the task of policing is in England and Wales. Remember, for our purposes, Scotland and Northern Ireland have been put on one side, not because their problems of policing are less, but because a deliberate limitation of the area of research better serves the purpose of this chapter.

It is useful to think of England and Wales as having approximately the same land area as the state of Michigan, but with a population of about 50 million as opposed to about 9.5 million. Because of tourism and sentiment, the instant image of Britain is one of redcoated soldiers, helmeted bobbies on foot patrol, and drafty castles; each visitor can add to this list. The real picture, from a police point of view, is one of an industrial society—now multiracial, with all the problems that involves—doing its best to preserve a long tradition of stability under democracy.

For example, citizens do not always "come quietly." The annual rate of officers reporting injury as a result of making arrests rose, in London alone, to just short of 3,000 in 1975.[4] But of course, as in the United States, there are variations in the risk factor so far as the officer is concerned, depending on the environment in which he works.

The patrol officer in the street, whether mobile or on foot, is unarmed except for a concealed truncheon. However, should an occasion require the use of firearms, these are available to trained and authorized officers on an *ad hoc* basis. Although property-crime patterns do not differ drastically from those in many parts of the United States, there is a significant difference in the matter of murders. The Home Secretary, responding to a question in Parliament, gave the total figures for homicide (murder, manslaughter, infanticide) for 1977 for the whole of England and Wales as 482.[5]

Before it is thought that this represents some kind of Utopia, the total number of indictable (serious) crimes reported to police in 1975 reached 2,105,631.[6] There is a steady annual increase occurring in crime, particularly in the areas of violence and juvenile crime. In relation to the latter, Sir David McNee, the present Commissioner of the Metropolitan Police, was reported in the British press in August 1978 as saying:

> It's quite frightening, and distressing, and the sooner society—parents, teachers, and social agencies—does something about it, the better.[7]

As to relationships with the public, although people in general think highly of their police—according to the opinion polls—attitudes also reflect the diminution of respect for authority that has been universally experienced over the last two decades.

In court, even though the police officer generally feels that he is fairly treated and well supported, provided that he himself is in the right,

[4]Great Britain, Her Majesty's Stationery Office, *Report of the Commissioner of Police of the Metropolis, 1975,* Appendix IV.

[5]*Police Review* (England), Vol. 85 (June 23, 1978), 940.

[6]Great Britain, Her Majesty's Stationery Office, *Report of Her Majesty's Chief Inspector of Constabulary, 1975,* p. 1; and *Metropolis Report,* Appendix 13, p. 103.

[7]*Daily Express,* London, August 27, 1978.

he does contend that soft penalties and overconcern for the rights of the accused have eroded respect for the law. Few have expressed this more clearly than Sir Robert Mark, former Commissioner of the Metropolitan Police:

> You must make up your minds what you really want. Absolute unrestricted freedom for the individual, with all that implies? Freedom to rob, freedom to steal? Freedom to break into shops and houses? Freedom to intimidate minorities by threats and violence? Do not think I am exaggerating when I say that this is part of the price you will pay increasingly for the continued enjoyment of liberty without responsibility. You can compensate the victim of criminal violence, you can provide free medical care for those who suffer it, you can encourage crime prevention and insurance to lessen the hardship arising from crime, but you will not reduce crime until you recognize that it is no longer enough for every citizen to play a negative part in law enforcement. The surest and quickest way to reduce crime and achieve a more humane and enlightened penal system is to increase the likelihood that the guilty will be convicted. If you are not willing to do this, you cannot hope to achieve any real progress in reducing crime, or changing society's object in dealing with criminals. It is for you to decide.[8]

Apart from crime, political demonstrations and trade disputes are always part of the British scene, and now racial disturbances make increasingly heavy demands on police manpower. Canceled leaves and the likelihood of injuries do not improve the morale of the patrol officer, particularly if he is married.

This brief picture is not intended to dramatize the situation, merely to be realistic. The difficulties of police work are universal. On the credit side must be added the fact that the work attracts good people, and that the conditions of service, protected as they are by national legislation, offer an excellent career, either laterally or promotionally.

THE ORIGINS OF THE RANK SYSTEM

To examine the origins of the rank structure, and how the military titles arose in the first place, is not merely an excuse for an excursion into history. It is necessary because of the criticisms of police management styles and structures that have become fashionable since the establishment of the Presidential Commission on Law Enforcement and the Administration of Justice. Various writers have expressed themselves on this theme, the essence of which is that the monolithic, military, self-perpetuating style of management that has been prevalent in the police is counterproductive to progress. Mas-

[8]Sir Robert Mark, *Policing a Perplexed Society* (London: Allen & Unwin, 1977), p. 43.

low, Herzberg, McGregor, and others have been frequently quoted in support of this contention. As a result, remedies such as the modification of uniforms, team policing, the abolition of rank emblems, and the changing of titles have all been either contemplated or adopted with varying degrees of success. As the flurry of innovation dies down, perhaps we are beginning to realize that the intention is more important than the trappings, and that it does not matter what you call it, or how you dress it up; people will soon know whether or not you are doing what you are paid for.

It all started when Sir Robert Peel, having steered his Metropolitan Police Act through Parliament in 1829, selected two commissioners and gave them the task of setting up the police organization in Metropolitan London. They established a police office in a courtyard known as Scotland Yard.

However, by 1829, quite a considerable body of police already existed in London, what with the Bow Street horse and foot patrols, the parish watch and constables, and the river police. The "peelers" or "bobbies" were superimposed on this system for the first few years, until it died away. The mounted patrols and the river police were absorbed into the regular police structure.

Col. Charles Rowan was a regimental soldier of considerable experience, and his fellow commissioner, Richard Mayne, was a lawyer. They made a formidable team. It was only natural that Rowan should draw heavily on his military background in planning the Metropolitan Police organization. He had in mind the company, platoon, and section formation of his army days. In the British Army, the command ranks for these formations would have been, and still are, respectively, captain, lieutenant, and sergeant. Rowan and Mayne, while maintaining the general idea, created the following structure: For the company, they substituted the division and placed in charge of it the superintendent. For the platoon, they substituted the sub-division and called the officer in charge an inspector, a rank borrowed from the Bow Street patrols. Then, finally, they put the sergeant in charge of the relief, or shift. (The title of sergeant, in fact, may not have been purely military; it occasionally crops up in descriptions of the policing arrangements of the times.)

This description of the allocation of ranks contains some simplifications (see Table 7-2), but it does give the broad approach taken by Rowan and Mayne. What they achieved was an amalgam of the military and the civil: military formations and civilian titles. Military organization also made itself felt in other ways. General orders, police orders, and an instruction book for the guidance of sergeants and constables were quickly published. The instruction book ensured that all constables and supervisors were aware of the discipline code and the duties that were expected of them. In addition, sergeants were issued a drill book, and expected to put the constables through their "turnings," as the foot drill

TABLE 7-2

Rank Structure in the British Police

England and Wales Outside London	Metropolitan Police, Scotland Yard
	The Commissioner
	Assistant Commissioner
Chief Constable	Deputy Assistant Commissioner
Assistant Chief Constable	Commander
Chief Superintendent	Chief Superintendent
Superintendent	Superintendent
Chief Inspector	Chief Inspector
Inspector	Inspector
Sergeant	Sergeant
Constable	Constable

was described. And, in the manner of posting sentries, after posting their men, the sergeants marched them onto their beats. At the end of the tour of duty, they would collect and inspect all reports. Once again, we are made aware of a civilian organization, dressed in blue but subject to a severely military way of life.

Miller makes a most interesting comparison of the life and times of the New York Metropolitan Police with that of the Metropolitan Police in London. He makes the point that the London policeman, although pledged to serve the community, was separated from it by the severity of the discipline code.[9] On the other hand, the bobby was also very fortunate in that he had no political bosses, so he was able to carry out his duties without undue pressure.

THE ROLE OF THE SERGEANT IN A DEVELOPING POLICE SYSTEM

The foregoing is sufficient to indicate the origins and work of the sergeant in those far-off days. It must have been arduous but straightforward. As police forces developed throughout the remainder of England and Wales during the nineteenth century, the role of the sergeant was essentially the same wherever he worked. However, certain factors have arisen over the years that are crucial in considering the role of the sergeant today. These will be analyzed in turn.

[9] Wilbur R. Miller, *Cops and Bobbies* (Chicago: University of Chicago Press, 1977), p. 151.

Police Discretion

Because of the quasi-military structure, it is very easy to equate the constable with the private soldier, whereupon the sergeant falls easily into place in the organization. But, of course, the sergeant has never had any more authority under the law than the constable, and neither has his chief officer. In the street, making an arrest, one is no better than the other. In England and Wales, as the police gained the trust and acceptance of the public, they became accustomed to using discretion and were expected to do so. In the Metropolitan Police, a passage in General Orders stated that instructions could not be provided to cover every situation, that much depended on the initiative of the individual officer, and that in the use of that initiative lay his claim to future advancement. It was not the sergeant or the inspector who was revered or reviled by the public; it was the constable on his beat or patrol. This was bound to affect the military relationship imposed by the discipline code. The constable was, after all, despite his miserable salary and appalling working conditions, an officer of the crown. All this happened gradually, of course, but the paradox of the man at the bottom having the same authority as the man at the top has complicated the role of the sergeant ever since.

Police Mobility and Radio

Apart from the independence of the officer in the street in enforcing the law, another major complication of the role of the sergeant was the advent of the patrol car and the radio dispatch system. With the car came a wider range of action, and wider still when the officer was getting his instructions not from the sergeant, but straight from the station. The gap widened.

Supervision of Reports

At one time, a constable's worst moment was handing in his reports to his sergeant. Even more than constant direct contact with his men in the street, this told the sergeant of the quality of the work being carried out. He could retrace the incident, criticize the quality of the contents, order a rewrite, and generally exercise control over the situation. However, with the passage of the years, sheer volume of work has changed the format of reports and altered administrative systems. The worst critic of an officer's work may now be the secretary in the office. The paper must move on, and there is no time to be too fussy unless something is radically wrong.

Education and Management Approaches

Over the years, the standard of education of both the public and the police officer has greatly increased. Coupled with that, as elsewhere in the world, attitudes toward authority have changed. Thus, management styles have had to alter and staff associations have had a large say in all kinds of policies.

Development of Policing Policies

The most illuminating spotlight of all on the role of the sergeant has been provided by experiments with policing methods. The first of these was the Aberdeen Team Policing system, which appeared in 1949. This approach, well documented in the literature of American policing,[10] represented a breakthrough from the old set formula of laid-down beats and laid-down times. The sergeant was provided with a team of constables and deployed them in a given area at his own discretion, but in accordance with the problems of time and area. The idea aroused great interest in Britain, and soon, versions were in use in a number of forces. The Metropolitan Police used this system or modifications of it for a number of years. That it was not an unqualified success was due to two main factors. First of all, manpower proved to be a stumbling block. The essence of any system of this sort is to keep the team intact and up to strength. Second, the quality of the supervisor, always paramount, is critical in team policing. Police officers generally work on their own, priding themselves on being their own bosses. Like many who are loosely supervised, they may, within limits, vary the type and times of their workload. But put them in a group, and these rugged individualists require management of a high quality to keep them pulling in the same way at the same time.

However, the potential of the basic idea was recognized, and the second principal approach, the Unit Beat system, sought to combine the best of both worlds by giving the individual officer autonomy and responsibility to make decisions, but with help when required, by backing him up with the detective, the crime collator at the station, and the sergeant.

THE SERGEANT

The Sergeant under the Law

There is little real difference in the overall function of the sergeant between the police of the United States and their British counterparts. Sergeants supervise in the station and in the streets, and are to be found performing various administrative tasks. They are the first-line supervisors of the Criminal Investigation Department of each force. Sergeants are also to be found as police duty instructors in the regional training schools situated

[10]Samuel G. Chapman, *Police Patrol Readings,* 2nd ed. (Springfield, Ill.: Charles C. Thomas, 1972), pp. 374–444.

throughout England and Wales. However, the legal framework in which the sergeant in England and Wales operates is different in a number of ways, and requires discussion.

It was indicated before in this chapter that the sergeant is, in law, a constable, and is appointed to this ancient office on joining the police:

> I, _____ of _____, do solemnly and sincerely declare and affirm that I will well and truly serve our Sovereign Lady the Queen in the office of constable, without favour or affection, malice or ill will; and that I will to the best of my power cause the peace to be kept and preserved, and prevent all offenses against the persons and properties of Her Majesty's subjects; and that while I continue to hold the said office, I will to the best of my skill and knowledge discharge all the duties thereof faithfully according to law.
>
> The declaration has to be made:
>
> (a) In the case of the Metropolitan Police, before the Commissioner, or an Assistant Commissioner of Police for the Metropolis.
>
> (b) In any other case, before a justice of the peace having jurisdiction in the area.
>
> Having been appointed, the officer has all the powers and privileges of a constable throughout England and Wales. [Police Act 1964 S.19][11]

However, one must not read too much into the declaration and its attendant power. This does not indicate a nationalized police force, or a state police. It does provide a reminder that the constable or any other officer is above politics and serves the people as a whole. So far as the power to act is concerned, its advantages when making an arrest in another jurisdiction are obvious. But it does not mean that when officers go on vacation and become bored, they will make a sortie into the nearest town and start issuing tickets, or making traffic stops. Their reception would be dubious, to say the least.

In addition to their basic authority as police officers and first-line supervisors of the shift or relief, sergeants in England and Wales have another very important function. In those two countries, there are no prosecutors at the county, district, or city level such as there are in the United States. There is just one Director of Public Prosecutions at the national level. This is an appointed office. The policy is that the Director's office will be informed of all criminal cases of a particularly sensitive or serious nature, and will, subject to the circumstances, exercise the right to prosecute them. Thus, the police well know that the papers will have to go to the Director's office in all cases of murder, for one example, and in the same way, should a complaint against police involve a criminal charge, he will have to be informed. The result of

[11]E.R. Baker and F.B. Dodge, *Police Promotion Handbook, No. 3* (London: Butterworth, 1975), p. 334.

this is that the police prosecute their own cases before the courts. If the case is a minor one, or if no complications are expected, the uniformed officer in the case will deal with it. Otherwise, a lawyer on the staff of the department, or retained for the purpose, will act for the police. Obviously, when the case goes to trial, the police must be legally represented.

All this throws a heavy responsibility on the sergeant on duty at the desk. When a prisoner is brought in, there are the usual matters of care, safe custody, and searching to be dealt with. But unless there are special arrangements in force, it is the responsibility of the sergeant to decide (1) whether the offense for which the person has been arrested is one for which the law allows arrest without warrant, and (2) whether there is some credible evidence to support the charge.

Should the charge be drunk and disorderly, there is little difficulty. But in the case of theft, burglary, or robbery, the law in England presents pitfalls just as it does in the United States. In such a case, the CID officer at the station has the specialist training to ensure that the charge is good in law and will follow it to court. However, when all is said and done, it is the responsibility of the sergeant to ensure the correct procedure initially. The document on which he enters the charge obviously differs in form but not in spirit from force to force. It goes to court with the defendant at the initial hearing and forms a permanent record throughout the proceedings, whether they end in conviction or acquittal. It can well be appreciated that the training of the sergeant in this area prior to his promotion is regarded as most critical.

The last remaining duty of the desk sergeant toward the prisoner is in the matter of bail. The prisoner must be bailed, having first given due regard to the seriousness of the offence and his likelihood of turning up at court, and will be released either on his own recognizance or upon that of a surety.

The Sergeant as Supervisor

Having dealt with the legal and ministerial authority of the sergeant, it is now time to turn to the role of that rank within the police organization. The general picture of the British organization in the minds of Americans is one of formality at the very least. Americans might also expect a severe standard of discipline, conformity, and bureaucracy. Whether this is at all true of other aspects of British life, it is certainly not true of the police service. In fact, the very similarity of the ingredients that make up police work in both countries tends to produce correspondingly similar organizational patterns and problems.

For example, we find the same kind of people doing the same kind of job within a basically similar kind of criminal justice system, at least so far as common-law principles are concerned. The police officer in England and Wales tends to be drawn from the upper working class or lower middle class of the population, and brings to the service all the strengths and weaknesses, pride and prejudices, of that section of the people. A number of studies have been done on why a person joins the police. None have shown any good reason to suppose that such a career choice is due, in Britain any more than in the United States, to markedly authoritarian tendencies. Recruit selection processes include, of course, personality tests that seek to isolate this factor and weed out the unsuitable. The training and probation system are also effective filters in this respect.

Police recruits present a picture of ordinary people seeking a steady career. They are the kind who value law and order and tend to be conservative in their approach to life, like to be with others, and like to pursue a physically active life with a spice of adventure. Once the officer is in the street, the authority and discretion that the public vests in the police, together with the rigors of everyday contact with all sections of the population, very quickly produces a young person who is alert, impatient, critical, and action-oriented. Cynicism quickly replaces idealism, and the paradox arises, common to both cultures, of youth in authority. It is in this climate of action and feeling that the sergeant has to exercise supervision over his shift of both male and female officers. (The Sex Discrimination Act of 1975 ensures that there is no separate establishment for women, and they are therefore an integral part of the patrol force.)

It is a sensitive job for the sergeant. He or she will have to be "first among equals" in order to be accepted. The first hint that absence from the scene of an incident is due to tardiness or incompetence will quickly be seized upon. On the other hand, too zealous an attention to the work of the officers in the street will be just as bitterly resented. The sergeant will, of course, be expected to be the buffer between the shift and higher authority. It is unlikely that either will be completely satisfied.

Age, too, enters into the picture. In order to allow officers of potential to progress quickly, promotion to the rank of sergeant can arrive in the early twenties. This appointment is not lightly conferred, because the recipient is under scrutiny from the younger officer on the one hand, and from the experienced officer on the other.

These are perennial difficulties, unique neither to culture nor to organization. Obviously, they are overcome only by the creation by good management of a climate of loyalty and respect for professional ability. It is most important that the sergeant is not used as a scapegoat by those above him to divert attention from weaknesses in role definition, planning, or administration generally.

This brings us to the next point. It has already been stated that the evolution of policing has complicated the role of the sergeant beyond the simple lines of demarcation possible in earlier times. Although he or she is still the first-line supervisor, the broadening of the role of the constable has chipped away at that concept. There is no problem at all in defining the role

TABLE 7-3

Devon and Cornwall Constabulary
Promotion Board System—Constable to Sergeant

The Devon and Cornwall Constabulary has an authorized establishment of 2,673 officers. From that number, the Chief Constable is entitled to promote 428 to the rank of sergeant.

Police Promotion Regulations made under the Police Act of 1964 dictate that for a Constable to be promoted to the rank of Sergeant, he must:
(a) have passed the qualifying written examination; and
(b) have completed two years service in the police force.

The selection of Constables for promotion to Sergeant rank in the Devon and Cornwall Constabulary is achieved annually by the following method.

Each year applications are invited from Constables who are qualified for promotion to Sergeant, and who wish to be considered. Some 450 Constables are currently qualified.

Vacancies for Sergeants average approximately forty a year, depending upon retirements, resignations, and the promotion of existing Sergeants to Inspector rank.

Each officer who makes application appears before the Preliminary Promotion Board. The total recommendations of all the Preliminary Boards are then scrutinised by a Headquarters Review Panel consisting of two Assistant Chief Constables.

Consequent upon the recommendations and the subsequent review, a list of candidates for interview by the Final Board is then drawn up.

In 1977, 298 officers were interviewed by the Preliminary Boards, as a result of which 109 went forward to the Final Board to compete for forty-five places.

The Final Board, comprising two Assistant Chief Constables and a Chief Superintendent, interview the candidates and from them choose a selected list.

This list is then submitted to the Chief Constable for approval, and is then published in General Orders in alphabetical order. In fact, the list is compiled in order of merit, but that order of merit is confidential information.

Source: Ch. Insp. W.D. Webber of the Personnel Department, on the authority of the Chief Constable.

of the sergeant in a tactical situation; it is that of close supervision and instant obedience to orders by those under his control. But the expansion of the "service" role of the constable into the community calls for quite a different concept of supervision.

The police service in England and Wales has been very conscious of the need to specify the role of the sergeant. The Working Party on rank structure set down the duties and responsibilities of the rank, and the training programs prepared by the Police Central Planning Unit at Harrogate In Yorkshire for use at the Home Office regional training schools gear their objectives to those ends.

The digest of the sergeant's course stresses the concept of the "front-line manager" and looks at the task of the sergeant as falling within three areas:

1. Supervision: stressing welfare and team spirit.
2. Training: putting theory into practice, and developing the constable, even beyond the probationary period.
3. Administration: the sergeant is the leader of a section in an organization consisting of many sections.

Essential to these three concepts are the notions of communication, leadership, delegation, and deployment. Here is what one chief constable says to newly promoted sergeants:

> I appreciate your problems, your worries, your staff difficulties, the never-ending demands on your time and patience; the constant stream of paper, directives, requests, orders, complaints and demands.
>
> I repeat, you are the most important rank in the Force—the CORNERSTONE. I rely on you. You should be as proud of your Section as I am of the Force as a whole. You should seek to protect the good name and reputation of your Section.
>
> There must be no lack of cohesion, or lack of a feeling of "belonging to," among the PCs in relation to their Section.
>
> You must ensure that your Section is a complete unit, not a conglomeration of PCs out on beats.
>
> A team is a thing that you must aim for. If you are a leader, you will have your men in such a frame of mind that they will look upon you as their leader, and that they are one of a team and not individuals.

This extract was chosen not only because it provides an example of an approach to management, but also to provide the reader with a feeling for the paternalism that has long typified English county policing.

Leaving behind the concepts of management, it is time to turn to some of the actual duties and responsibilities that are laid down for the patrol sergeant:

1. The sergeant posts constables to their beats, patrols, posts, and traffic points, etc., arranging adequate coverage to meet local needs, and allocates refreshment times and reliefs.
2. He briefs constables on all relevant information, including complaints, crime, traffic, court attendance, school crossings, etc.
3. He ensures that his constables are properly dressed and equipped, usually issues personal radios, and may allocate police vehicles.

4. He allocates enquiries such as warrants and summonses.

5. He accounts for the shift and checks reports at end of shift.

6. He may be one of the first at, and will attend or be called to, all serious incidents; e.g., fatals, crimes, sudden deaths.

7. He deals personally with the more difficult or complicated enquiries; e.g., referees for licensing, firearms, or naturalization, applicants for the police service, etc.

8. He makes recommendations regarding the siting of school and pedestrian crossings, etc.

9. He liaises with the collator, crime prevention officer, CID regarding crime trends.

10. He takes command at all major incidents in his area until the arrival of a senior officer.

11. He may on occasion prosecute minor offenses at Magistrate's Court.

12. He gives individual advice and attention to probationers in his unit, and allocates a wide variety of work to them; advises and instructs confirmed constables.

13. He submits progress reports.

14. Although he has no executive powers in respect of welfare matters, he will know his men and be available for advice and consultation.

15. He has the right to give orders and expect obedience, and can deal with minor disciplinary infringements by means of a warning; reports more serious matters to his senior officers.

16. He is responsible to the law of the land for the way in which he carries out his duties.

Discipline

As a police officer, the sergeant is subject to the discipline code and the complaints procedure and, of course, as a supervisor has an added responsibility to see that they are adhered to. The procedure in both instances is governed by the Police Act of 1964 and regulations made under that act, so there is uniformity throughout the country in the way they are applied. For example, should an officer appeal against the decision of a disciplinary board, the ultimate appeal authority is the Secretary of State for Home Affairs.

A few examples of offences against the discipline code are given below. The reader may find they have a familiar ring.

Discreditable conduct: manner prejudicial to discipline, or likely to bring discredit to the police service

Neglect of duty: e.g., leaving a beat or place of duty

Corrupt or improper practice

Drinking on duty

Improper dress

Additionally, an officer is required to devote his whole time to the police service, and moonlighting is not allowed. American officers should note that taking a meal break in any eating place such as a restaurant while on duty is not allowed. Facilities are provided at police stations for this purpose.

Under the regulations, the Chief Constable or his deputy may suspend an officer on report of a possible disciplinary or criminal offense. Most allowances, except for rent, cease during suspension.

Should an officer be found guilty, punishment may be dismissal, requirement to resign (alternative to dismissal), reduction in rank, reduction in pay, a fine, a reprimand, or a caution.[12]

Regarding complaints from members of the public, the sergeant has no discretion to deal with the matter at his level, however trivial. Talking about the incident to a supervisor is very often as much as a person wishes to do about it, but since 1964, all complaints must be recorded in the Divisional Complaints Book.

For comparative purposes, the question must be asked at this stage, is the British police sergeant operating in an environment of strict discipline in which every infraction calls for action? The answer is no. The sergeant is, as always, the man in the middle. As we have seen, his subordinates hold a responsible public office and wield considerable authority. The discipline code may have to be used, and used with firmness, but only as a last resort. The sergeant who is always running to his superiors with fresh offenders will be regarded as failing in his duty. He must be able to make decisions at his level, and since he will be on probation for one year after promotion, his qualities in this respect may be judged. It may well be the most testing rank that an officer will hold. In a large force, he will inevitably be leading many men older, more experienced, and more able on the street than he is. His loyalties must extend both upward and downward. The British police officer is no more forgiving than his colleagues elsewhere when he scents weakness.

Selection and Training

The sergeant, whether man or woman, will have joined the police as a constable between the ages of 18½ and 30, subject to satisfactory standards of education and health. A woman will be at least 5' 4" in height, and a man 5' 8". Both will have had the opportunity of joining either direct from school or another occupation, or from the police cadets.

The probationary period lasts for two years and commences with a ten-week course at a regional training school. This is followed by further in-service training and attachment on returning to the officer's own force.

---

[12]Baker and Dodge, *Handbook,* p. 385.

TABLE 7-4

Devon and Cornwall Constabulary
Training System for Sergeants

1. The Devon and Cornwall Constabulary has an establishment of 428 sergeants, ranging in age from 23 years to 55 years, which is the upper limit for retirement, and in total police service from 5 years to 30 years.

2. Training is given to all sergeants as soon as practicable following their promotion to that rank. The programme of a formal training course lasts for three weeks and is prepared on a national basis by the Central Planning Unit of the Home Office. Courses are held on a regional basis, which has the advantage that officers entering a supervisory rank for the first time have the benefit not only of attending a course but also during that course of associating with colleagues and contemporaries from other police forces in their region. The course is job-related, intensive, and concentrates on improving the professional competence of the student and highlighting his responsibilities as a leader. The first week deals almost exclusively with the management side of sergeants' responsibilities. Weeks two and three deal with other legal and professional subjects which are regarded as essential tools for the rank.

3. In the Devon and Cornwall Constabulary experienced sergeants return to the Training College every five years whilst serving in the sergeant rank, for a two-week refresher course which up-dates their professional knowledge and enables them to review developments in tactical leadership. These courses are also arranged on a regional basis, although some forces do organise their own refresher courses for sergeants and may well, therefore, give them additional training at shorter intervals than the five years quoted as appropriate for this force.

4. The courses referred to in the preceding paragraphs deal with the general responsibilities of the sergeant's rank. Any sergeant who is employed on specialist duties which require him to receive training specifically appropriate to those duties, will be sent on an appropriate course.

Further training and assessment will continue throughout the probationary period, culminating in a final course and examination in police subjects.

National police regulations state that an officer may sit for the promotion examination on completion of two years' service. He is then eligible for selection to the rank of sergeant. Once he has passed the sergeants' examination, there is nothing to stop an officer sitting for the inspector's examination. However, success in these examinations is no guarantee of promotion; the average officer is not ready for the rank of sergeant until he has at least four or five years as a constable and proved his worth to himself and his colleagues.

A few exceptions are allowed so that outstanding talent may not be held back, and every year a number of constables who have achieved top scoring in the promotion examinations go before a national selection board. Those who are successful attend the National Police College for a course of professional studies lasting for one year. If successful, the officer automatically becomes a sergeant, and then an inspector after one year of probation. In 1975, 264 candidates were initially interviewed under this scheme, of whom 26 were recommended for the course. You can see that while there is such an avenue for promotion, it is quite rightly kept extremely selective.[13]

There are far fewer college graduates in the British than in the United States police. In part, this represents the national picture of the college population. But it is often felt that the police could attract a bigger slice of the educational cake. Accelerated promotion of the type mentioned above is offered to a few university graduates every year, but not at the expense of quality. Only twelve of these attended the Special Course at the Police College in 1975, having proved that they possessed the aptitude for active police duty.

Further Career

Our sergeant, having found his way through the regular system of passing the examination, proving himself on duty, and achieving his promotion after about four years, has certain career prospects open to him that form part of his motivation for his job.

If he or she is not one of the few who achieve accelerated promotion by means of the graduate entry scheme, or by being considered for the Special Course at the College, then the ordinary avenue of success is the examination for promotion to inspector, together with selection judged on performance.

The National Police College, situated at Bramshill, about 35 miles from London in the county of Hampshire, was instituted just after the Second World War and sited in its present location in 1961. It provides command training for the ranks of inspector up to chief officer. Incidentally, it has a close relationship with the United States; in addition to the continuing presence of American police officers in the courses, there is a system of exchange professorships with John Jay College of Criminal Justice in New York. Conversely, British police officers attend the FBI Academy at Quantico, Virginia.

An added attraction for students in the inspectors' courses is the possibility of obtaining a college scholarship. If successful, the officer will attend university full-time on full pay in order to obtain his degree. The opportunity is limited, however, to about 25 officers per year.

[13]Chief Inspector's Report, p. 32.

TABLE 7-5

Sergeants' Course

For Newly Promoted Sergeants at Regional Training Schools

Week No. 1

Day	1	2	3	4	5	6	7
MONDAY	ASSEMBLY including personal introductions by means of oral autobiographies.		Overview of Course	Introduction to Management P1		The Individual P2	
TUESDAY	Motivation P3		Morale P4	Duties and Responsibilities of the Sergeant P5	Case Study 1	Communication P6	
WEDNESDAY	Leadership P7	Delegation P8	Deployment P9	Deployment Exercise (briefing) E1	Deployment Exercise (presentation) E1	Case Study 2	Private Study
THURSDAY	Personnel Assessment & Staff Appraisal P10 and P11		"Manhunt" (film)	"Manhunt" (discussion)	Probationary Training P12	On-the-Job Training P13	Case Study 3
FRIDAY	Police & Public P14		Discipline and Complaints P15		Case Study 4	DISPERSAL	

Day	1	2	3	4	5	6	7
MONDAY	Researching the Law P16		Discussion	Checking of Files P17	Prosecution of Minor Offences P18	Checking of Files E2	
TUESDAY	Discussion	Betting, Gaming and Lotteries P19	Liquor Licensing P20		Licensing Applications P21	Licensing Exercise E3	Private Study
WEDNESDAY		Controlled Drugs P22	Raids— Overview P23	Raids—Roles P24	Raids—Roles P24	Discussion	
THURSDAY	Discussion	Public Disorder and Trade Disputes P25		Private Study	Major Incidents P26	Traffic Control and the Sergeant's Roles at Major Incident P27	
FRIDAY	Major Incident Exercise E4				Discussion	DISPERSAL	

Day	1	2	3	4	5	6	7
MONDAY	Charge & Bail P28	Care/ Custody Prisoners P29	Children & Young Persons P30	Discussion	Case Study 5	Drink and Drive P31	
TUESDAY	Discussion	Case Study 6	Safe Custody of Police Property & Lost/Found Property P32	Forensic Science P33	Accident Investigation P34	Stolen Vehicle Branch P35	Collator P36
WEDNESDAY	Regional Crime Squad P37	Duties of Sergeants at Scenes of Crime P38	Crime Exercise E5	Crime Exercise E5	Crime Exercise E5	Identification P39	
THURSDAY	Handling Firearms P40	Explosive Devices P41	Discussion	Crime Prevention P42	P N C P43	Research and Planning P44	Welfare P45
FRIDAY	Force Admin. & Finance P46	Case Study 7	Discussion	Review of Course	DISPERSAL		

A sergeant who aspires to one day become the chief constable of a police force will not only have progressed through the long and arduous process of professional training; he will also have had experience in a number of different forces, and have achieved high standards in each. Lateral mobility is expected in the higher ranks. It is not necessary at the sergeant stage, but opportunities are offered from time to time and are encouraged. An officer thus transferring will not lose his pension rights.

Internal mobility within a police force is also feasible and expected for career development. In these days of larger police departments, this is made easy. Outside the Metropolitan Police in London, it has been the practice for many years to transfer officers from the detective branch to uniform, and vice versa, on each promotion. This has increased professionalism and averted many of the sectarian jealousies and lack of communication that may result from specialization in one field or another.

CONDITIONS OF SERVICE

The direction in which the police of England and Wales, and indeed the whole of England and Wales, have been moving over the years is to allow for local autonomy where it is necessary to preserve the community nature of policing, yet to establish national standards in those areas where it is necessary for the efficiency of the police service and the interests of the public as a whole.

As we have seen, the provisions of the Police Act of 1964 and the regulations made under it draw the lines of demarcation between what is central and what is local. Among those aspects that it is felt must be uniform across the country are conditions of service. Although no one is ever satisfied (particularly in respect to pay and allowances), it is necessary that every attempt should be made to provide a secure base for the individual in his or her working life. This seems to apply with especial significance in the police service, where the strains and exigencies of the work are particularly evident.

The Police Council and the Police Federation

As the Boston police had their strike in 1919, so did the British police; the Metropolitan Police alone in 1918, and seven forces in all in 1919. The reasons were the same in all these cases: membership in a police union as a means of obtaining satisfactory working conditions.

The strike in 1919 was not supported by the majority of officers, because the government had already granted a pay increase and the setting up of a representative body. However, as so often happens, those who were determined to force through the idea of a police union gained support to a total of over 2,000 officers nationwide. Troops were called in in the north of England, and blood was shed.[14]

What came out of this was a greater measure of centralization for the police, particularly in the matter of pay and conditions of service. Very significantly, representation from within the service was to be achieved by the Police Federation, which exists to this day. It provides for representation for all ranks up to chief inspector. Over the years, associations have also been provided for superintendents and chief officers, so that all ranks of the service are represented.

The Police Federation is not a union. No serving officer may join a union, and to strike is illegal. It is a legal body, catered for by act of Parliament, and provides means whereby the views of the ranks about the welfare and efficiency of the service can be brought to the attention of both senior officers and the government. The election of representatives, meetings, conferences, and committees are all laid down by regulations and provide a ladder of representation that finally reaches the Home Secretary if necessary.

The peak of the representation process is reached by means of the Police Council for Great Britain:

> The Police Council originated in 1919 when the Police Act of that year introduced it as a body with whom the Home Secretary could consult on matters of pay, allowances, pensions and conditions of service whenever these matters were under review for the purpose of new regulations being made. . . . The Police Act 1964 put the new but non-statutory Police Council on a legal footing and provided:
>
> (a) that it should consider matters relating to hours of duty, leave, pay, allowances, clothing, equipment and pensions;
>
> (b) that the Home Secretary should furnish it with any draft Regulations on these subjects and consider representations on them made by the Council;
>
> (c) that any disagreement between himself and the Council on any such matter should be referred to arbitrators.[15]

What is of particular interest in discussing the role of the sergeant is that the Police Council consists of an official side and a staff side. The official side comprises representatives of both central and local government, while the staff side is composed of 27 representatives of all ranks in Great Britain, from the Commissioner of the Metropolitan Police (Scotland Yard) to the constables and sergeants. If agreement cannot be reached, the Prime Minister refers the matter to three arbitrators for a final decision.

[14]Critchley, *History of Police,* p. 189.
[15]Baker and Dodge, *Handbook,* p. 357.

The discussion above of the representative machinery is of necessity somewhat truncated, but it has been included because it relates essentially to participative management. There is an opportunity for all officers to make an impact if they so desire, at the ultimate level of government. The system is, of course, not free from the sort of difficulties that are inherent in the process of representation. In most of the areas referred to, it seems to work well. When it comes to pay and allowances, however, the matter becomes heated, and arbitration has had to be sought.

Before the reader looks too enviously upon the Police Federation, staff associations, and Police Council, it is highly relevant to look at some of the things said at the 1978 Federation Conference:

> We are asking that the police service have the right to strike. . . . We seek to achieve the status of an independent trade union for the police representative body. We seek the same rights and benefits available to all other workers under existing legislation, including the Trade Union and Labour Relations Act 1974, and the Employment Protection Act 1975. . . . In his address to the conference, Eldon Griffiths spoke about changes in the Federation. "Your representative organization had best continue to be statutory. There are drawbacks to be sure, but never forget the advantages of being the only staff association to be set up by Parliament, and which therefore can operate, not by muscle, but by right. . . . Frankly, I cannot foresee any government or any parliament agreeing to a trade union if that means the right to strike." Any government that had to face a police strike would build up a second police service on which it could count in all circumstances, a state security force to maintain public order, he said. This would lead to two tiers of policemen, one of them parliamentary, and this was not the road for us to take in Britain.[16]

Allowances

In addition to his salary, which as we have seen may go to arbitration at a national level, the sergeant will have a number of allowances such as rent, overtime, and plainclothes. The last two of these do not need explaining, but the first does. On joining the service, a police officer is entitled to free accommodation, and this will continue whatever rank he attains. That accommodation may range from single person's quarters to a house or apartment. Should officers live in their own houses, or be paying rent or a mortgage, they are entitled to a tax-free allowance. This allowance is calculated to provide accommodation appropriate to the status of a police officer in the community.

[16]Quoted from remarks by Jim Jardine, chairman of the Federation, in *Police Review* (England: May 26, 1978), pp. 772–73.

Pension

Except for the highest ranks, an officer must retire at age 55 or at 30 years service, whichever comes first. The pension may be taken after 25 years, when it is 50 percent of salary; it is two-thirds when taken at the completion of service.

Honors and Awards

Next in line to salary, promotion, and pension is the question of recognition for good work done. An officer's recognition for his performance on duty ranges from a commendation from his senior officers, magistrate, or judge, to a knighthood conferred by Her Majesty the Queen. Of course, there are officers who never achieve any of these things and still do a good job.

Twice a year, at the New Year and on her birthday, the Queen publishes an Honors List, which bestows awards on her subjects for distinguished service, both civil and military. The police are included in this list, of course, and the awards may range from a knighthood for the Commissioner of the Metropolitan Police, or one of the chief constables, or yet again the Chief Inspector of Constabulary, down the line to a British Empire Medal for a sergeant or constable. Should none of these come the way of the officer, the Queen awards a Long Service and Good Conduct Medal at 22 years' service, in recognition of public service. However cynical, a police officer has the feeling of being part of a larger family when he receives this award.

SUMMARY

It is hoped that this chapter will provide a broad overview of the life and times of the police sergeant in England and Wales, dwelling on the human areas and highlighting those aspects that should be of especial interest in a comparative view.

Enormous care, effort, and goodwill have gone into the making of the police service in England and Wales, as in the remainder of the United Kingdom. The object has been excellence of service to the public and good working conditions for its members. There is a high degree of pride. Yet the service faces severe challenges in the future, which will test it to the utmost. The hackneyed phrase about a police force being only as good as the society in which it exists is none the less true for being trite.

The maintenance of law and order ranks with National defence as a primary task of government. It is an essential condition of a nation's survival and happiness.

Royal Commission on the Police, 1962

ACKNOWLEDGEMENTS

Grateful acknowledgements are due to the following persons who found the time to supply information and material in order to ensure that this chapter reflects current thought, practice, and sources.

JOHN C. ALDERSON, Q.P.M., F.B.I.M., Barrister at Law, Chief Constable, Devon and Cornwall Constabulary

ARTHUR HAMBLETON, C.B.E., M.C., Q.P.M.. D.L., Chief Constable, Dorset Constabulary

JOHN ENGLISH, Director, Home Office Central Planning Unit, Harrogate, Yorkshire

Chief Inspector W.D. WEBBER, Personnel Department, Devon and Cornwall Constabulary

Inspector KENNETH MILLER, Training Branch, Metropolitan Police, New Scotland Yard

CHAPTER EIGHT

The Management of Stress

by Sydney W. White*

THE PROBLEM

As a leader, the police supervisor has a twofold responsibility for the management of stress. First, he should learn to become aware of the sources of stress in his own life and the methods by which they can be eliminated or controlled so they do not impair his effectiveness on the job, or the quality of his personal and home life. Second, he should learn to recognize and deal with job stress affecting his subordinates if he is to be a successful supervisor. The two aspects are closely interrelated, since many of the stress variables affect both officers and their supervisors, just as many stresses of supervisors are shared by higher levels of police management.

The relationship of stress at the supervisor and subordinate levels is always interactive; the highly stressed supervisor will by his behavior tend to increase the stress felt by his subordinates, and vice versa. Recognition by the first-line supervisor of these interacting effects and of his dual responsibility is an important step toward learning to manage stress.

Although it has received scant attention until recent years, stress is probably one of the most serious threats to individual health and well-being that exists in this country today. For example, cardiovascular disease, long known to be stress-related, accounts for more than half of all deaths in the

*Mr. White, presently in practice as an organization consultant, has had extensive experience in industrial management.

United States.[1] Stress has also been implicated as a causative agent in kidney disease, diabetes, arthritis, and skin ailments, and is suspected as a contributing cause of certain types of cancer.[2]

Before considering how the police supervisor should proceed to manage stress, it will be helpful to consider what is currently known about the nature, causes, and effects of stress in daily life.

Stress may be defined in various ways, depending on what facets seem most important to the situation being studied. Perhaps the broadest description is to say that stress is "essentially reflected by the rate of all the wear and tear caused by life."[3] In this sense, it includes physiological, psychological, and social manifestations in personal and family life as well as in the working environment. But this concept is too general to be of much practical value. We know that everyone tends to wear out with age; what can be more helpful is better knowledge of how stress operates in particular situations, and the ways in which its premature ravages can be avoided.

A more specific attack on the problem was begun by scientists interested in determining how the body maintained its defenses against potentially damaging conditions in the natural environment. Over 100 years ago, a French physiologist, Claude Bernard, discovered that despite exposure to great heat or cold, a man tended to keep fluctuations in his body temperature within a very narrow range. From this finding he theorized that the ability to maintain the *milieu interieur,* as he called it, is an important characteristic of all living creatures. He attributed this ability to the action of glands in producing certain vital chemicals, and to the action of the nervous system in regulating blood flow and other bodily processes. Later, Walter B. Cannon at Harvard observed the effects of hunger and thirst, and strong emotions such as fear and rage, on the secretion of adrenalin, and formulated the concept of homeostasis—the power of the body to stay the same despite threatened attack or even actual tissue damage.

These discoveries set the stage for Hans Selye, the world's leading authority on stress, to develop his theory of the *general adaptation syndrome.* Selye found in the course of experiments with animals, carried out over many years, that stress develops through three stages: (1) the alarm reaction, (2) the stage of resistance, and (3) the stage of exhaustion.[4] During a normal life, we go through the first two stages many times in the course of facing demands and fulfilling activities required of us. The last stage will occur when resistance ebbs after a prolonged fight against injury or illness. Selye called the stress-producing agents "stressors," and

---

[1]U.S. Department of Health, Education and Welfare, *Monthly Vital Statistics Report, Annual Summary for the U.S.,* Vol. 8, No. 13 (1970).

[2]Hans Selye, *The Stress of Life* (New York: McGraw-Hill, 1978), p. 271.

[3]Ibid., p. xvi.

[4]Ibid., p. 1.

showed by experiments with animals the effects produced by severe stressor action. Whether the stress was physiological (prolonged immersion in ice water) or psychological (tying the animal up), the results were the same—enlarged adrenal glands and peptic ulcers—if the experiment was continued for even a few days.

In the case of man, the maladaptive defense reactions to prolonged stress will eventually result in one or more of the so-called "diseases of adaptation." These include such well-known illnesses as heart attack, stroke, peptic ulcers, or a nervous breakdown, as well as a host of others that are not so common. But there are many earlier signs of stress, and heeding them by changes in activity or behavior can allow us to prevent significant damage to our bodies. The following list, although not exhaustive, gives a number of common stress indicators:

1. Pounding of the heart
2. Dryness of throat and mouth
3. Inability to concentrate
4. Tendency to tire easily and to feel stale
5. Feelings of dizziness or weakness
6. Feelings of tension and being "keyed up"
7. Feelings of generalized anxiety
8. Trembling or shakiness
9. Insomnia
10. Sweating
11. Frequent need to urinate
12. Stomach upset, indigestion, diarrhea
13. Migraine headaches
14. Pain in the neck or lower back
15. Loss of appetite or excessive appetite
16. Increased smoking, drinking, or use of drugs or medications
17. Nightmares
18. Accident-proneness
19. Depression[5]

These signs of stress can apply to anyone; specifically, they can be used as reliable indicators of police job stress, and they apply to police supervisors. There is considerable evidence that police work is a high-stress occupation.[6] Results of a field study of police administrators showed that they

[5]Ibid., pp. 174–77.

[6]William Kroes, Bruce Margolis, and Joseph Hurrell, "Job Stress in Policemen," *Journal of Police Science and Administration,* Vol. 2, No. 2 (June 1974); and Martin Reiser, "Some Organizational Stresses on Policemen," *Journal of Police Science and Administration,* Vol. 2, No. 2 (June 1974).

were affected to a greater degree by stress than their subordinates were.[7] A study in Tennessee revealed that the suicide rate for policemen was the third highest among 24 occupations in the state that had significant suicide rates. The same study also showed that policemen were being admitted to general hospitals at a significantly higher rate than people in other occupations, and that circulatory and digestive disorders accounted for a large proportion of their admissions.[8]

Another study, reporting on police stress from a psychiatrist's point of view, states:

> Psychological stress produces not only what is commonly thought of as being frank mental and emotional disturbance, neurosis and psychosis, personality regressions, brain damage-related problems known as organic brain syndromes, and so-called traumatic neurosis also known as combat neurosis, gross stress reaction, or transient situational disturbances often resulting from life and limb threatening situations or other line-of-duty crisis, but also produces a whole gamut of psycho-physiological disturbances, that, if intense and chronic enough, can lead to demonstrable organic disease of varying severity. A list of such psycho-physiological conditions that lead to medical and surgical conditions includes: psycho-physiological disorders of the skin such as neurodermatitis and atopic dermatitis; of the musculoskeletal system such as backache (the low back syndrome), muscle cramps, tension headache, stiff neck; psycho-physiological respiratory disorders such as bronchial asthma, hyperventilation syndrome; psycho-physiological vascular disorders such as high blood pressure, tachycardia; gastrointestinal disorders such as peptic ulcer, chronic gastritis, ulcerative and mucous colitis, constipation, hyperacidity, pyloric spasm, heartburn, irritable colon, gastroesophageal reflex; psycho-physiological genito-urinary disorders such as disturbances in urination, sexual functioning, impotency; and psycho-physiological endocrine disorders such as diabetes mellitus, thyroid disorders, adrenal disorders, pituitary disorders, menstrual disorders, and other sexual hormone disorders. There is also increasing evidence that the occurrence of industrial accidents themselves are often stress-related; this has been called the "accident process."[9]

CAUSES OF STRESS

Stress must be attributed basically to the involuntary reactions of our bodies to the demanding lives that we choose in present-day society. According to Walter McQuade:

---

[7]William Kroes, Joseph Hurrell, and Bruce Margolis, "Job Stress in Police Administrators," *Journal of Police Science and Administration*, Vol. 2, No. 4 (December 1974).

[8]Wayne C. Richard and Ronald D. Fell, "Health Factors in Police Job Stress," in *Job Stress and the Police Officer: Identifying Stress Reduction Techniques*, William Kroes and Joseph Hurrell, eds. (Washington, D.C.: U.S. Dept. of HEW, 1975).

[9]Jerome Jacobi, "Reducing Police Stress: A Psychiatrist's Point of View," in Kroes and Hurrell, in *Job Stress and The Police Officer*.

These reactions are rooted deep in the prehistory of the human species. Early man survived in a brutal world because, along with an elaborate brain, he had the mechanisms of instantaneous, unthinking physical response when in danger. Picture a primitive man, many thousands of years ago, lying in front of his cave after the hunt, digesting. Suddenly he felt the cool shadow of a predatory carnivore, stalking. Without thinking, he reacted with a mighty surge of bodily resources. Into his blood flashed adrenal secretions that mustered strength in the form of both sugar and stored fats to his muscles and brain, instantly mobilizing full energy, and stimulating pulse, respiration, and blood pressure. His digestive processes turned off at once so that no energy was diverted from meeting the threat. His coagulation chemistry immediately prepared to resist wounds with quick clotting. Red cells poured from the spleen into the stepped-up blood circulation to help the respiratory system take in oxygen and cast off carbon dioxide as this ancestral man clubbed at the prowling beast, or scuttled safely back into his cave.[10]

But today's manager cannot react physically in this way. He faces many threats in his job that cannot be solved by fight or flight. He must stay calm, even though under that forced calm builds repressed rage without any adequate target—except himself. It was not always thus. Stress as an important factor in disease is mainly a product of the twentieth century. Until then, heart disease was virtually unknown anywhere in the world, and as late as the 1920s it was still fairly rare in the United States. Peptic ulcers used to be primarily a woman's ailment; from 1850 to 1900, close to seven out of ten patients with perforated peptic ulcers were women. But from 1920 to 1940, nine out of ten were men.[11]

Other research has found great differences between individuals in their susceptibility to stress, and that personality differences in particular seem to be of great importance as causes of coronary heart disease in Americans. Drs. Meyer Friedman and Ray Rosenmann are heart specialists who have spent more than 30 years studying heart disease at hospital bedsides, in consulting rooms, and in the laboratory. They have found that people can be divided into two major personality types, which they designated Type A and Type B. They believe that Type A personality is the chief cause of premature coronary heart disease, which strikes so many American men in their thirties and forties. A Type *A* person has a behavior pattern characterized by:

Ambition

Intense drive

Aggressiveness

Competitiveness

Pressure to get things done

[10]Walter McQuade, "What Stress Can Do to You," *Fortune* (January 1972), p. 102.
[11]Ibid.

Habitually pitting oneself against the clock
Obvious restlessness

The extreme Type *A* is a tremendously hard worker, a self-confident person who likes to make decisions, and who likes to do more than one thing at a time, such as making business calls while waiting in his dentist's office. He smokes cigarettes and is not much for exercise—it takes up too much time. He will seldom wait in line for anything and may become very angry if he is delayed in traffic.

The sad fact about Type *A* is that he is about three times more likely to have a heart attack than Type *B,* who has the converse type of personality. Type *B* persons tends to have about the same background and ability as Type As, but their personality characteristics are in sharp contrast. Type *B* persons:

Seldom become impatient
Are not compulsive about use of time
Have more time for leisure
Are less competitive
Speak more quietly
Are not concerned with constant and rapid achievement
Take enough time to make decisions carefully

When Friedman and Rosenmann began to look at the personal data recorded for the two types at the beginning of their study, they found a number of interesting differences. Substantially more of Type *A* were smokers, and almost one-third more had a history of high blood pressure. This seemed to implicate personality Type *A* as a prime suspect in causing the higher rate of coronaries. It was also found that the incidence of heart attacks in parents of Type A subjects was about 20 percent higher than for Type *B,* suggesting that the parental behavior pattern may have been picked up by Type *A* as children.[12]

STRESS IN ORGANIZATIONS

Since stress always involves the interaction of person and environment, the extent of organizational stress depends on the characteristics of the organization and its members. As defined by Joseph McGrath, "There is a potential for stress when an environmental situation is perceived as presenting a demand which threatens to exceed the person's capabilities and resources for

[12]Meyer Friedman and Ray Rosenmann, *Type A Behavior and Your Heart* (Greenwich, Conn.: Fawcett Publications, Inc., 1974).

meeting it, under conditions where he expects a substantial differential in the rewards and costs from meeting the demand versus not meeting it."[13] It might be well to repeat the essential elements in this definition:

1. The individual's *perception* of an environmental demand
2. A demand that *threatens* to exceed his capabilities
3. Where he expects *important* rewards or costs from meeting or not meeting the demand

For there to be stress, the individual must perceive a threat that could result in important rewards or costs.

Relating those elements to a police organization, it can be said that every police supervisor's behavior is being observed each day by his subordinates, perceived as threatening or nonthreatening, and evaluated in terms of the rewards and penalties they see as involved. Since more attention is paid to the immediate supervisor's behavior than that of anyone else, it follows that his behavior is potentially important as a major stress-producing factor. Perhaps the real estate tycoon was thinking of his subordinates as he told visitors to his office, "I don't get ulcers; I *give* them." There is evidence that many leaders progress by learning how to manage stress, and that they have fewer hangups, breakdowns, or heart attacks than middle managers and workers.[14]

Of course, stress can arise from many factors over which the supervisor has little or no control. McGrath goes on to list six sources of stressful situations:

1. Stress within the person's system, which he brings with him, such as his perceptual style
2. Stress arising from interpersonal relations within the social environment
3. Stress arising from the physical environment
4. Task-based stress
5. Role-based stress
6. Stress intrinsic to the behavior setting, such as the effects of crowding or under-manning[15]

The police supervisor obviously has no control over the individual's perceptual style, nor does he usually have much to say about the physical environment, or the factors responsible for crowding or undermanning. But

[13]Joseph E. McGrath, "Stress and Behavior in Organizations," in *Handbook of Industrial and Organizational Psychology*, M.D. Dunnette, ed. (Chicago: Rand-McNally, 1976), p. 1352.
[14]Ogden Tanner and the editors of Time-Life Books, *Stress* (Alexandria, Va.: Time-Life Books, 1976), p. 29.
[15]McGrath, "Stress and Behavior," p. 1369.

he is closely involved with stress arising from tasks, roles, and interpersonal relations, and it is in these areas that stress management can be most effective.

Recent studies of police stress have found that organizational stressors have the strongest negative effects on police personnel, regardless of rank. Despite the difficulties and risks of patrol work, it is the threats from inside the organization that affect patrolmen most. As one officer stated it bluntly, "It's the idiots inside the department that really stress me, not those outside." When Kroes et al. asked 100 patrolmen in the Cincinnati Police Department what factors they considered "bothersome" about their jobs, they responded as follows:[16]

	% perceiving stressor as bothersome
Courts	56
Administration	51
Equipment	39
Community relations	38
Changing shift routine	18
Relations with supervisors	16
Nonpolice work	14
Other policemen, bad assignments, isolation/boredom, etc.	24

The findings from this study concerning administration policies and supervisory relations emphasized the vital nature of support for the officer:

Within the framework, administrative support becomes all-important. An officer is better able to cope with the stress he faces if he feels that his superiors know and understand his problems and are in his corner. It is clear that to some extent patrol car officers feel let down by the administration. Instead of the administration's taking some pressures off the officers, they often create new ones. Further, it is the administrator who appears to be responsible for equipment replacement and repair policies. As an added irritant, the officer is not asked to provide any professional input in decisions and policies that directly affect him. Thus, in several ways, the individual officer perceives that his own administration fails to treat him as a professional.[17]

[16]Kroes, Margolis, and Hurrell, "Job Stress in Policemen," p. 147.
[17]Ibid., p. 154.

A later study by Kroes et al. asked twelve captains and eighteen lieutenants from the same department about things that bothered them in their jobs. Job-stress categories mentioned by 10 percent or more of the respondents were as follows:

	% mentioning the category
Administration	60
Equipment/Manpower	37
Community relations	27
Courts	13
Changing shift routine	13
Ineffectualness	10

In discussing the results of the survey, the researchers drew some conclusions about these data:

> It seems apparent that a great deal of the administrator's psychological job stress stems from the fact that he is the "man in the middle." He is directly responsible to both the community and the police administration for his actions and the conduct and efficiency of his subordinates. When complaints are made, it is the administrator who must directly bear the wrath of the public and higher echelon supervisor. No matter how conflicting the demands of the community might be, the administrator must answer to their complaints. When he makes a wrong decision under the pressure of expediency, he will be held accountable for its consequences.

> Within this framework, the higher frequency of response to the categories of community relations, administration, courts, equipment/manpower, and work ambiguity take increased meaning. For example, in the area of lack of say in decisions and policies, the overwhelming complaint was that key subordinates were frequently detailed from their commands without prior consultation or knowledge. The predominant concern here was that the police administration expected them to be good supervisors and commanders, yet they were not consulted in matters directly affecting their jobs. The paradox is apparent to the administrator; he is responsible for law enforcement and the safety and conduct of his subordinates, yet he has little to say in the selection of his subordinates.[18]

[18]Kroes, Hurrell, and Margolis, "Job Stress in Police Administrators," p. 387.

In an interesting follow-up to these surveys, James Hillgren et al. polled 20 police chiefs and sheriffs at a law-enforcement seminar, asking them to identify stressors they thought were affecting their line personnel, and also those that weighed heavily on them as chief administrators. The major stressors they mentioned are listed below:

Major Stressors of *Line Personnel:*	*% of Respondents* *Mentioning Them*
Administration	90
Role conflict (conflicting expectations)	90
Double standard (for officers)	80
Courts	75
Peer-group pressure	70
Social exclusiveness	40
Home life	35
Public opinion vs. sworn duty	25
Supervisors	15

Major Stressors of *Chief Administrators:*	
Imposing discipline	90
Communication difficulties	85
Public vs. personnel (conflicting demands)	85
Performance/Conduct (of line officers)	80
Changes in law enforcement	60
Decision-making process	45
News media	35
Recruitment (pay of officers)	30
Limited authority (restricted by higher officials and laws)	20

In their comments on the survey results, these investigators also emphasized that many stressors originated within the organization, or as a consequence of its procedures. They said that "the demands of various political factions in the community permeate the police department," and that the chief administrator will not be able to relieve stress by supporting his police officers until city officials "concur that effectiveness and efficiency, rather than political considerations, should be the major criteria satisfied in administrative decisions."[19]

[19]James S. Hillgren, Rebekah Bond, and Sue Jones, "Primary Stressors in Police Administration and Law Enforcement," *Journal of Police Science and Administration,* Vol. 4, No. 4 (1976), 449.

STRESSORS IN POLICE AND OTHER OCCUPATIONS

In examining police job stress, there is a tendency by police personnel to consider all stressors as unique to police work. The fact is that policing has a number of stressors that are unique to that profession, but it also has many in common with other occupations. William H. Kroes discusses both categories in some detail. He believes that "the problem of administrative pressure on the individual worker is so ubiquitous across occupations that . . . almost universally in large organizations there is a very real communication gap between those at the top and those at the bottom. This gap may be due to the usual inefficiencies of bureaucracy in a large organization, or it may be due to the differences in conditions, influences, and factors that an individual must consider at different levels in the organization."[20]

As administrative stressors that police work has in common with other occupations, Kroes includes frustration caused by lack of participation in decision making, and the feelings of anxiety and alienation caused by lack of support of the police officer by his superiors. The result is to leave the individual not knowing where he stands and to cause loss of trust in his leaders.

Job conflict is a police stressor that is shared with other occupations, especially in larger organizational units. It may arise when the officer has to try and please too many bosses, or is pressured to bend the law in favor of influential people and their friends and relatives. Once again, the main source of the problem is police managements that either do not observe clear lines of responsibility or fail to back the officer when his decision is correct.

Kroes also deals with the twin stressors of job overload and job underload. Overload may consist of too many duties (quantitative overload), or duties that are too difficult (qualitative overload). The former is more often met with in crowded inner-city policing, where patrols are commonly understaffed in relation to the high crime rates, but may occur in any department with an inadequate budget. The latter typically results from requiring police officers to take responsibility for too many complex roles just because they are the only civil servants in the area when the need arises.

Job underload is a more insidious factor. It is only recently that the lack of stimuli caused by inactivity has been recognized as causing serious stress. "Private reports from policemen as well as documented research have shown that the need for action to avoid boredom is so great that policemen occasionally engage in marginal activities such as arresting or baiting drunks or hippies just to have something to do."[21]

---

[20]William H. Kroes, *Society's Victim—The Policeman* (Springfield, Ill.: Charles C Thomas, 1976), p. 10.

[21]Ibid., p. 25.

For policemen, the stress may be compounded on the night shift by the isolation of spending long periods alone, or by the monotony of patrolling empty streets. Hans Selye describes the deleterious effects of boredom and sensory deprivation:

> Normal function of the brain depends on constant arousal generated in the reticular formation by continuous sensory input. Hallucinations, which may cause accidents, have been noted in pilots, astronauts, and long-distance truck drivers, presumably because the monotony of their work acts as a form of sensory deprivation.
>
> Although complete sensory deprivation over a prolonged period is rare in daily life, a decrease in sensory input below the normal is a common cause of boredom.[22]

And on the topic of isolation and loneliness, he writes:

> It is a common impression that isolation increases alcoholism. Objective observations in rats showed that isolation raises voluntary consumption of alcohol when drinking water is equally available as an alternative choice. . . . Observations on confined puppies revealed that the presence of another puppy decreases the level of emotional distress and helps to maintain homeostasis. Most of the pertinent studies have been performed on mice, certain strains of which tend to become extremely aggressive in isolation and at the same time show a drop in blood eosinophils and characteristic changes in the brain content of adrenaline-like compounds. We can thus hypothesize that those changes may have an influence on the development of aggressiveness. Also the formation of gastric ulcers in fasting mice is facilitated by isolation.[23]

Shift Work

Police officers surveyed by Kroes et al. in Cincinnati mentioned changing shifts as a major complaint. Terry Eisenberg describes it as a source of psychological stress:

> Shift work characterizes law enforcement work scheduling. It is considered a significant stressor in that it has substantial adverse effects upon one's family life and possibly health. Changing shifts every month, three months, or whatever, is disruptive to one's personal and occupational styles. Adjustments become a demanding way of life. For example, the change from day shift to swings or midnights requires numerous personal and occupational modifications. Additionally, related issues previously addressed, such as hold-overs, court time, and

[22]Selye, *The Stress of Life,* p. 386.
[23]Ibid., p. 387.

late/untimely assignments, create a working environment which disallows both short and long-term planning regarding one's personal life.[24]

There is no doubt that shift work, particularly rotating shifts, is a major cause of stress both in police work and elsewhere. Philipp and Griew made an in-depth study of more than 100 shift workers at five plants in New Zealand and reported:

> In the present study, the areas in which there were the most, and the most severe, consequences of being on shift work proved to be very much the same as overseas. These were in its effects on the physiological, physical and psychological health of the workers on it, in the loss of social life, and in its far-reaching effects on domestic and family life, and on association and companionship with wives and children. These consequences were more severe for some workers than for others, and in most areas were most severe for men on fixed night shifts and for men on weekly and 6-day rotation.
>
> There were also many reported difficulties with eating and sleeping, and with adjusting to shifts and to shift changes. There were many reported difficulties with excessive fatigue, adverse moods, and with deteriorations in health. Separately, and more certainly together, these kinds of bodily disturbances may lead to less than effective performance of a man as a worker on the job, and as a father and husband at home. The costs of shift work to men and their families appear to be high. There may be much that can be done to reduce them.[25]

They believe that the long-term effects of shift work may be dangerous to the health of some employees:

> There are accepted medical and physiological contraindications for putting, or for keeping, an individual on shift work. The data in this report lend further support to recommending that no worker be placed more especially on rotating, or on fixed night shift, without a medical examination for his suitability for such kind of work. There are considerable grounds for also suggesting that there should be regular medical check-ups for all men on shift work. There should then be readiness on management's part to encourage a man to transfer off shifts, or not to come on them in the first place, when such examinations show that shift work would be, or has become, inadvisable for him.[26]

Mott et al. found that evening and night work create problems for certain time-oriented body functions, especially sleep, digestion, and elimination. They also confirmed that the amount of family difficulty caused by shift

[24]Terry Eisenberg, "Job Stress and the Police Officer," in Kroes and Hurrell, *Job Stress and The Police Officer*, p. 32.

[25]Eileen Philipp and Stephen Griew, "One Hundred Shift Workers," Research Paper No. 15 of the New Zealand Institute of Economic Research, Inc. (1970), pp. 90–91.

[26]Ibid., p. 93.

work was a function of the degree of the imbalance caused in the usual activities that the shift work interfered with. Afternoon-shift workers had most difficulty with the father role because of often not seeing their children for days at a time. Night-shift workers reported more difficulties with sexual relations and protecting the wife from harm. The temporal disruption of role behaviors occasioned by shift work interfered with the building of stable, shared family roles, impaired the adequacy of functional integration, and increased family strain and tension.[27]

Psychological reactions to shift work reported by Philipp and Griew were to the effect that the workers became irritable, anxious, and tense on afternoon, night, and rotating shifts; in addition, on rotating shifts they had time-oriented difficulties (felt confused, had no sense of time, and so on).[28]

Kroes states that the rotating shift pattern predominates in most police departments and that it tends to cause the most serious stress results. The interruption of diurnal rhythm cycles for sleep, digestion, heart rate, and the like is worsened by interaction with the social-psychological environment, and adaptation becomes difficult or impossible because of the rotating schedule of work hours. The result is often the fostering of marital and juvenile-delinquency problems.[29]

EFFECTS OF STRESS

A number of symptoms may appear in the behavior of police officers as results of stress overload:

Use of excessive force

Resort to excessive sick leave

Claims for faked injuries, or excessive claims for actual injuries

Excessive drinking in spare time

Getting out of touch with family, causing spouse to call station to inquire or complain about him

Continual behavior requiring minor disciplinary action

Off-duty injuries

Involvement in vehicle accidents

Behavior requiring frequent internal investigations[30]

[27]Paul Mott, Floyd Mann, Quin McLaughlin, and Donald Warwick, *Shift Work* (Ann Arbor: University of Michigan Press, 1965), p. 17.

[28]Philipp and Griew, "One Hundred Shift Workers," pp. 42, 49.

[29]Kroes, *Society's Victim,* pp. 31–33.

[30]Dennis L. Rowlison, "Management Considerations to Combat Police Stress," *Michigan Police Journal,* Vol. 53, No. 1 (January 1978), 4.

In the short term, the responses of individuals to job stress are manifested in the forms of behavioral strains, of which there are several common categories.

Tension

When job requirements, the expectations of self or others, or the compulsive action of his own drives cause a person to act at high speed for an extended period, a frequent result is tension. The term itself suggests physical stretching or straining, but most job tension probably results from suspense, excitement, anger, fear, or anxiety. Patrol activities are fraught with potentially tense situations that an officer must approach, often with little or no idea of the situation he will be confronted with. Doubts and uncertainties tend to raise heart rate and blood pressure and to keep him keyed up physically and mentally so that he is prepared for whatever swift and powerful action may be necessary to apprehend a suspect, or stop a fight. Walter Cannon first described many of the changes the body makes under the energizing influences of emotional excitement: the cessation of visceral processes, thus freeing the energy supply for other parts of the body; the shifting of blood from the abdominal organs to the organs immediately essential to muscular exertion; the discharge of extra blood corpuscles from the spleen; the deeper respiration; and the mobilizing of sugar in the circulation—all for the purpose of making the organism more effective in the violent release of energy that may be necessary.[31]

But suppose that neither fight or flight is called for. Suppose that instead of a fight, there is merely a long-drawn-out family argument, or that instead of a "burglary in progress," there is but another in a series of false burglar alarms. The bodily systems are mustered to face a threat, but the situation does not call for the kind of physical release that would serve to dissipate the resulting tension. In ancient days, the tension could be worked off in the exertion of the hunt, or perhaps a hand-to-hand battle. In today's well-regulated society, neither the challenges nor the ways of meeting them are quite so simple. For a long time it has been considered bad form to club a business adversary, and the tension of competition has no traditional outlet. This unrelieved buildup results in much of the strain response to job stress.

The usual examples of stress in police work tend to be dangerous patrol situations, but these are but a minor part of the strain-producing factors facing police personnel, especially those in supervision. The organizational job stresses discussed earlier are much more likely to cause tension, and unfortu-

[31]Walter B. Cannon, *Bodily Changes in Pain, Hunger, Fear and Rage* (New York: D. Appleton, 1929), pp. 225–26.

nately, they also occur much more frequently, so the tension they engender may become chronic. As McQuade points out, the situation with regard to managers is particularly acute:

> Management jobs carry more risks than most. In a detailed study done for NASA at the Goddard Space Flight Center, the investigators from Ann Arbor found that administrators were much more subject to stress than engineers or scientists. Responsibility for people, French explains, always causes more stress than responsibility for things—equipment, budgets, etc. The rise in serum cholesterol, blood sugar, and blood pressure among ground managers is much greater during manned space flights than during flights of unmanned satellites. Whatever their assignment, the administrators at Goddard, as a group, had higher pulse rates and blood pressures, and smoked more, than the engineers or scientists. Medical records revealed that administrators also had suffered almost three times as many heart attacks as either the scientists or the engineers.[32]

Anxiety

One of the commonest responses to the stress caused by a perceived job threat is anxiety—a state of uneasiness or apprehension about future happenings whose course seems unpredictable. The person may be anxious about a specific matter such as an internal affairs investigation that is pending, or he may have a general feeling of dread, of impending trouble, without being able to pinpoint the source of his discomfort. The latter feeling is sometimes labeled "floating anxiety," described by Selye as a state of stress in which "we are afraid, although we do not know exactly what we are afraid of."

Among new supervisors, anxiety often develops as a result of the new responsibility for people that comes with the job. Not infrequently, the anxiety level becomes so high, especially if they have not had adequate presupervisory training, that they cannot tolerate it, and request return to a nonsupervisory job.

Depression

This state is physiologically opposite to anxiety, being accompanied by slower heartbeat and breathing and lowered blood pressure. Some researchers have found that when organisms are placed in situations where nothing can be done to escape or control a dreaded event, their level of a potent brain hormone decreases and they become depressed. The anxiety felt when the outcome of events was uncertain is replaced by a mood of resigned helpless-

[32]McQuade, "What Stress Can Do," p. 134.

ness when it is repeatedly found that the result will be bad and that nothing can be done to avoid or control it.

One might think that police, as action-oriented professionals, would have little susceptibility to depression. To date, the evidence about its frequency among policemen is somewhat mixed. In a survey of 23 occupations, police personnel scored sixth lowest on a measurement of depression.[33] But a self-report questionnaire completed by the officers in one medium-sized department indicated that fewer than one-third of them never felt depressed while at work.[34] A study that was made of adolescents and college students yielded data that could be useful in screening applicants to eliminate those prone to depression. The findings were that those who became depressed periodically were usually overconscientious, idealistic, serious-minded, and unrealistic in the standards and goals they set for themselves and others.[35] People with these traits might become disillusioned rapidly in police work, especially if, as is common with police recruits, they began their careers with somewhat romantic notions about the policeman's role.

There is also evidence that depression may result from the stress of low peer support. Moos found in a survey of military training programs that low support by officers was associated with hostility, whereas low peer cohesion was associated with depression.[36]

Perhaps the saddest result of depression, and one that has long been linked with it in clinical studies, is suicide. The rates of suicide among police were reported to be the second highest (47.6 per 100,000) among 36 occupations in the United States in 1950. A more recent study of mortality statistics for the state of Tennessee in 1972–74 shows annual suicide rates for police to be the third highest of those in all occupations tabulated (69.1 per 100,000).[37]

From the standpoint of the supervisor, the most important factor affecting depression is support:

> One feature which distinguishes between occupations which are high and low on depression is the extent to which others at work are seen as supportive. The occupations with the highest scores on depression also have the poorest supportive relations with others at work, while the occupations with the lowest

[33]Robert D. Caplan, Sidney Cobb, John R.P. French, R. Van Harrison, and S.R. Pinnuau, *Job Demands and Worker Health* (Washington, D.C.: U.S. Government Printing Office, 1975), p. 329.

[34]Sydney W. White, "Policework and Stress" (unpublished study for doctoral dissertation, Michigan State University, 1977).

[35]John LaPlace, *Health* (New York: Appleton-Century-Crofts, 1972), p. 25.

[36]Stewart Kiritz and Rudolph H. Moos, "Physiological Effects of Social Environments," *Psychosomatic Medicine,* Vol. 36, No. 2 (March–April 1974), 110.

[37]Richard and Fell, "Health Factors," p. 80.

scores on depression generally have very good supportive relations with others at work.[38]

The role of supervisory support in successful management of stress will be dealt with later in more detail, but the foregoing evidence of its value in preventing or alleviating depression should be noted by everyone interested in effective police management.

Psychosomatic Complaints

A brief definition of psychosomatic complaints is that they are physical disorders caused or influenced by the emotional state of the individual. Until recently, they were virtually ignored by the medical profession and generally neglected as a subject for serious research. But as more and more studies have explored the relation between psychological stress and various diseases, the realization has come that many somatic complaints are in fact early manifestations of the effects of stress. Such complaints as dizziness, fainting, headaches, backaches, nausea, stomachaches, fast heartbeat, shortness of breath, insomnia, and nightmares are examples of disorders that may be the visible or felt responses of the body to job or other stress. Obviously, some of these may result from accidents or bacterial action, but the chronic complaints with no evident cause are now considered in most cases to be stress-related, and as such they not only cause suffering but also impair job performance.

Evidence of a linkage between stress and somatic complaints in work settings has been found in recent research. In one experiment, the salaries of female clerks were supplemented on certain days by piecework bonuses, which gave them the opportunity to increase their earnings considerably on those days. Their physical and mental conditions were measured by means of questionnaires and by urine samples that were analyzed for stress hormones. Increased production with no higher rate of errors was reported under the piecework condition, but along with it came many reports of increased pain in arms, shoulders, head, and back, and much higher fatigue. Even more significant was the evidence from the urine analysis, which showed that the proportions of the stress-causing hormones—adrenalin and noradrenalin—had increased by one-third on the piecework days.[39]

This relationship between speeded-up work and stress seems logical, but it is surprising that too slow a work pace can also cause strain. There is an optimum range of stimulation for the human organism, below which stress can be caused by boredom and inactivity. It must always be remembered that

[38]Caplan et al., *Job Demands*, p. 135.
[39]Alan McLean, "Concepts of Occupational Stress; A Review," in *Occupational Stress,* Alan McLean, ed. (Springfield, Ill.: Charles C Thomas, 1974), pp. 5–6.

this range will vary from person to person, because of individual differences in innate characteristics, different life experiences, and the differential effect of work environment; but the point is that the person who perceives his role as too isolated or monotonous will be stressed and may develop somatic complaints as fast as his overworked peers. Donald Hebb at McGill University in Montreal demonstrated the exceedingly stressful nature of complete isolation by immobilizing blindfolded students in bed in darkened, sound-proofed rooms. They found the experience unbearable after several days. Even more severely stressed were subjects suspended in a tank so as to counteract gravity and shielded from any sensations of sight, sound, or feeling through their skin; none of them could endure this stimulus-free environment for more than six hours.[40]

The effects of understimulation, then, are in many ways similar to those of overstimulation. The person begins to perceive things that are not there, because he cannot handle a level of stimuli outside his normal range. He "feels," "sees," or even "hears" things that cannot be confirmed objectively. It is almost as though, lacking normal sensory input, the body creates its own, in the fashion of a solitary child who invents his own companions when he lacks a playmate.

It is vital for a supervisor that the distinction between this type of behavior and deliberate malingering be understood. The person with psychosomatic backache may feel it every bit as much as someone who has injured his back in a fall; he is not trying to deceive anyone. But since there are no strained or torn ligaments, it will not get better by natural healing processes over a period of time. However, if the stressor causing it is removed, it may get better, as if by a miracle, overnight.

Job Dissatisfaction

Measurements of job dissatisfaction usually ask the person how satisfied or dissatisfied he is with a number of job elements that are then totaled to arrive at an overall score. One of the most thorough studies of job dissatisfaction as a strain variable was carried out by Caplan et al. at the University of Michigan. They questioned more than 2,000 men in 23 occupations, including policemen, and correlated their answers with findings on stress variables. They found that job dissatisfaction was most strongly influenced by underutilization of skills and abilities, simple and repetitive work, low participation in making decisions that affect one's work, job insecurity, and poor social support from one's immediate superior and from others at work.[41] (Police were found to be fifth lowest in job dissatisfaction of the 23 occupations studied.)

[40]Tanner et al., *Stress*, pp. 25, 28.
[41]Caplan et al., *Job Demands*, p. 202.

These factors in job dissatisfaction were in turn attributed to a number of stress causes. Underutilization of abilities usually creates boredom and is part of a larger factor that the study showed was the greatest single cause of stress and strain—poor fit between the individual and the job. In police work, the supervisor often has no part in choosing his subordinates, but he is usually an important influence in evaluating their performance, which should bring out the degree of job fit and suggest the corrective measures necessary to remedy this problem. Simple and repetitive work should be less of a problem in police work than in industry, and probably accounts in part for the lower dissatisfaction of policemen shown by the comparative data in this survey. At the same time, the supervisor must recognize that many police routines are monotonous and boring, particularly on night shifts, and may contribute to job strain.

With regard to participation in decision making, the reaction of many police supervisors is that since they themselves have minimal participation, there is no way they can improve this situation for their subordinates. But where this is the case, the supervisor can still encourage his officers to give him input and listen carefully to what they have to say. He will then be better prepared to contribute to decision making when the opportunity arises.

The problem of stress caused by job insecurity is not as serious for police personnel as for industrial workers, but it can still be a nagging source of strain for some officers, especially at certain stages of their careers. The new recruit will often feel very insecure until he has become familiar with the environment and routines and is accepted by his peers. The new supervisor typically has some problems adjusting to his new status and responsibilities, and the change in relationships with his former buddies. An officer transferred to a new and unfamiliar assignment will often ask himself whether he has a future in this kind of work. In each of these examples, the supervisor of the person involved should recognize the possible strain being undergone and take the lead in alleviating it. In doing so, he will also be dealing in the best possible way with the last factor mentioned by Caplan et al.—poor social support from the immediate supervisor. Some police organizations are still inclined to favor the "sink or swim" school of supervision inherited from the old military tradition, but being tough with subordinates was never used by good military leaders as a substitute for looking after the needs of their men, and it is completely outmoded even in the military today. Good training has always meant that, in addition to telling the neophyte what lies ahead and imparting the skills necessary to handle his new assignment, the leader will also give him encouragement and support during the novice period and later. This is an important factor in developing esprit de corps in any group, so it is not surprising that it also promotes higher job satisfaction.

An interesting study of job satisfaction in blue- and white-collar groups found that high levels of job satisfaction in both groups tend to be associated with low rates of death from coronary disease. Since the data are correlational, the researchers caution that a cause-and-effect relationship cannot be inferred. Nevertheless, they raise the distinct possibility that changing people's work environments so as to raise their level of job satisfaction may thereby lower their risk of coronary disease.[42]

Physiological Effects

There is a danger that by treating stress and strain effects under separate psychological and physiological headings, the view that mind and body are independent of one another may be reinforced. Kenneth Pelletier points out that this belief has tended to prevent clear thinking about health and illness in the past:

> Throughout the history of the healing professions, two clear polarities are evident. On the one hand there is a philosophical and clinical orientation which essentially dismisses all psychological factors and considers both disease and health maintenance to be based on purely physical considerations. In contrast and reaction to this is an equally extreme point of view which maintains that all physical illness is the end product of some psychological shortcoming on the part of the individual. . . . One common misconception in both of these orientations is their separation of mind and body as totally discrete entities.

He goes on to explain that neither of these extreme views will suffice to explain the onset of disease:

> An individual needs to be considered physiologically, psychologically, and spiritually, with the intent of gaining as much understanding as possible about his relationship with his total environment. This environment includes his family, peers, job situation, living society, as well as his childhood background, which has formed a significant part of his present character.

The modern healing professions are evolving a new approach, which recognizes the interaction between each individual and his psychosocial environment:

> Mind and body function as an integrated unit, and health exists when they are in harmony, while illness results when stress and conflict disrupt this process. . . . Consideration of the whole person emphasized the healing process, the

[42]S.M. Sales and J. House, "Job Dissatisfaction as a Possible Risk Factor in Coronary Heart Disease," *Journal of Chronic Diseases,* 23 (1971), 861–73.

maintenance of health, and the prevention of illness rather than the treatment of established disorders.[43]

It is absolutely vital to grasp this integrated view of mind and body in relation to both causes and effects of stress and strain in order to understand the processes involved and to be able to take the broadest possible approach in considering the many strategies available for coping with stress. The physiological signs of stress that we shall consider next will probably appear in conjunction with psychological and behavioral indicators and should be weighed with them in deciding on strategies for managing stress.

Blood pressure. One of the commonest physical effects of stress is an increase in the blood pressure. If the stress is chronic, the blood pressure will remain to some extent elevated, and if the elevation is marked, the condition is known as hypertension. In present-day society, it is estimated to affect at least 25 million Americans, making it one of the commonest diseases of our time.

Although experimental confirmation of the role of stress in hypertension is lacking, there is strong evidence implicating it. It is known that the body reacts to trauma or to threats by preparing for "fight or flight," and that part of that preparation consists of the release of powerful hormones into the circulatory system that increase blood pressure to assist the body in any strong action needed. Unfortunately, the action required in modern culture is not the kind to permit the violent movements that would work off the effects of the arousal.

Police work is an outstanding example of a profession that has many threats and frustrations to meet but can seldom take physical action to resolve them. When physical discharge of tension is not possible, there is a tendency for blood pressure to remain somewhat elevated, perhaps because the threat cannot be completely removed. When this condition of tension without release occurs many times, the result may be that blood pressure remains permanently at a level somewhat higher than normal. The muscles constricting the blood vessels remain tense, hence the term hypertension. This narrowing of arterial walls, in conjunction with the accumulation of cholesterol deposits on the inside of the arteries, may lead eventually to the blocking of a coronary artery, which brings on a heart attack.

Turning to the experimental evidence about blood-pressure levels in police personnel, there is some indication that they are indeed higher than for other occupations. In a study evaluating physical-fitness programs for police officers, it was found that middle-aged officers had an average diastolic

[43]Kenneth R. Pelletier, *Mind as Healer, Mind as Slayer* (New York: Dell Publishing, 1977), pp. 10–12.

blood pressure before exercise training about 10 percent higher than the average for middle-aged men in other occupations.[44] Another study of police in a medium-sized department yielded virtually the same results.[45] Both systolic and diastolic blood-pressure levels for police personnel aged 40 to 49 years were approximately 10 percent higher than the average for seven other occupations.[46]

Heart rate. The increase in pulse rate with the onset of physical or emotional stress is perhaps the easiest effect of all to demonstrate, as it is obvious to anyone who has felt the blood pound in his body as a result of rage, pain, or fear. Less well known is the fact that if stresses become chronic and cannot be dissipated by action, when they must be inhibited or suppressed time after time, the heart rate will not return all the way down to normal but will become permanently elevated to some extent. In the study of police personnel in their forties referred to above, the average pulse rate was approximately 5 percent higher than for comparably aged members of seven other occupations.

Cholesterol levels. It has long been known that cholesterol levels in the blood become elevated during periods of stress. Selye suggests that the increase in cholesterol is a reliable measure of stress and is comparatively easy to estimate.[47] Cholesterol is a fatty alcohol manufactured by the body and is also present in certain animal-derived foods, such as eggs, meat, and dairy products. When there is an excess of it in the body, it is deposited in the arteries and becomes the main component of atherosclerosis-producing plaques.[48]

In a coronary heart disease study of 3,500 subjects over a period of years, Rosenmann et al. found that there was an increased risk of heart attacks among subjects with abnormally high cholesterol levels only when the subjects exhibited Type A behavior patterns.[49] In another experiment, a group of volunteers sorted ball bearings to the accompaniment of distracting criticism, noise, and light, thus imitating important stresses commonly found with industrial activity. The results confirmed that increased cholesterol levels are readily induced even by a work situation that is not real but simulated, and

[44]Michael L. Pollack and Larry L. Gettman, "Coronary Risk Factors and Level of Physical Fitness in Police Officers," *Proceedings of the 83rd Annual Conference of the International Association of Chiefs of Police* (1976).

[45]White, "Policework and Stress"

[46]Caplan et al., *Job Demands,* pp. 145–46.

[47]Selye, *The Stress of Life,* p. 172.

[48]John LaPlace, *Health,* p. 485.

[49]R.H. Rosenmann, M. Friedman, R. Straus, M. Wurm, C.D. Jenkins, and H.B. Messinger, "Coronary Heart Disease in the Western Collaborative Group Study," *Journal of the American Medical Association,* Vol. 195, No. 2 (1966).

of short duration and moderate intensity.[50] A study of 22 men under work-loads at NASA used a telemetric record of heart rates and a daily measure-ment of cholesterol levels for three days. Both subjective and objective work overload were found to be positively related to heart rate and to choles-terol.[51] Sidney Cobb reports that cholesterol level and certain personality dimensions were related to role responsibility:

> Cholesterol level is associated with the self-report of time spent exercising responsibility for others' futures, but only in those who are high on the first two Type A personality dimensions mentioned above, to wit: Involved Striving and Persistence. We have, then, modest evidence that responsibil-ity for persons, particularly for their futures, rather than for things, contrib-utes to coronary disease risk among those who are overly conscientious. Furthermore, there is in Caplan's work ample evidence that this quality of being conscientious is associated with responsibility. Therefore we might say that the conscientious person is encouraged to take on responsibility for people and their futures, is rewarded for it with increased status and in-come, and usually pays a price by way of increased risk of myocardial in-farction.[52]

Another study by John French, of what he called person–role fit—the degree to which the person's skills and abilities match the demands and requirements of the job, and to which the needs of the person are supplied in the job environment—showed significant relationships among this vari-able, cholesterol, and systolic blood pressure.[53]

It would appear from the foregoing that cholesterol levels are a useful indicator of strain and may be a precursor of heart trouble if the strain is chronic. It also appears that these strains are more likely to occur in areas in which a supervisor has direct responsibility for people, or for the fit between men and their jobs.

Smoking. Although the decision to begin smoking is usually made dur-ing adolescence, an increase in smoking is often associated with increased job pressures. Excessive smoking, like overeating and too little exercise, is also widely recognized as a common manifestation of emotional stress.[54] Hans

[50]Alan McLean, "Concepts of Occupational Stress," p. 5.
[51]Robert L. Kahn, "Conflict, Ambiguity, and Overload: Three Elements in Job Stress," in McLean, *Occupational Stress*, p. 59.
[52]Sidney Cobb, "Role Responsibility: The Differentiation of a Concept," in McLean, *Occupational Stress*, p. 64.
[53]J.R. French, "Person–Role Fit," *Occupational Mental Health*, Vol. 3, No. 1, 15–20.
[54]Henry I. Russek, "Stress, Tobacco, and Coronary Disease in North American Professional Groups," *Journal of the American Medical Association*, Vol. 192, No. 3 (1965).

Selye lists increased smoking as one of the self-observable signs of danger, by which a person can recognize that he is experiencing undue stress before he suffers evident damage.[55] A study done in the National Aeronautics and Space Administration by Caplan gave evidence that smoking is significantly associated with responsibility for persons and for things, both of which are stress variables.[56] Alan MacLean also comments on the relationship between work overload, smoking, and cholesterol in the following passage:

> Work overload has been related to both excessive smoking and increased levels of cholesterol (French & Caplan, 1971). These authors noted that both quantitative and qualitative overload correlate with job-related threat. The number of cigarettes smoked, a much publicized factor of heart disease, also increases with increases in the actual number of phone calls, actual visits and meetings a person has (as tallied by each person's secretary). The correlation between cigarette smoking and this measure of quantitative work overload is .58.[57]

The statistics for policemen who smoke, gathered by Caplan et al. in their study of job stresses for 23 occupations, indicate that the percentage who are smokers (49.5) and the number of cigarettes smoked per day (23.9) are not significantly different from the means for all the occupations studied. However, the smoking quit rate for policemen is less than 60 percent of the average quit rate for all 23 occupations in the sample. Caplan suggests that, since the nicotine level in cigarettes may increase the smoker's ability to tolerate stress, high stress levels in an occupation may make it difficult for its members to quit.[58] If this is true, it is ironical, because smoking also tends to heighten tension and thus may add to the very problem it was meant to help solve. Therefore, it may be hypothesized that although fewer policemen quit because smoking helps them to tolerate stress, they might have somewhat lower levels of stress to contend with if they did not smoke at all.

There has also been some research indicating that nicotine in smoke stimulates the nervous system to release the stress hormone norepinephrine, which pushes up blood pressure and releases fatty substances like cholesterol.[59]

[55]Selye, *The Stress of Life,* p. 176.

[56]R.D. Caplan, "Organizational Stress and Individual Strain," (doctoral dissertation, University of Michigan, 1971).

[57]McLean, *Occupational Stress,* pp. 7–8.

[58]Caplan et al., *Job Demands,* p. 142.

[59]Tanner et al., *Stress,* p. 142.

MANAGING STRESS

It is easier to identify the factors that cause stress and strain for supervisors and their subordinates than it is to give answers that will result in elimination or substantial reduction of them. Corrective action may depend on factors in the outside environment that are not susceptible to change by police supervisors, or indeed by anyone. Or stress causes may lie with policies, practices, regulations, orders, or traditions over which the supervisor has no control. Finally, the management of stress may depend on the elimination of old habits and the development of new ones by supervisors and officers alike, and we all know how difficult it is to change long-established attitudes and behavior patterns.

At the same time, a proper perspective requires us to recognize that change is an inevitable part of life, and not merely a reaction to environmental forces. Rene Dubos points out that man has a choice:

> The response that a particular person makes to a given situation is conditioned by his past; his evolutionary and experiential backgrounds sharply delimit the range of conditions within which his responses can be successful. But experience shows that human beings are not passive components in adaptive systems. Their responses commonly manifest themselves as acts of personal creation. Each individual person tries to achieve some self-selected end even while he is responding to stimuli and adapting to them. . . .
>
> Human life is thus the outcome of the interplay between three separate classes of determinants, namely: the lasting and universal characteristics of man's nature, which are inscribed in his flesh and bone; the ephemeral conditions which man encounters at a given moment; and last but not least, man's ability to choose between alternatives and to decide on a course of action.[60]

Coping with stress can be considered to take place in three stages:

1. Eliminating, neutralizing, or reducing stressors at their source
2. Intercepting and dealing with stressors before they reach the individual
3. Reducing the effect of stressors after they become sensory input

First-stage measures included outside environmental changes, such as controls over noise and air pollution, or organization changes to eliminate or mitigate stressful policies, operations, or roles. An example of second-stage coping measures is physical relocation of personnel, to protect those vulnerable to specific stressors or to ward off the effect of potentially stressful situations. In the third category belong such actions as attitude-change programs, desensitization and biofeedback training, and relaxation and medita-

[60]Rene Dubos, *Man Adapting* (New Haven, Conn.: Yale University Press, 1965), pp. xviii–xix.

tion programs, which either change the individual's perceptions of threatening stimuli or offset the strain effects on his system. Also included in this category are measures to build up the person's ego strength and physical fitness so that he is better able to withstand the effects of stress.

THE SUPERVISOR'S ROLE

In most organizations, the immediate supervisor is by far the most important influence in determining the impact of stress on the subordinate. The extent to which the supervisor can significantly affect subordinates' stress will obviously depend partly on some factors that are difficult for him to control, such as the selection and training of subordinates, the ways in which roles are structured and tasks are arranged, the amount of interference by higher authority or his peers in dealing with his men, and the physical arrangement of facilities. But much more important than these influences in determining stress loads are the supervisor's basic attitudes toward his officers—the care, guidance, fairness, consideration, competence, and social support he demonstrates day by day and hour by hour in his dealings with them.

The following sections will deal with measures that the progressive supervisor can consider for adoption in order to reduce stress and strain in the part of the organization where he has responsibility and influence. Since the final effects of stress are losses in productivity, efficiency, and effectiveness, and ultimately illness and disease, the value of the immediate supervisor's role in promoting both individual and organizational health can hardly be overestimated.

A Stress Model

The accompanying model (Figure 8-1) represents a set of theoretical concepts that have so far had only limited verification in field studies. Nonetheless, it will serve to illustrate the major variables that are important in stress management. Methods by which the police supervisor may exercise influence over stress variables are discussed in the following sections.

Objective Environment

Many police supervisors might disclaim responsibility or influence in this area, feeling it is outside their jurisdiction. But "objective environment" refers to events or stimuli outside the individual, not outside the department, and it is inherent in the supervisor's job that he controls to an important degree the number and quality of stimuli affecting the subordinate. Much of

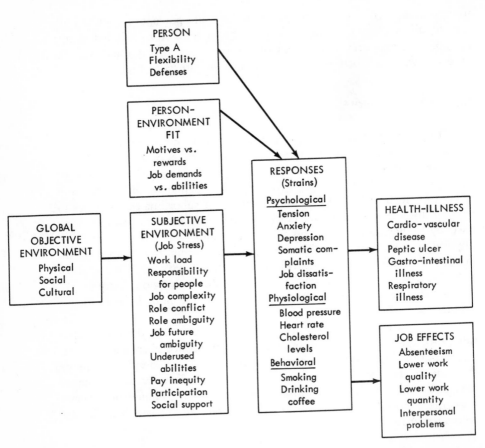

Figure 8-1. A theoretical model showing the sources and effects of job stress in organizations

Source: Adapted from Robert D. Caplan, Sidney Cobb, John R.P. French, R. Van Harrison, and S.R. Pinnuau, *Job Demands and Worker Health* (Washington, D.C.: U.S. Government Printing Office, 1975).

what follows will deal with the ways in which he can use this strategic position to reduce or mitigate stress and its effects on his men.

The Person

Here the supervisor might also feel that he had no responsibility; obviously, he is not responsible for the personality his subordinate has developed since early childhood or the traits he has inherited from his parents. But he does have, or should insist on having, considerable responsibility for choosing new subordinates, or at least for deciding which recruits have the qualities required for retention in the department and which ones should be transferred or advised to try another career, after a reasonable probationary period. For example, armed with knowledge of the stress-prone nature of the Type A personality, the alert supervisor will look for this pattern in a recruit and, if he finds it, consider whether it can be modified. If not, he may conclude that the person will not make a good officer as far as stress resistance is concerned.

Several of the Type A characteristics have been found to condition the effects of job stresses on strain, including physiological strains and risk factors in coronary heart disease.[61] The same study also revealed that the degree of flexibility/rigidity of the individual's personality and his need for social approval also had strong effects on the relation of job stress to individual strain. It can thus be appreciated that the responsibility of the supervisor in choosing and evaluating these qualities in his new subordinates can have very important effects in this area of personal qualities and the ability of the individual to withstand stress.

Person–Environment Fit

The model in Figure 8-1 hypothesizes that lack of fit between the individual's personality and his job environment may be an important predictor of strain resulting from two possible kinds of discrepancies: those between the demands of the environment and the individual's ability to meet them, and those between the individual's needs and the environmental supplies to meet those needs. Both kinds are measured by asking the person questions about the environment he perceives on the job and the environment he desires.

The responsibility of the supervisor is a key factor in ensuring good job fit. He is in an unexcelled position to evaluate the subordinate, to get to know his strengths and weaknesses, his desires and aversions, which determine much of the stress load he will have to bear in that job. To judge fairly, the supervisor must observe the behavior of his subordinates carefully, being ready at all times to listen to their reactions, comments, and complaints. He must try them out in different situations to see how they develop by adaptation and experience in their assigned roles. Finally, he must consider and reach a judgment as to whether they are making a satisfactory fit with the job requirements so that their stress load will not be too heavy. If there is a misfit, the supervisor must consider what corrective action should be taken for the benefit of the individual and the organization.

[61]Caplan et al., *Job Demands,* p. 14.

Trojanowicz found a consensus across ranks in one department that the probation period should be used more effectively to determine which new sergeants are not functioning effectively. If, after counseling and retraining, the sergeant still cannot do the job, he should be demoted rather than transferred.[62] Caplan states that the effects of poor fit are likely to be felt most strongly as dissatisfaction with workload, boredom, and overall job dissatisfaction.[63] These are clues that the immediate supervisor can watch for and he can then tell by listening to his people whether, and in what regard, there are discrepancies between their abilities and needs and the demands and opportunities of their jobs. Often the remedies lie with the supervisor in the form of training or rearrangement or reassignment of duties, to make the job more interesting or less onerous or to better equip the officer to handle difficult aspects of his work. In some cases, of course, none of these actions will be sufficient and it will be necessary to arrange transfer to a more suitable position.

Altering the Subjective Environment

It was mentioned earlier that stress arises from people's subjective perceptions of threats in the stimuli they receive from the outside global environment. But people can learn to perceive stimuli in a less threatening light. Often they do this themselves as the new and strange becomes the old and familiar. But some situations and events are too disturbing for them to adjust to on their own, and may become even more disturbing unless they learn to deal with them adequately. For example, some officers find it very difficult to deal with rudeness, insolence, and hostility from the public without displaying anger, although their training has warned them against showing signs of provocation. When their supervisor learns this by asking them how they feel in different situations and listening carefully to their replies, he should recall his own feelings when this first happened to him and make suggestions to help the officers deal with this type of stress. If further help is needed, the supervisor can arrange for special training, perhaps making use of simulated role playing, which has been found to be a useful technique for training police to handle difficult street situations.[64] Whatever the method employed, the supervisor must have a firm conviction that the officer's perceptions can be changed and that he is the best person to see that this is done effectively.

[62]Robert C. Trojanowicz, "Perceptions of the Role of the First Line Police Supervisor" (unpublished research study, Michigan State University, 1977).
[63]Caplan et al., *Job Demands*, p. 199.
[64]A.P. Goldstein and M. Sorcher, *Changing Supervisory Behavior* (New York: Pergamon Press, 1974).

Job-Stress Variables

There are a great number of potential stress variables in police work about which little can be done directly, by either the officer or his supervisor, at least on their own initiative. Such factors as the high-stress environments in urban ghettos, line-of-duty crisis situations, negative public image, and treatment of police officers by the courts cannot be changed by the action of an individual supervisor. However, a number of other job stresses that are more important in the daily lives of officers and supervisors *can* be reduced by individual action, particularly action by the supervisor. It is these that will be dealt with in the following sections.

Workload. Workload stress may be caused by either quantitative or qualitative factors, and by either an overload or an underload. One usually thinks first of heavy and difficult tasks causing stress, but the boredom of inactivity or of tedious, repetitious, and dull tasks can also be stressful. The word "overqualified" used to describe an unsuitable job applicant is of fairly recent vintage, but it points up a problem of increasing importance in an era of better-educated candidates, when many jobs have had much of the need for initiative and ingenuity automated out of them. Nowadays, police officers and supervisors often complain bitterly that they spend half their time filling out forms, which they see as a boring or frustrating substitute for the public service and law-enforcement functions they were hired and trained to perform.

The supervisor can make things less stressful for his subordinates by showing them the quickest ways to dispose of paperwork, by not being petty or perfectionist in reviewing completed forms, and by allowing them to be completed when the officer is not tired and prone to error. The supervisor must also be quick to press for simplification or discontinuance of information that is required in too much detail or has become obsolete. Where the paperwork is really necessary, the supervisor should explain the value of it to his men, for there are few chores as stressful as a task that is not only unpleasant but thought to be unnecessary.

Overload in work quantity can be justified only in conditions of real emergency, and if these seem to be occurring too regularly, there is need for the supervisor to review his unit's operations to determine and correct the conditions responsible. Assignments perceived as too difficult are more often the result of inadequate training than of inadequate abilities, and the careful supervisor will refrain from blaming the subordinate for poor performance until he has made sure that sufficient instruction and practice have been given.

Lack of participation. Over and over again in police organizations, one finds dissatisfaction and stress caused by the adoption of new policies, procedures, regulations, and orders without any prior consultation with the ranks who are charged with the responsibility of carrying them out. Trojanowicz sums up the feelings in one police organization:

> The consensus among ranks is that sergeants don't usually encourage input from their officers because it is not viewed as either a part of their job or a desired activity in a semimilitary organization.
>
> In the final analysis it depends on the sergeant. Some sergeants feel it is a sign of weakness to ask the opinions of their officers, because they think the officers will view this as the sergeant not having all the answers. Effective training could help the sergeant understand that soliciting input from officers is not a sign of weakness but an indicator of concern for their officers and respect for their opinions.[65]

In interviewing a number of supervisors and officers in one police department, I found that a recurring source of dissatisfaction was the extra work caused by adoption of a computer-based reporting system. They had been told that the new system would result in a reduction of paperwork and welcomed the change for this reason, but were disappointed to find that the new system required more paperwork from them than before. Many of them felt that if they had been consulted before the new system was introduced, the result would have been different.

In industry, a great deal of attention has been paid in recent years to the problems of poor morale resulting from worker alienation, monotonous and boring work, and lack of personal involvement or of any sense of ownership of the processes being used. In an effort to get workers interested and involved, and in order to improve attendance and the quantity and quality of output, programs of job enlargement and job involvement have been started in recent years. Along with these, there have been some programs to allow the workers to participate in decision making, particularly when operations are being started or old ones changed. One model of a participation system is the Scanlon Plan, named after a union representative who started it to help save a foundering steel plant. It goes beyond job enrichment by encouraging suggestions from employees and by setting up joint worker–management committees to review and screen the suggestions and discuss their implementation. It also provides for group bonuses to be paid from productivity savings. Studies that have been made of the operation of this plan show that participation

[65]Trojanowicz, "Perceptions."

in decision making was significantly correlated with job involvement and motivation of workers.[66]

Job enrichment programs are recommended for police work by Kroes, who deals directly with the objections by police administrators that they do not apply to policing:

> The police administrator may feel that this is all well and good but it does not apply to policing—to assembly lines or automobile manufacturing maybe, but not to policing; this is not so. Policing is actually one of the most fertile fields for the introduction of job enrichment. And some departments have actually done so in a minimal way. Witness the new approach of assigning an officer full responsibility for an area. That is, the officer not only acts as patrolman but detective, too. He receives more job satisfaction by being able to take a case through to completion. He is no longer quickly replaced by investigative personnel to return to the humdrum of radio calls. The success of this approach can be seen in the words of one patrolman, who, in speaking of his fellow officers, states . . . 'it gives them a sense of accomplishment, that they are doing more than just taking reports after a crime has been reported. They are receiving credit for the arrests instead of someone else. Before they started this policy, many officers were disgruntled, but since then the morale of the men has risen sharply.'[67]

Kroes also points out that there is a two-way payoff for participation in that both the individual and the organization stand to gain from it:

> When an officer is assigned responsibility for a task or has exceptional knowledge or experience in an area, he should be involved in the decision-making process related to that area. The organization gains because they obtain the use of a resident expert and the individual gains in that his sense of professionalism and stress-coping ability are enhanced.[68]

Social Support

The extent to which officers lack support by police management also indicates an area in which unnecessary stress is being imposed through poor communication or faulty organization. No doubt there are sound reasons for many of the failures to back up the officer's field decisions, and for the internal investigations which set one man against another, and in which, to quote the words of one officer the writer has listened to:—"They investigate every complaint from the public without even talking to you first, and when

---

[66]Carl F. Frost, John H. Wakeley, and Robert A. Ruh, *The Scanlon Plan for Organization Development: Identity, Participation, and Equity* (East Lansing: Michigan State University Press, 1974).
[67]William H. Kroes, op. cit., p. 107.
[68]Ibid., p. 104–105.

they do, you are held to be guilty unless you can prove yourself innocent. Talk about stress! That's the worst kind you can get when it comes from your own people."

Obviously, police management does not subject the ranks to this sort of grueling procedure in order to produce these reactions from them. Perhaps the pressures from City Hall, politicians, newspapers, and the public force them to handle investigations this way so that charges that the police are brutal or that the facts are being covered up cannot be substantiated. But are the ranks being made aware of the need to protect the whole organization in this way? And were the consequences in stress and strain throughout the organization fully considered? Any sound organization with well-trained personnel can withstand heavy pressures from outside without cracking, but when the stress comes from inside, its members are much more vulnerable. This is particularly true in the police culture, where, lacking positive feedback from the public, officers must turn to their peers for necessary social support. If they are accused and feel rejection by people within their own ranks, the effect can be devastatingly stressful, because they may feel both a sense of betrayal and a sense of desperation, that they have nowhere else to turn.

Social support can also refer to the day-to-day relations on the job between the officer and his immediate supervisor, or with other people at work, or with the officer's spouse, friends, and relatives. Caplan et al. found that poor social support from one's immediate superior and from others at work is associated with high job dissatisfaction,[69] and this finding was also borne out by the results of a national random-sample survey of the work force of the United States.[70] The Caplan study also found that high levels of depression in workers were influenced by poor social support from the supervisor and others at work.[71] As a result of these findings, they recommended that changing the social environment to provide more support from one's supervisor and one's co-workers is an important feature in reducing stress and promoting psychological well-being. They suggest, however, that training a supervisor in the area of human relations by traditional programs may not change his actual behavior back on the job. A training program by which a supervisor and his boss and his boss's boss can all receive training at the same time is more effective in producing substantial changes in supervisory practices.[72] This technique sounds promising, because it addresses itself to the common complaint made by training program participants that they liked the program but wished that their boss could take it as well.

[69]Caplan et al., *Job Demands*, p. 197.
[70]R. Quinn, S. Seashore, R. Kahn, T. Mangione, D. Campbell, G. Staines, and M. McCullough, *Survey of Working Conditions: Final Report on Univariate and Bivariate Tables*, Document No. 2916–0001 (Washington, D.C.: U.S. Government Printing Office, 1971).
[71]Caplan et al., *Job Demands*, p. 210.
[72]Ibid., pp. 210–11.

In a report on the role of the first-line police supervisor, Trojanowicz found that all ranks except command officers alluded to the lack of backing and support from the administration. He stated that officers obviously want a supervisor they can talk to, rely on, and get answers from in reply to their questions. Complimenting an officer when he has done a good job is also helpful in providing positive reinforcement and helping motivate the officer to continue to do a good job.[73]

Role conflict. Situations in which officers are caught between conflicting orders are primarily the responsibility of the immediate supervisor to control or eliminate. People must be able to rely on administrators for a clear and stable set of instructions consistent with organizational protocol. In situations in which the norms of rule orientation and universalism are weak, role conflict and job-related tensions are almost twice as prevalent.[74]

Role conflict has been found to correlate more consistently than any other stressor with anxiety, irritation, and depression.[75] Most supervisors would not be surprised by this, because they have been caught between conflicting demands themselves. The solution lies in making clear to the officer the general line he is to take in dealing with such situations, and the fact that he will be backed to the hilt if he follows this line. By patient reiteration of the recommended procedure, he can be taught to follow it without suffering the tugs and pulls between conflicting demands that are so stressful.

Role ambiguity. The question of being certain about what is required on the job, and clear about what others expect, is another one that must be answered by the immediate supervisor. Because of the wide range of discretionary authority wielded by the officer in the field, he is peculiarly vulnerable to reprimand and censure for making mistakes or exceeding his authority. All the more reason why he should be clear in his mind about how his supervisor wants him to handle a given situation, so that he will not feel threatened by lack of support for his decision. A supervisor who takes the time to listen to his men and to correct any mistaken impressions they may have early in the relationship will strengthen their impressions about what is expected of them and help dispel the doubts and uncertainty that cause this type of stress.

Shift changes. Earlier in this chapter, the findings with regard to the stress effects of shift work in police work and in industry were reviewed.

---

[73]Trojanowicz, "Perceptions."

[74]Daniel Katz and Robert L. Kahn, *The Social Psychology of Organizations* (New York: John Wiley, 1966), p. 329.

[75]Caplan et al., *Job Demands*, p. 85.

There has not been sufficient study given this topic in police work, but what recommendations there are lean toward adoption of a voluntary system in which officers could choose their preferred shift. Kroes says that some police chiefs maintain that this would leave insufficient trained personnel for certain late shifts, but then he gives an example of a police department in which it worked quite satisfactorily.[76] In one department I know of, rotating shifts were replaced by fixed shifts staffed on the basis of choice for a year at a time, with seniority the guiding factor where not all choices could be accommodated. This system has operated satisfactorily for a number of years. In another case, rotating shifts were discontinued in favor of fixed shifts but command staff made some of the shift allocations in order to strengthen less popular shifts. This arrangement has not been in operation long enough for an accurate assessment of its long-term effects, but it appears that most officers strongly prefer it to the rotating shifts.

The recommendations of Mott et al. were that the fixed-shift system was a better arrangement than the rotating shift for the well-being of the worker. Management often contends that the rotating shift is less expensive to operate because it requires less manpower, but this may be a shortsighted conclusion in view of the deleterious effects of rotating shifts on worker health. Management and workers should get together to try out different shift combinations before deciding which arrangements are best suited to their combined needs.[77]

From the standpoint of the supervisor concerned with minimizing stress on his officers, it seems clear that the best system is to let them choose their own shift as far as possible, at least after they have had enough time on each shift to familiarize themselves with the work it requires and the conditions that must be fulfilled. It might also be wise to insist that the spouse be consulted before a final decision is made by the officer, because the high stress certain shifts may produce in families will reflect negatively on the officer and his performance.

Organizational Approaches

The foregoing discussion of stress management has dealt with certain common variables, mainly psychological, that are responsible for much of the individual stress suffered in police work, and it has suggested certain behaviors and actions for supervisors to take to eliminate or minimize stress and strain effects. But if department cooperation can be obtained, it would be much preferable to consider launching an overall stress-management pro-

[76]Kroes, *Society's Victim,* p. 103.
[77]Mott et al., *Shift Work,* pp. 308–15.

gram that would enlist the services of the whole organization simultaneously to make a concerted attack on the problem. Such a program would include identifying the major stressors, developing ways of eliminating or alleviating them, implementing the most promising programs, and establishing a feedback system to monitor their effectiveness and to make whatever changes become necessary as the program unfolds.[78] Although an outside consultant might be helpful for the initial study and recommendation phase of a stress-management program, its ultimate success will really depend on the strength and lasting nature of the department's support for it, and therefore on how convinced the administration is of the advantages to be gained from it.

Individual Stress Management

Regardless of the fate of overall organizational stress-management programs, a number of steps that each individual can take to manage stress can pay off in greater satisfaction and effectiveness, in both his job and nonjob life. In the final analysis, the individual must learn to control his own behavior so as to accomplish his personal objectives at the least cost to himself and his family in strain and illness.

Self-image. Perhaps the most important first step a person can take is to be aware of the extreme importance of his self-image as the basic value that largely determines the extent to which he is threatened by the psychological variables discussed, as well as a number of others that were not touched on. The individual's perceptions of incoming stimuli as threatening or nonthreatening is first of all dependent on how much regard he has for himself. To put it another way, if your own opinion of your worth is solid and unassailable, then you will not be threatened by the opinions or actions of others and will be able to influence your thoughts and feelings so as to avoid perceptions that might otherwise cause stress, strain, and eventually illness.[79] It is no coincidence that two of the variables dealt with above, social support and participation, are very much affected by feelings of self-worth and desire for approval by others. When this desire becomes a need, the person is admitting that the views of others about him are more important than his own. If this happens, he is extremely vulnerable to emotional stress in every phase of job and personal relationships, since it is impossible to go through life without incurring a great deal of disapproval. This does not mean that a person must develop a shell of indifference to the wants, needs, and desires of others; it means that he must pay attention first to the things that are fulfilling for him, always remembering that he is unique, different from every other person on

---

[78]Kroes, *Society's Victim,* pp. 103–7.
[79]Wayne W. Dyer, *Your Erroneous Zones* (New York: Avon Books, 1977), pp. 238–39.

the planet, and he must put his own uniqueness first. As Polonius told his son in *Hamlet:*

> This above all: to thine own self be true,
> And it must follow, as the night the day,
> Thou canst not then be false to any man.

Although this is sufficient counsel for the individual worker, the supervisor must also take responsibility for the performance and accomplishments of his subordinates if he is to succeed. He can only succeed through their efforts, so he must carefully consider what kind of psychological environment they require if their efforts are to be nurtured and developed to the fullest extent. More than anything else, this means getting to know each person's strong interests and aversions, the things that reward him and those that set his teeth on edge. The supervisor must ask himself questions about each subordinate, such as, How much work load is right to keep him from boredom without overloading him? What tolerance does he have for complex or ambiguous assignments? How much social support does he need? Does he like to have input into, and be consulted on, decisions that will affect him? What will a shift change do to his family life? Which people does he work well with, and which not so well?

There is still a lingering tendency on the part of some police supervisors to disregard this kind of individual treatment as coddling, and unsuited to the paramilitary traditions of police organizations. The members of this old school were taught to do exactly as they were told, without asking questions. Any deviation was a sign of weakness, to be eliminated. Small wonder then that they do not favor treating subordinates as individuals. What they have failed to notice is that the day of automatic, unquestioning obedience in organizations (including the military) has passed. More important, they are not aware that good leaders, including great military leaders such as Eisenhower and Montgomery, always paid attention to the needs of their men, because they realized that it produced better morale and, hence, better results. The successful military leaders have always realized that to threaten men is to demonstrate weakness. The newer method is to justify authority on the basis of personal qualities as well as role criteria.[80]

Physical fitness. One individual approach that holds great promise for stress management is emphasis on personal physical fitness. In recent years, there has been growing recognition that a carefully planned and consistently

[80]M. Janowitz, "Changing Patterns of Organization Authority: The Military Establishment," *Administrative Science Quarterly,* Vol. 3 (1959), 490.

maintained fitness program may be one of the best ways to counteract the tensions, anxieties, and somatic complaints generated by occupations that are psychologically stressful but do not allow for the physiological outlets through hard physical labor that were an integral part of the life of our forebears. Evidence shows that the introduction of proper physical activity may delay or avert the development of such conditions as hypertension, emphysema, and heart disease. Most physiologists agree that greater longevity and greater enjoyment of life can be achieved through activity and physical fitness.

Among the benefits of exercise are the following:

1. Increased size and strength of heart, enabling the organ to pump more blood with each beat and to rest longer between beats, a possible saving of 10,000 to 40,000 beats per day.
2. Increased size and pliability of blood vessels, reducing blood pressure and cutting down on cholesterol levels in the blood.
3. Expansion of the blood supply, hemoglobin, and blood plasma, streamlining the body's waste removal system and allowing more oxygen to saturate the muscles and other tissues, and reducing fatigue and building endurance.
4. The creation of networks of new blood vessels and capillaries (increased tissue vascularization) in the cardiac and skeletal muscles, thereby improving the flow of oxygen to all parts of the body.[81]

A healthy and physically fit body cannot guarantee mental well-being, but it is less quickly overcome by emotional stress. Furthermore, a strong constitution and good health can contribute to a more positive outlook on life, which does influence one's mental well-being. Vigorous activity can help the body adapt to strain and can prevent its being overwhelmed by mental stress.[82]

A series of experimental exercise programs was implemented using police personnel in Dallas in order to evaluate the physiological effects of running and weight training on officers. The results indicated significant improvement for both young and middle-aged runners in working capacity, cardiovascular function, body composition, strength, and muscular endurance.[83] Another report by the same researchers states that police officers between 36 and 52 years of age were found to be at higher risk for coronary heart disease and lower in physical condition than the normal population. They suggest that their results support the need for physical fitness and

---

[81]LaPlace, *Health,* p. 305.

[82]Ibid., p. 307.

[83]Larry R. Gettman and Michael L. Pollack, "Evaluation of Physical Fitness Programs for Police Officers," *Proceedings of the 83rd Annual Conference of the International Association of Chiefs of Police* (1976).

preventive medicine programs for police officers.[84] An article in *The New York Times* of June 2, 1978, says that U.S. companies see "the profit in physical fitness," and that "corporate fitness programs are multiplying almost as fast as brands of running shoes." The article quotes one company vice-president to the effect that the expenditure of $2.5 million for a fitness center for salaried employees was "very much a business proposition," and "intended to be cost-effective." Others label their fitness programs as aimed at the executive group, because they are under the most pressure and have the most stress. Still other fitness directors claim that absenteeism is down and significantly fewer days are being lost through illness since their programs were begun and that productivity and morale have improved. Another study, at Tel Aviv's Wingate Institute, showed that when it comes to functioning under the pressure of mental tasks such as important decision-making, "the physically fit person has a definite advantage."[85]

Even if the medical arguments are set aside, it is useful to consider the role of exercise in working off stress and strain effects:

> Exercise relieves tension. Fitness enthusiasts call exercise the best tranquilizer known. And it makes sense. Stress is the body's response to danger or challenge; the heartbeat quickens, adrenalin rushes in, the senses leap to attention. This is called the "fight or flight" response, and it's a marvelous survival instinct that has been programmed in humans for millions of years. Unfortunately, we still experience this response today when there's no one to fight and nowhere to take flight, and the stress has nowhere to go. It stays inside the body in the form of ulcers, headaches, or psychosomatic illness. Vigorous exercise, such as running, swimming, or clobbering a tennis ball, is fighting and fleeing—or doing what the human body was intended to do. And out flows the tension.[86]

Meditation. This is a method of coping with stress that has been used in the East for many centuries under such names as yoga and Zen. The meditator focuses his attention on an object or a word, or opens up his attention by placing himself in a state of undistracted receptivity to external and internal stimuli. By either means, he gains mastery over attention, and the results in terms of control over body functions can be quite spectacular. The characteristic pattern of physiological change during meditation includes the slowing of pulse, respiration, galvanic skin reaction, and brain-wave activity to an extent indicating a state of deep relaxation.

However, the real advantage of meditation as an agent of stress control is the carryover into the person's daily activities. Meditators have been found

[84]Pollack and Gettman, "Coronary Risk Factors."

[85]John E. Gibson, "What Decisions Tell about You," *Family Weekly,* June 18, 1978, p. 12.

[86]Don Akolin, "I Was a 49-pound Weakling," *Insider* (Knoxville, Tenn.: 13–30 Corporation, 1977), pp. 5–6.

to be more stable psychologically and less anxious, because meditation helps them maintain a low arousal state. If a person can learn to respond to stressful stimuli, to which a fight-or-flight response would be inappropriate, by inducing a state of relaxed, non-aroused physiological functioning, he will be able to avoid the consequences of a prolonged stress reaction. There is also evidence that, with sufficient training, the ability to substitute a low-arousal state for the normal response to a stressful situation can become habitual.[87]

Biofeedback. Another method for relief of stress is biofeedback, although it is so new that no precise definition of it has yet been agreed upon. In this technique, a selected physiological activity, such as the heart rate, is monitored by an instrument that measures it and "feeds back" the resulting information to the person generating it.[88] For example, by sitting quietly and repeating a few autosuggestion phrases to himself while watching his heart rate on the instrument, a person can quickly learn to change the rate of his heartbeat as he desires. Other bodily processes subject to control in essentially the same manner include blood pressure, brain waves, muscle tension, and skin temperature. Muscle biofeedback has been reported as effective in reducing anxiety, tension, chronic headaches, hyperactivity, stage fright, insomnia, alcoholism, drug abuse, depression, asthma, hypertension, intestinal disorders, and muscle spasm.[89]

The ultimate biofeedback may be through monitoring of brain waves, by which people can learn control over complex brain functions. For example, people with irregular brain functions such as epilepsy or psychosis can learn to generate brain states that reduce both physical and emotional distress. Methods are also being developed to produce brain states conducive to tranquillity and creativity.

Although the reality of biofeedback is well established, its use in stress management is only beginning to be developed and has been limited so far mainly to a process of desensitization. As the subject receives muscle biofeedback, he visualizes as vividly as possible a variety of stressful situations, while attempting to maintain the relaxed muscle tension or to reduce quickly the increased tension resulting from the visual image. He is then encouraged to transfer his tension-control learning to real-life stressors, and to learn to relax after stressful situations.[90]

As the subject becomes more skillful at producing the relaxation results, he becomes aware of the effects he is producing, such as sensations of lightness and warmth in his limbs, while excluding certain thoughts from his

[87]Pelletier, *Mind as Healer.*
[88]Barbara B. Brown, *Stress and the Art of Biofeedback* (New York: Harper & Row, 1977), p. 3.
[89]Ibid., pp. 54–55.
[90]Ibid., p. 97.

mind. He can then learn to verbalize these feelings as an aid in controlling them and to use that control in life situations where he wishes to relax or to offset stress effects.[91]

SUMMARY

This chapter has presented evidence about the importance of stress in police management. The nature and causes of stress, particularly in police organizations, were explored, and the effects of a number of behavioral strains, illnesses, and impairment of job performance were considered. Steps that can be taken by the police supervisor to manage stress in his own activities and those of his subordinates were outlined. A model of the sources and effects of stress in organizations was presented, followed by discussion of the various elements of the model as they relate to police work. Finally, a number of individual stress-management techniques that have shown promise in recent research were described.

The key role of the police supervisor in recognizing stress symptoms in his personnel and in taking effective action to limit and control their negative consequences was emphasized. His efforts will be reflected in better health and greater job satisfaction for his people, and in improved performance and attainment of organization goals.

[91]Ibid., p. 98.

CHAPTER NINE

The Sergeant as a Reflection of His Department and Community

As this book has tried to show, the environment of the first-line police supervisor is a complex one. This chapter will focus on the need for departmental and community support if the sergeant is to be an effective leader. The police sergeant may be highly educated, well paid, and able to handle stress; equipped with the latest technological devices for fighting crime; and given the most comprehensive, up-to-date training. But without support from his department and his community, he cannot be completely effective.

THE NEED FOR DEPARTMENTAL SUPPORT

Department support will both improve the sergeant's attitude about himself and make firmer the *psychological contract* he has with his subordinates and his employers.

The Psychological Contract

The psychological contract is an implied relationship that is essential to organizational functioning. It materializes immediately upon the person's joining the police department and affects his morale, motivation, job satisfaction, and job performance.

Huse and Bowditch define this relationship as:

. . . the mutual exchange and reciprocation between the individual and the organization. This includes the influence process for mediating conflict between the goals of the organization (large system) and those of the employee (subsystem). This psychological contract stipulates that material wages and "psychological income" be given to the individual, who in turn makes a commitment to work toward the goals of the organization. It constitutes the sum total of the expectancies perceived by both the individual and the organization about their relationship.[1]

Other, more basic elements inherent in the psychological contract are described by Spencer:

The interdependence in needs and expectations between the individual and the organization is immense, with the lives of the two inseparably intertwined. The individual brings certain skills to the organization, along with his ability to learn and an undefined degree of commitment. The organization, in turn, undertakes some defined and some undefined responsibilities to the individual.[2]

The psychological contract, then, is a dynamic phenomenon in the ongoing process of individual–organization interaction. Its effects extend throughout the entire period of affiliation of the employee with the organization he has chosen to become a part of.

Because the nature of the contract affects the employee's motivation, performance, and job satisfaction, it is incumbent on police department administrators to understand its implications with regard to these factors. Certainly, if recruitment and selection are the first task of an organization, then the motivation of people toward a high level of performance is its second, and equally important. The sergeant's psychological contract with his department must be firm because he is the link that translates and interprets departmental policies, procedures, and orders. It is mandatory that he be committed to carrying out those duties to the best of his ability. Conversely, the department has to support him and back him up in his delicate role of "man in the middle."

Application of the contract. The psychological contract between the department and the sergeant—indeed, between the department and all employees—is implemented, from the department's point of view, largely through the concept of authority, inasmuch as the employee's decision to join the organization implies the commitment to accept that organization's au-

---

[1]Edgar F. Huse and James L. Bowditch, *Behavior in Organizations: A Systems Approach to Managing,* 2d ed. (Reading, Mass.: Addison-Wesley, 1977), p. 77. (The section on the psychological contract was written by Roger W. Watson, Michigan State University, 1978.)

[2]Hollister Spencer, "Designing Commitment into the Organization," *Personnel Journal,* Vol. 5, No. 12 (December 1972), 892–97.

thority system.[3] In the same way, the contract between the sergeant and his subordinates implies the legitimacy of the sergeant's authority, by virtue of his being the first-line management representative of the department. If the sergeant is perceived as merely a "super patrol officer" with little department influence or authority, this contract will have little meaning.

Etzioni has identified the following types of authority exercised by organizations over their employees:

1. *Coercive authority* which rests on the application, or threat of application, of physical sanctions.
2. *Remunerative authority* is based on control over material resources.
3. *Normative authority* rests on the allocation and manipulation of symbolic rewards (i.e., esteem, prestige, acceptance, positive response, etc.).[4]

From the standpoint of the sergeant, his psychological contract with the department is implemented through his perception that he can influence the department sufficiently to ensure that he will not be taken advantage of—that is, that he is able to affect the authority structure directly, to change situations if necessary, and to have input into the decision-making apparatus.[5] The sergeant's involvement can range from minimum participation, in which he does just enough to get by, to complete moral commitment to the department and its policies and goals.[6]

Given the inherent necessity for an authority structure in the department, it is mandatory that all officers, including sergeants, consent to that authority. But this consent hinges upon the department's upholding of the psychological contract it has with its officers. If the department fails to live up to the contract and, at the same time, cannot coerce the officer to commit himself to department goals, then the officer will most likely leave or "semiretire"—perform minimally. Such "psychological retirement" is even more devastating to the department than is regular employee termination.

Scott, in studies of employee termination, demonstrated that the dysfunction of the psychological contract was a major factor in labor turnover:

> Prospective employees who are attracted to a company often have certain expectations as to the roles they will perform and the way they will be treated. If these preconceived ideas turn out to be unrealistic, with result-

[3]Edgar H. Schein, *Organizational Psychology*, 2d ed. (Englewood Cliffs, N.J.: Prentice-Hall, 1970), pp. 12, 13.

[4]Amitai Etzioni, *A Comparative Analysis of Complex Organizations* (New York: The Free Press, 1961), pp. 5, 6.

[5]Schein, *Organizational Psychology*, p. 13.

[6]Etzioni, *A Comparative Analysis*, pp. 9–11.

ing frustration and disillusionment on the job, early termination is frequently a consequence.[7]

Thus, the problem of motivation and organizational incentives or rewards is best understood as a complex bargaining situation between the department and officers, involving the decisions of whether to join the department in the first place, how hard to work, and how creative to be; feelings of loyalty and commitment; expectations of being taken care of and of finding a sense of identity through one's departmental role; and a host of other decisions, feelings, and expectations.[8] If the department's psychological contract is consistently broken with its officers because of favoritism, inconsiderate treatment, lack of backing, and unreasonable manipulation, then the sergeant will have a difficult time influencing his supervisees to do a good job. Hence the need for a firm psychological contract that is honored by both parties. The sergeant as middleman can be the force to keep both sides honest, ensuring the fulfillment of the psychological contract.

A number of social scientists and organizational theorists have expressed the importance of the psychological contract in terms of individual commitment to the organization's goals and policies in return for expectations of rights, privileges, and employment longevity.[9] However, there are exceptions to this theoretical generalization. Drucker contends that the first concern of the organization must be for profitability and productivity, not for the welfare of its employees:

> A legitimate government is a government that rules in the interest of its subjects. But that the enterprise cannot possibly do. The first concern of the enterprise must be for profitability and productivity, not for the welfare of its members. The members are not the citizens for whose benefits the institution exists. They are a group of claimants—a very important group of claimants, but no more important than other groups such as consumers. They must be definitely subordinate to the claim of economic performance: profitability and productivity.[10]

Drucker's contention notwithstanding, workers do remain with organizations. Within the job situation, two sets of factors—motivators and maintenance factors—influence a worker's decision to remain on the job. Motiva-

[7]Richard D. Scott, "Job Expectancy—An important Factor in Labor Turnover," *Personnel Journal*, Vol. 51, No. 5 (May 1972), 360–63.

[8]Schein, *Organizational Psychology*, p. 15.

[9]Ken Jennings, "Employee Loyalty: Relationship between Theory and Practice," *Personnel Journal*, Vol. 52, No. 10 (October 1973), 863–71.

[10]Peter F. Drucker, *The New Society*, 2d ed. (New York: Harper & Row, 1962), p. 99.

tors have to do with job satisfaction; examples are achievement, recognition for achievement, the work itself, responsibility, and growth or advancement. Maintenance factors, which are extrinsic to the job, may include the department's philosophy and policy, the orientation and operation of working conditions, salary, status, and security.[11] These factors are all present in, and operate in the maintenance of, the psychological contract at one time or other. The sergeant, even without having complete control over the work environment, can play a major part in seeing that the motivators and maintenance factors are present and operate fairly.

Dysfunction of the contract. In the foregoing discussion of the nature and application of the psychological contract is the implication that the department/officer relationship is maintained as long as there is at least some satisfaction with the terms of the contract. However, for a multitude of reasons, the contract often weakens and dissolves during the course of this relationship, and the perceptions of the department's work environment become cynical. Several of the 300 line officers interviewed in the survey mentioned earlier stated that they did not want to become sergeants because of the grief they had seen sergeants go through once they assumed their supervisory position. Several officers felt that their departments did not live up to the psychological contract with the sergeants— the job was supposed to be influential, important, and meaningful, but in reality, sergeants were merely "super patrol officers." Likewise, they felt that the department did not fulfill its contract with the line officers, because without committed and motivated supervisors, line officers lose a necessary element in the work environment. When the psychological contract is broken, or even perceived to have been broken, long-lasting reverberations are sent throughout the department, causing damage that will take much effort to repair.

In some police departments, the psychological contract includes rewards to employees based on loyalty, with seniority often being used as an informal index of loyalty. Such rewards appear to contradict the emphasis of much of the current motivation literature. Rewards for longevity, since it is often associated with incompetency, may cause serious morale problems among the more competent members of the organization, with the possibility of accompanying declines in productivity.[12] Such departments often exercise their power coercively, displaying overadherence to established policies and procedures, encouragement of organizational loyalties, and intolerance toward those who deviate from established institutional norms. Such an organi-

---

[11]Huse and Bowditch, *Behavior in Organizations,* pp. 95, 96.

[12]Thomas Rotondi, Jr., "Personality Implications of Organizational Identification," *Personnel Administration,* Vol. 35, No. 3 (June 1972), 24–28.

zational climate emphasizes total departmental identification to the detriment of creativity, innovation, updating, and constructive criticism.[13]

In all fairness to police departments, it should be noted that the department is frequently not the initiator of the weakening or breaking of the psychological contract. Research and pronouncements emphasizing the responsibility of the department to the employee are frequently addressed in the literature of organizational behavior and personnel management; but missing from many of these texts, at least explicitly, are concepts of the employee's responsibility to the organization. Traditionally, "a fair day's work for a fair day's pay" was assumed to be the standard for determining and evaluating that responsibility. However, one must question whether this notion is a sufficient or meaningful measure, especially in an environment of complex, dynamic organizations vying for survival and growth.[14] Measures of what constitutes a fair day's work are often lacking.

Given these factors, police departments in today's dynamic environment must continually be aware of and address the need to deemphasize the coercive nature of the psychological contract and reemphasize policies encouraging interpersonal competence—autonomy, flexibility of goals and operations, creativity, and the like—in order to successfully attain employee commitment to the department and its goals.[15] When competence is the measure of worth, the sergeant's job will be much easier, because he will have reference points with which to measure his supervisees, reducing claims of favoritism and increasing officer motivation and morale.

Police departments have not always kept pace with progressive organizational administrative concepts. The reasons for this are many, and very often complex. Mark identifies the following as some of the reasons why police organizations have been slow to adapt and change:

> Exacerbating the perplexities and complexities of police organizational change is that it is occurring in a sea of uncertainty—in a society uncertain of its own direction, under economic stress and dislocation, with a considerable degree of dissensus, with individuals under severe tensions, groups in conflict, volatile pockets of racial polarization, people in fear of crime, easy accessibility to and rampant use of firearms, and, in the wings, the ever-lurking threat of nuclear holocaust. . . . Compounding the difficulties and dilemmas of comprehensive police change in the United States are the extreme fragmentation of its policing system, the proliferation of local and county jurisdictions, and the concrete realities of metropolitan regions that transcend state lines and function as entities more viable than each of their

[13]Ibid.
[14]John P. Loveland and Jack L. Mendleson, "Employee Responsibility: a Key Goal for Managers," *Human Resource Management,* Vol. 13, No. 1 (Spring 1974), 32–36.
[15]Rotondi, "Personality Implications."

separate parts, their viability, however, diminished by the different laws of the states overlapped.[16]

Also serving as a formidable barrier to progressive organizational change in the police organization, and directly affecting the sergeant's ability to supervise imaginatively, is the organizational structure itself. Its paramilitary nature incorporates virtually all elements of the traditional organizational structure: chain of command, authority, and communication; formal division of work, based on task specialization; prescribed rules and regulations; and a pyramidal arrangement of its hierarchy, with decision-making power centered at the top. Mark addresses this structure from the perspective of its impact upon the members of the organization:

> This predominant outlook embraces the doctrine of close supervision of subordinates and increased manpower to meet the problem in police administration and ineffectiveness in operations that surface.[17]

The influence of the paramilitary structure has an immediate effect upon the new member of the organization. The depersonalization—dramatically symbolized by the number assigned to him, and the uniform—and the requirement to suppress individual opinions and forms of conduct often quickly demoralize him. In examining specific factors that produce a demoralizing effect upon the police officer, Goldstein identifies the following:

> Once on the job he is rewarded for conformity and for nonthinking compliance with departmental directives and may be severely disciplined for minor infractions of petty rules. He may be shifted about, often at great personal inconvenience, to meet the needs of the agency. He is often used in ways that suggest all officers are interchangeable and that their physical presence is more important than any distinctive skills or abilities they bring to the job. His superiors tend to maintain an aloofness that greatly inhibits open communication outside the chain of command. He is frequently kept in the dark on matters that directly involve him. He must grab at straws for recognition.[18]

Under these conditions, if the police officer does not become discouraged and leave, it is almost certain that, in time, management policy and often the pressures of the first-line supervisors and peers will dilute much of the ability, potential, and enthusiasm he had upon entering the field. The psychological contract will be weakened and finally broken.

[16]Arthur Niederhoffer and Abraham S. Blumberg, *The Ambivalent Force,* 2d ed. (Hinsdale, Ill.: The Dryden Press, 1976), p. 356.

[17]Ibid.

[18]Herman Goldstein, *Policing a Free Society* (Cambridge, Mass.: Ballinger Publishing Co., 1977), p. 260.

Many police officers do leave. In a 1973 survey of factors related to personnel turnover, Teske found:

> Of twenty-four law enforcement agencies in Texas responding to a question-naire concerning personnel status during 1973, 79 percent perceived the rate of personnel turnover as a problem. Moreover, 33 percent of the agencies indicated that they experienced difficulty in finding enough qualified personnel to fill allotted positions. Among the twenty-four agencies, a total of 628 person-nel left the agencies during 1973. Moreover, 83 percent of those left for reasons other than retirement, disability, or death. Furthermore, the greatest proportion of individuals apparently leave within the first five years.[19]

In addition to contributing to the high turnover among police person-nel, the dissatisfaction experienced by the new officer manifests itself in other ways as well. Niederhoffer found that officer cynicism regarding superior–subordinate interaction, organizational discipline, organization effectiveness, and department rules and regulations was highest among those officers with two to twelve years service.[20] All these factors affect the psychological con-tract and make the sergeant's job more difficult.

Conclusion. If the primary indicators of psychological-contract dysfunc-tion within a police department are employee dissatisfaction and early turn-over, then a study of the literature of police organizations reveals a significant problem in the interrelationship of the organization and its members. In order to recruit and maintain the best possible police officers and provide an environment where the sergeant can effectively do his job, organizational change is needed.

Although some changes have taken place in recent years, there does not appear to be sufficient experimentation and reassessment of traditional organ-izational principles and attitudes and their effects on police departments. In general, too many departments appear unwilling to abandon outmoded con-cepts, to work in close collaboration with community agencies, or to encour-age personnel, especially sergeants, to show initiative or offer suggestions. This prevailing attitude must change if the police are to meet the changing conditions of police service.[21]

The progressive police administrator who enthusiastically seeks the goal of organizational change needs to be aware that, by its very nature, such change is a slow, difficult, and often painful process, some aspects of which

[19]Raymond H.C. Teske, Jr., "Factors Related to Personnel Turnover in Law Enforcement Agencies," *The Police Chief,* Vol. 43, No. 4 (April 1976), 62–65.

[20]Arthur Niederhoffer, *Behind the Shield: The Police in Urban Society* (Garden City, N.Y.: Double-day, 1967; Anchor books, 1969), pp. 199–226.

[21]Edward Eldefonso, *Readings in Criminal Justice* (New York: Glencoe Press, 1973), p. 138.

cannot be artificially induced. It takes many years to change attitudes, to develop competence, to shape operating philosophies, and to win support for a new approach to performing old functions.[22] It also takes community political leaders who are interested in quality law enforcement—not just favors for special interest groups.

Notwithstanding these limitations and conditions, change is essential, and it can be brought about. In working toward it, mutual cooperation and support among administrators and rank-and-file officers is vital, with the sergeant as the link. In their common quest for an improved, responsive organization, they will develop more meaningful and viable psychological contracts in the process of interaction. An agreed-upon psychological contract that is honored is the very least the sergeant must expect from both his department and the officers he is supervising. When either or both groups disregard the contract, the sergeant's role of middleman will become frustrating and anxiety-provoking, his leadership ability will be neutralized, and his supervisory mission difficult to achieve.

The Department's Responsibility

Not only does the department have the responsibility to provide the atmosphere and the tools for goal achievement; administration must constantly ask itself what more it can do to improve the sergeant's effectiveness. Two questions should be kept in mind: How could the preparation for sergeants be improved? and, What should be done with a sergeant who is not functioning effectively?

Preparation of the sergeant. In the survey taken of 300 officers, a majority of them were found to feel that a good patrol officer does not necessarily make a good supervisor, and that promotion to that rank should be related to the role requirements of the sergeant position, not to those of the patrol-officer position.

This points up the necessity of a well-defined job description, not just to provide reference points for the person already in the position but as a guide to determine if prospective candidates will be able to handle the job once they are promoted. The idea that anyone can be a supervisor with proper training is simply not true, and the department has the responsibility to ensure that only competent, motivated line officers are promoted to first-line supervisors.

Table 9-1 shows the responses most often given to the question, How could the preparation of sergeants be improved? Although the responses

[22]Goldstein, *Policing a Free Society,* p. 309.

TABLE 9-1

How Could The Preparation For Sergeants Be Improved?

Patrolmen	Detectives	Sergeants	Lieutenants	Command
Experience is the best trainer.	Need a course to teach the role of the sergeant.	Have him go with an experienced sergeant for an extended period of time (30 days).	Have new sergeants ride with experienced sergeants for an extended time (30 days).	Send him away to school so he can make the break.
Teach management and supervisory theory and principles.	Need leadership course.	Send to management schools.	Don't need training—it's a matter of personality and experience.	Teach him the role of decision making.
Teach interpersonal relations and communications.	All new sergeants should have investigative experience.	The sergeant trains himself by patterning after a role model.	Send to supervision school.	Need at least a two-week training course.
Give him a job description and let him know what his role is.	Courses in management theory and practice.	Train several officers prior to a promotion and then pick the best.	Send sergeant away to school and remove him from the organization.	Most of the training now is informal.
Schooling in law and departmental procedures.	More on-the-job training.	Tell the sergeant what his role and authority are.	The sergeant should train himself.	The sergeant should understand his role.
Require college training.		How to be a good sergeant can't be taught.	On-the-job experience is the best.	Expose him to interpersonal-communication classes.
Have training transfer program for sergeants.		Let sergeant work with a captain or above.	The lieutenant should do the training.	Attend management programs.
Assign new sergeant to experienced sergeant.		On-the-job experience is the best trainer.	College courses in management should be required.	
Need a better selection process.		Send to Interpersonal Communication course.	Better use of the probation period.	
Teach sergeant how to use his authority.		Have retraining and constant updating.		
Have refresher courses.		Train on how to go from a doer to an observer.		
Give him feedback so he knows how he is doing.				
Give him the authority and then let him alone.				
Teach leadership.				
Teach how to identify strengths and weaknesses.				
Train in both administrative and field aspects.				

Note: Responses are listed in the order of importance as stated by the particular group of respondents.

TABLE 9-2

What Should Be Done With a Sergeant Who Is Not Functioning Effectively?

Patrolmen	Detectives	Sergeants	Lieutenants	Command
Reassign him to an inside job.	Make better use of the probation period.	Counsel and help him understand his role.	Transfer him to another unit.	Counseling.
Demote him.	Use years of experience for promotion to sergeant and not testing.	Give him more training.	Use the probationary period better.	Training.
Find a slot in the organization for him.	Demote him.	Transfer him to a position where he won't do any harm.	Find out why he isn't doing the job and then help him.	Transfer to another division.
Give him more training.		Make better use of probation period.	Retrain him.	Use the probationary period better.
Counsel him—find out what the problem is.		Tell him directly why he isn't cutting it.	Do the following in order: talk to him; train; "chew out"; transfer; fire him.	Define his role better.
Improve the screening and promotion procedures.		Assign him to an experienced sergeant.		Reprimand him.
Make better use of the probation period.		Find an appropriate slot for him.	Explain his role to him better.	Have strong administrators who can make difficult personnel decisions.
Put him with a successful senior sergeant.		Give him time to adjust without pressure.	Demote him.	
Reward patrolmen with higher pay, and then they won't feel they have to make sergeant to be successful.		Have better testing and selection procedures.		
Don't make the same mistake by promoting him again.		Have the lieutenant talk to him.		
		Don't reward the "screw-up" sergeant with a daytime job.		

Note: Responses are listed in the order of importance as stated by the particular group of respondents.

255

vary, overall they indicate that adequate and continuous training is an essential part of the psychological contract.

Assistance to the ineffective sergeant. In the same way, the department is responsible for identifying and helping sergeants who are not functioning effectively. The responses of the 300 officers interviewed to the question, What should be done to a sergeant who is not functioning effectively? are shown in Table 9-2.

One area of major consensus across ranks was that the probation period should be used more effectively; the officers felt it should be understood that those who don't function properly during their probation period will revert back to their previous rank. As one stated, "The department doesn't want to demote a sergeant during the probation period because they don't want to admit they made a mistake."

The majority of the officers, regardless of rank, said that the sergeant who is not functioning effectively after having passed the probation period should receive counseling and retraining to become more effective. Then if the sergeant still cannot do the job, he should be demoted rather than transferred from one unit to another. There are both advantages and disadvantages to transferring an ineffective sergeant out of one unit and into another. It rids the unit of a problem, but it may create difficulties for the unit he is transferred to. Transferring a problem employee from one unit to another is just a short-range solution and will ultimately create more problems than it solves.

The department cannot focus all its hostility on the ineffective sergeant and blame him totally for his incompetence. It has the responsibility to do all it can to help him be more effective; that should be a part of the psychological contract. Just as it is the sergeant's responsibility to counsel his supervisees on both job-related and personal problems, it is the department's responsibility to counsel the sergeant who is having personal or job-related problems. In like fashion, the sergeant's superiors should give him day-to-day feedback and not wait until the situation has gotten out of hand.

The sergeant needs compliments and reference points just as his supervisees do. Compliments on a job well done do not cost a thing, but they are a long time coming in some police departments. One captain stated, "You can't compliment the sergeant, because then he will start to slack off. You have to keep him tense to produce." Conversely, in many cases, the ineffective sergeant is allowed to continue on the job and is protected by the administration rather than counseled to correct his behavior.

In summary, the sergeant cannot be effective if he does not have the support of his department. The psychological contract works both ways, and as long as there is general consensus between the department's administration and the officers, there will usually be at least a tolerable working relationship between the sergeant and his supervisees. The psychological contract between the sergeant and his officers will usually reflect the general tenor of the department's administrators. If they can be trusted and have a well-defined mission with minimal political interference and manipulation, then the psychological contract will usually be fulfilled and an atmosphere will prevail that will facilitate supervisees' receptiveness to supervision by the sergeant.

THE NEED FOR COMMUNITY SUPPORT

Just as the sergeant needs the support of his department to be effective, so does he need the support of his community. And just as the sergeant's attitude and actions will reflect those of the department's administrators, his behavior will generally replicate what is expected of him by the community.

There are those who believe that the sergeant, being the lowest manager in the organization, is insulated from community pressures and expectations. This is not the case. The first-line supervisor who is close to his supervisees and constantly available to help if needed is keenly aware of community expections. When a citizen asks to talk to a supervisor to inquire why an officer is "harassing citizens with tickets when he should be spending his time chasing crooks," the sergeant feels the "bite" as much as his officers.

Community expectations are directly related to the department's mission and role expectations, and these are ultimately reflected in the department's job descriptions. The job description is then, ideally, translated into action via the patrol, investigative, and special police functions.

The community that views its police department as a vehicle for the power structure will cause problems for the sergeant. In this atmosphere, he will have to explain to new officers why some people get tickets and some do not, why some drunk drivers are handled one way and some another, and why some people are processed through the courts and others are not.

This is not meant to portray every community as riddled with sinister forces. Communities vary in what they expect of their police; some are free from such corruption, some are infested with it, and first-line supervisors have to deal with the political dynamics of their own communities. This is their environment.

THE NEED FOR REFERENCE POINTS

It has been mentioned frequently in this book that the sergeant needs reference points with which to properly guide his subordinates, to give him measures for judging them, and to provide an orientation so that he may be evaluated. At first glance, the problem of identifying common reference points seems unmanageable, because of the pressures and pulls on the sergeant from his superiors, his supervisees, and the community, as well as the dynamic nature of policing itself.

By using the matrix method of analysis, however (to be discussed later in the chapter), community and department expectations can be visually identified, and input from line officers, the sergeants themselves, their supervisors, and community residents can easily be solicited. The product of this process is a definition of the sergeant's role, from which a job description follows. Adequate functioning should reflect the expectations stated in the job description.

The ultimate goal is to define the sergeant's responsibilities, authority, and accountability in the best way possible, with the understanding that community and department expectations are constantly changing, police work is dynamic, and the capabilities of sergeants vary. All these factors considered, it is still possible to define the sergeant's role by developing reference points and guidelines. A well-defined role will facilitate the fulfillment of the psychological contract and lead to organizational goal achievement, with the sergeant as the vehicle linking policy to action.

The Sergeant's Role Definition

Police supervision cannot be appropriately discussed unless the expectations of the sergeant as leader can be linked to the organizational role requirements. The supervisor cannot be objectively evaluated unless he knows what is expected of him, and he cannot measure his performance unless he has the reference points provided by a clear role definition. In the final analysis, management techniques like "management by objectives" or some other approach to increasing efficiency will be meaningless if there is no adequate role definition. Too often in contemporary police departments, role requirements of supervisors are not defined in such a way that they can be easily translated into a job description. In many cases, the job description is merely a general statement of responsibilities, with little mention of the span of authority or a method of accountability. For example, the following is a typical description of the role of the sergeant in field operations:

Supervision in Field Operations The Department is an organization with an assignment of responsibility and accountability throughout the rank structure. To the degree that a senior officer is responsible and accountable for the performance of his junior, he must be granted commensurate authority in order to properly discharge his supervisorial responsibility. Field supervision begins with the senior policemen of the Department, and it is upon them that the primary burden of training and supervising less experienced officers is placed. A field sergeant is the first level of full time supervision and it is his primary responsibility to guide, train, direct and motivate those over whom he has control. A field sergeant is not normally expected to engage in law enforcement operations except in a command or supervisory capacity.[23]

Even though the quotation above alludes to authority, responsibility, and accountability, it does little to define the extent and scope of the authority and responsibility or to specify the mechanism of accountability except to say, "throughout the rank structure." In the survey of the 300 police officers, the major criticism the sergeants voiced was the lack of a clear role definition. In more serious field operations, such as a man with a gun, a barricaded gunman, or a traffic stop with a carload of suspected drug dealers, sergeants are often expected to call for higher command assistance and advice even though their job description usually refers to their responsibility and authority in these areas. The common remark heard from sergeants was, "The department allows us to be in charge in situations that the senior patrol officer can handle, but in more serious situations, I have to call for help from a lieutenant or higher."

The sergeants also mentioned the inconsistent behavior of the lieutenants and captains. Some of the upper command are comfortable enough to stand back and observe, allowing the sergeant to make decisions and direct the field operations. Others are not satisfied with doing their paperwork; because "policework is in my blood," they feel they have to be involved in any occurrence of consequence. Such overinvolvement of upper command in situations where the sergeant could handle the problem is often in departments with inadequate job descriptions for sergeants, since their job descriptions for lieutenants and captains also leave a great deal to be desired. As a result, some upper command do not know when to take charge of a situation and when to let the sergeant handle it.

There is also the problem of the insecure chief who has difficulty delegating authority and wants one of his high-level administrators on the scene to report what is going on—especially in politically sensitive areas like gambling, prostitution, and bribery involving influential citizens.

The point is that the job description cannot merely say that the department is "an organization with an assignment of responsibility and accountability throughout the rank structure." The situation is much more complex than that; it depends on the behavior of the sergeant's immediate supervisors, the willingness of the upper command to delegate authority to the sergeant, and the overall political climate of the community. When upper command cannot delegate authority and the influential citizens in the community are given special favors, then job descriptions will be vague and sergeants will

[23]National Advisory Commission on Criminal Justice Standards and Goals, *The Police* (Washington, D.C.: U.S. Government Printing Office, 1973), p. 607.

think of themselves as merely "superpatrolmen." They will tread softly so as not to make critical misjudgments, "psych out" superiors to determine what they really expect, and play it safe rather than concentrating on being effective guides, trainers, overseers, and helpers for supervisees.

Another description of the role of the sergeant states:

> The sergeant stands between the administrative and command groups who develop plans and order them into operation and the officers who are engaged in carrying out the procedure. In this position he has important responsibilities to both groups. To subordinates he must interpret the purpose of the plan, explain its desirability, and instruct and assist in its execution; for superiors he must be alert to discover evidence of the success or failure of the plan, to detect weaknesses and to recommend changes to meet actual needs which may fluctuate as a result either of the effectiveness of the program or of changed or unanticipated conditions.[24]

This is an appropriate attempt to portray the importance of the role of the sergeant in interpreting policies and covering problem areas. It does not, however, allude to the necessity to include the sergeant in policy development, even if he is limited to reacting to it before it is implemented. As has been pointed out several times in this book, the sergeant's role must extend beyond the rhetoric that he is the "grease that makes the organization wheels turn."

The results of an inadequate role definition. Without adequate guidelines, the sergeant will have little direction and may spend more time playing organizational games of survival than effectively doing the job. McMurry lists some of the "rules of the organizational game" when the first-line supervisor is not operating effectively:

> No one initiates trouble in his department or unit—makes complaints to top management, asks embarrassing questions, or otherwise "rocks the boat."
>
> No one reports the inadequacies or derelictions of anyone else in the unit, even though that person may be flagrantly incompetent, obviously an alcoholic, or openly dishonest.
>
> Troublemakers (i.e., those who will not join the group's conspiracy) are, when possible, transferred out of the unit, given unpleasant assignments, or made so uncomfortable socially that they leave voluntarily.
>
> The chief executive and those closest to him (the "they" encountered in most employee ideologies) are often regarded as common enemies to be deceived, misled, and bamboozled in every way possible short of threatening the job security of the participants in the conspiracy. This not only makes for group

[24]O.W. Wilson, *Police Administration,* 2nd ed. (New York: McGraw-Hill, 1972), p. 16.

solidarity, but also gives the subordinates a goal toward which to strive: the embarrassment or frustration of their supervisors. Generally, the participants use the age-old technique of "passive resistance"—the order is accepted deferentially, but then nothing happens.[25]

McMurry also mentions that pressures and stress can get to the point where the supervisor behaves inappropriately. This can be for many reasons, such as personal problems, physical sickness, or other non-job-related matters; but in many cases, it can be the result of ambiguities that are due to an unclear or abbreviated role definition and job description. All of us need reference points in both our personal and work environments. When reference points are vague or inconsistent, anxiety and tension may prevail. McMurry lists some of the overt signs that show the supervisor is reacting to stress and pressure. He may:

Be reluctant in backing up and supporting his subordinates, even when they are clearly in the right;

Refuse to accept responsibility for his own mistakes;

Take a two-faced attitude toward his subordinates, praising them to their faces and criticizing them behind their backs;

Play favorites, since their support is needed;

Make promises he does not intend to keep;

Be indecisive and evasive when asked even a simple question;

Seek scapegoats for his mistakes among his subordinates;

Be a petty tyrant;

Show inconsistencies in his day-to-day interpretation of company policies;

Make it clear that he has no interest in, or respect for, his subordinates;

Never praise, but always criticize, his subordinates to inflate his own ego;

Discourage creative thinking and suggestions;

Become frightened and disorganized in emergencies;

Be resentful of constructive suggestions from his subordinates;

Keep his subordinates uninformed about company plans and projects;

Operate a disorganized, disorderly, and dispirited department;

Never let a subordinate really know where he stands;

Set a poor personal example regarding rules and regulations.[26]

Not all these tendencies may be the result of an inadequate job description, but they are indications of some kind of conflict; and that conflict is often the

[25]Robert N. McMurry, "Clear Communications for Chief Executives," *Harvard Business Review* (March–April 1965), p. 134.
[26]Ibid., p. 137.

result of confusing and vague expectations due to the lack of a well-defined role.

The Sergeant's Job Description

In addition to the statements made earlier relative to the sergeant's job description, it must include a specific list of responsibilities, the scope of authority, and the specific line of accountability in all situations. Mention can also be made of the approximate percentage of time that is to be spent on each activity (see Chapter 5). All this, of course, will depend on the specific job assignment of the sergeant; a patrol sergeant has different job requirements from those of a sergeant assigned to a special operations section, or a sergeant assigned to administer a grant. And the job description will also depend on such factors as the size of the department, the jurisdiction (state, municipal, county), and the types of problems and needs of the particular community.

The following is an example of a job description for a uniformed patrol sergeant in a medium-sized police department:

Title: Sergeant
Division: Uniform Patrol
Purpose: To provide first-line supervision over Uniform Patrol officers

Organization Position:
Uniform Patrol Sergeant has direct authority over all Uniform Patrol officers as well as Police Cadets assigned to that division. Additionally the Sergeant has direct authority over Corporals and/or Detectives while performing activities directly related to or effecting the Uniform Patrol function. The Uniform Patrol Sergeant is directly responsible to the rank of 2nd and 1st Lieutenants within the Uniform Patrol Division.

Responsibilities
Provide two-way communications between the patrol officer and the department administration.
Provide for the patrol officer's explanations and insights regarding new departmental policies and procedures.
Provide for and monitor the implementation of new as well as established departmental policies and procedures.
Provide the patrol officer with a ready source of job-related knowledge.
Enthusiastically promote the goals of the department and constantly strive to upgrade the morale of the uniform patrol officer.
Require acceptable standards of both work quality and quantity from the uniform patrol officer.

Regular Duties

1. Verbally recognize officers for excellent work in the field.
2. Initiate written recommendations for commendations of officers who have performed "above and beyond the call of duty."
3. Verbally reprimand officers when and where appropriate.
4. Initiate suspensions when and where appropriate.
5. Provide on-the-job training:
   a. Point out officers' errors.
   b. Provide the proper alternatives.
6. Oversee a variety of calls, as set forth in departmental policies, such as:
   a. Abductions
   b. Accidents involving police vehicles
   c. Armed robbery
   d. Bank alarms
   e. Bomb calls
   f. Civil disturbances
   g. Dead on Arrival (D.O.A.) calls
   h. Drownings
   i. Fatal and serious Personal Injury accidents
   j. Felonious assaults
   k. Homicides
   l. Incidents where officers sustain injuries
   m. Labor disputes
   n. Mentally ill subjects
   o. Miscellaneous alarms
   p. Breaking and entering
   q. Shooting/stabbings
   r. Suicides
   s. Towed vehicles
   t. Water incidents where boat is requested
7. Ride with subordinates while on patrol for portions of shift.
8. Disseminate information concerning:
   a. New departmental policies/procedures
   b. Warrants
   c. Special attentions
   d. Attempts-to-locate
   e. State, federal, and local bulletins
   f. Update court decisions

   g. Complaints to be signed

   h. Subpoenas

9. Check on officers' appearance at line-up and throughout tour of duty.

10. Randomly check victims'/complainants' references to how the officers handled their contact (quality control measure).

11. Advise officers who have complaints to sign the following day prior to end of duty tour.

12. Authorize replacement of worn or defective equipment for officers.

13. Check out vehicles and other equipment to officers at start of shift.

14. Supply "communication center" with daily assignment sheet.

15. Check in officers, vehicles, and equipment at the end of shift.

16. Properly dispose of officers' activity at the end of the shift:

   a. Sign all traffic citations.

   b. Check activity sheets for completeness.

   c. Check accident reports for accuracy and completion.

   d. Check & initial all reports of investigation.

   e. Forward all written materials to shift basket.

17. Issue work assignments:

   a. District patrol

   b. Beat patrol

   c. Special assignments

18. Draw up daily assignment sheet.

19. Update time-book recordings:

   a. Duty time

   b. Sick time

   c. Leave days

   d. Court time on/off duty

   e. Vacation time

   f. Comp. time (taken/accumulated)

   g. Paid overtime

20. Be available to assist officer wherever and whenever needed.

21. Perform any other duties as designated by their superior officers.

Periodic Duties

1. Supervise scheduled rollcall video tapes.

2. Write performance evaluations on officers (6-month intervals).

3. Investigate complaints against officers.

4. Review officers' monthly activity printouts.

5. Supervise special assignments:

   a. Parades

b. Visiting dignitaries
6. Formulate monthly leave-day schedules.
7. Inspect vehicles.
8. Inspect lockers.
9. Inspect district log books.
10. Present confirmation certificates.
11. Update and disseminate callback sheets.

This job description, although more complete than those provided in many departments, still does not specify the approximate amount of time the sergeant should spend each month on each activity. But more important, the sergeant's authority must be commensurate with the listed responsibilities. For example, number 4 under "Regular Duties" states that the sergeant will "initiate suspensions when and where appropriate." First, the specific kinds of situations should be stated, with examples—drinking on duty, illicit contact with members of the opposite sex while on duty, and so on. Then, in practice, when the sergeant makes the decision to suspend, he should not be publicly "second-guessed" by the administration or have the suspension immediately countermanded by his superiors.

As another example, regular duty number 6 calls for the sergeant to oversee a variety of calls; but in the case of, say, an armed robbery, if the lieutenant or captain immediately comes on the scene and takes over, using the sergeant as an errand boy, then the sergeant's authority is not commensurate with his listed duties. Furthermore, after the sergeant gets directives from the lieutenant or captain, the chief might arrive on the scene and give conflicting orders. The sergeant, reluctant to say that the lieutenant told him to do otherwise, for fear of antagonizing his immediate superior, may end up by trying in future situations to make himself scarce. The ultimate result will be the administration's exasperated complaint that "we can't get our sergeants to make decisions."

In addition to having the job description of responsibilities consistent with the authority needed to carry them out, the job description has to be constantly updated to fit contemporary organizational and societal problems. Other areas of responsibility that might have been mentioned in the sample description are these:

Counsel officers who have marital problems.
Counsel officers whose wives are under stress over disagreement with them.
Counsel officers who have problems with their children.
Interview members of an officer's family to locate source of problems.
Review general or special orders for adequacy, scope, and validity of content.

Review grievances from departmental personnel.

Determine, as result of interviews with officers, whether psychological testing is required.

Complete questionnaires to supply police-related data to FBI, IACP, etc.

Record information in personnel files.

Assign training responsibilities to senior officers.

Coordinate establishment and maintenance of "continuing investigation" activities of homicide, robbery, burglary, theft, etc.

Assist persons in completing required reports.

Transfer paperwork to proper divisions or agencies.

Update duty roster.

Investigate legal claims against the department.

Conduct community meetings on police-related issues.

Review traffic activity data.

Review manpower distributions by district to establish equitable workloads.

Instruct by using demonstration methods.

Review officer termination-of-employment reports.

Assign officers to make public appearance on behalf of department.

Review and evaluate departmental policy.

Serve on promotion review board.

Supervise record-keeping operations.

Make speeches to interested organizations.

Review and evaluate work flow and work delegation.

Review training documents, aids, and materials.

Establish rapport with judges, district attorneys, and other officials.

Determine program performance requirements.

Evaluate attainment of learning objectives during a lesson.

Review and evaluate training programs.

Attend professional conferences and meetings (IACP, TPA, etc.).

Develop training documents (lesson plans, training plans, tests, etc.).

Review books, magazines, and other literature to collect information relative to a specific problem.[27]

This list not only adds completeness to the job description; it places emphasis on important areas in which the sergeant should be involved— namely, *personnel guidance and counseling, training, planning,* and *community involvement.*

[27]Doug Goodgame, "Training Priorities for First-Line Supervisor in Municipal Law Enforcement: A Contrast of Opinions," *Journal of Police Science and Administration,* Vol. 6, No. 2, 193, 194.

Summary. The sergeant's job description must include a discussion and description of the first-line supervisor's role requirements, which is ultimately reflected in the department's job description. A supervisor in any organization needs reference points so that his performance can be evaluated, and guidelines to help him do his part to help achieve organizational objectives. An important part of the description of a leader, defined in Chapter 4, was the ability to produce results. Results can be measured only in relation to the expectations the organization has of the sergeant. The device used to objectively evaluate results or organizational expectations is the job description.

Even more important than a precise and complete listing of responsibilities is the department's willingness to complement the listed responsibilities with enough authority so that they can be fulfilled and the sergeant made to feel that his job is important, that he has an impact on how his department operates, and that he has influence on the psychological contract.

The job description is not a magical document that automatically produces organizational results. It is a means to provide guidance and reference points for the sergeant. The department's backing of the sergeant by giving him the necessary authority is the real test of whether it means what it says. A well-defined job description, backed by an organizational commitment to provide the necessary authority, will contribute to an accountability structure that will be definite, with each organizational level knowing what its part is in the operation. This will reduce duplication of activity and counteract interference by higher command officers in functions that belong with the sergeant.

Realistically, however, for the department to operate this way, the chief executive must feel secure in his position, have a positive self-concept, and be allowed to run his department with a minimum of political interference and negative involvement by influential community citizens and groups.

THE MATRIX METHOD FOR ROLE CONSTRUCTION

The necessity of a role definition for the sergeant from which a specific job description can evolve should be obvious by now. However, when more than one person or group has ideas about what should be included in it, a role definition is not easy to develop. In the case of a police sergeant, the people concerned would be the community residents, the department administrators, the sergeants themselves, and the sergeants' subordinates. All these people have different orientations and therefore different concepts of what should go into the sergeant's role definition. Even though including the views of all these people would seem to make the process unduly complex, it will in the long run reduce possible conflicts between these groups.

What must be done is to develop a process to coordinate their ideas and blend their input in such a way that there will be a common orientation to role definition.

Defining the role of the line police officer is difficult enough; traditional police functions and methods are currently being challenged as it is, which contributes to the police officer's feeling of frustration and abandonment by the community. For the sergeant, who is expected to be the readily available "computer terminal" for his subordinates, mitigating their problems and answering all their questions, such feelings are often compounded. Not only must he deal with his officers' feelings of frustration in certain situations; his department expects him to be "military" in dealing with problems. The line officer's role, even with its uncertainty, provides more reference points and security than that of the sergeant, who must combine the discretion of the line officer and the administrative flexibility of a supervisor. In addition, he must be constantly sensitive to his superiors' expectations, his supervisees' desires and perceptions, and the views of the community residents who ultimately precipitate the necessity for his decisions.

The Effect of Social Changes

Watts and Free have reported on an attempt to get the opinions of average citizens on what can be done to reduce the crime rate.[28] Various solutions were proposed and respondents were asked to list their preferences. Responses showed a generally perceived need for stricter parental discipline, a citizen responsibility. However, none of the remaining preferred solutions promoted community involvement or citizen action, even though the most popular solution recommended was "cleaning up social and economic conditions in our slums and ghettos that tend to breed addicts and criminals." Respondents were proposing that this overwhelming task be left to the "professionals"!

The present tendency in the face of high crime rates is either to blame or to strengthen the professional crime-fighting element. Without citizen involvement, however, there can be no hope whatsoever for improvement. The Task Force on Community Crime Prevention of the National Advisory Commission on Criminal Justice Standards and Goals makes the assumptions that:

1. Citizen apathy and indifference contribute to the spread of crime;
2. Private and public agencies outside the criminal justice system influence rises and declines in crime rates; and

[28]William Watts and Lloyd A. Free, eds., *State of the Nation; A Report by Potomac Associates* (New York: Universe Books, 1973), pp. 118–20.

3. Community crime-prevention efforts include demonstrable benefits for existing institutions and agencies organized toward the achievement of other primary goals.[29]

Without citizen initiative, cooperation, and involvement, more crimes will be committed, more will go undetected, and the inability of the "professionals" to cope with these increases will in turn encourage lawbreakers to persist in illegal activity.

Before the growth of our complex urban communities, much crime was effectively prevented through informal normative influence. Even if someone did come in contact with a formal community agency such as the police, the matter was often handled informally, because the police officer on the beat knew his community and its residents.

At the same time, through this same informal process, the public exerted varying degrees of control over its public service agencies. In effect, the citizens were a part of the role-definition process. The sergeant knew what was expected of him as the supervisor, because he had close contact with his community and knew what its needs and expectations were and what resources were available for problem solving.

Contributing to the community was important both on and off the job, and the effective sergeant encouraged his supervisees to be an active part of their community. The sergeant and the line officers, in partnership with the community, had solid role definitions, even if they were not always translated into written job descriptions. Even though the line officer and his sergeant did receive pressure from special-interest groups, ordinary residents also had their say, because of the natural, informal communication process.

Today, however, the situation is greatly changed. The complexity of urban life, the vastly increased mobility of the public, and the substitution of radio and television for personal communication are among the factors that have alienated people from each other as well as from their public agencies. And the police, as part of the greater society, share in these changes. Their work has been specialized often to the point of being done with impersonality and dispassion, largely dehumanizing it; police officers often do not live in the communities they serve, which cuts down on their ability to empathize with the citizens, understand their life styles, and exert informal influence on them; and an alienated community is reluctant to become involved in crime prevention and detection.

The result has been not only a decrease in the ability of the police to deal with crime, but also a change in the community's input to the line officer's and sergeant's role definitions. Today, this input is by a formal process from the businesspeople and politicians. These are, of course,

[29]National Advisory Commission, *Police.*

legitimate sources; but they can very often represent special interests, insulating the officer from the greater part of the public with which he has to deal. And what is more important, the ordinary citizen must be protected against the power and influence already in the hands of special-interest groups; the very nature of our democratic society demands equal input from all citizens.

A Model for Action: Normative Sponsorship Theory

There has been much discussion in criminal justice in recent years about the need to more specifically define the role of the line police officer. The process usually breaks down when the element of discretion is introduced into the discussion, with the advocates for a flexible police role arguing that the effective police officer is one who has discretion and is able to use it when appropriate. Because discretion is such an intangible—nearly undefinable—characteristic, little progress can be made in standardizing the role definition by specifically putting the line officer's role expectations down in black and white.

Hence, either of two paths is taken—leave the role definition loose, recognizing that discretion is a real and necessary part of the line officer's role, or, at the other extreme, standardize that role to the point where a clerk could do the job.

A meaningful and workable compromise is to adequately define the role of the line officer's supervisor, the sergeant. In this way, guidelines are set for police action as viewed from the immediate supervisor's perspective. The line officer still has discretion, but within the sphere of the sergeant's supervisory role. With an adequate role definition, the sergeant is able to monitor, oversee, coach, advise, suggest, answer questions, and counsel. Because he is not caught up in the day-to-day activities as the line officer is, he has a more expansive perspective on the "big picture," reflecting community needs yet adhering to the legal mandates of his department.

The key, then, is not overdefining the role of the line officer but adequately identifying the factors that relate to his effective supervision. This can be accomplished by using the method of *normative sponsorship.* The discussion of the environment of the first-line police supervisor is irrelevant without recognition that the basis of his effective operation depends on a carefully analyzed role definition that includes input from all relevant groups.

The normative sponsorship theory approach to role identification and definition and job description has been used in community problem solving. The theory was originated and developed by Dr. Christopher Sower. Simply stated, normative sponsorship theory proposes that a role definition will be sponsored only if it is normative (within the limits of established standards) to all persons and interest groups involved—in this case, the police department administrators, the sergeant's supervisees, the sergeant, and community residents.

In the initiation of a consensus role definition, it is of major importance to understand how two or more interest groups can have sufficient convergence of interest or consensus on common goals to bring about the agreed-upon role definition. Each group involved and interested in having input into the role definition must be able to justify, and hence legitimize, the role definition within its own patterns of values, norms, and goals. The more congruent the values, beliefs, and goals of all participating groups, the easier it will be for them to agree on the role definition. They need not, however, have the same reasons for their involvement or acceptance of a group goal.[30]

Whatever the areas of consensus between groups with different normative orientations, it is important not to deny the concept of self-interest, because it cannot be expected that all groups will have common or similar motivations for desiring input into the sergeant's role definition. Self-interest is not dysfunctional unless it contributes to intergroup contest or opposition and diverts energy that should more appropriately be directed at problem solving. In other words, the fact that the police department administrators, community residents, the sergeants, and their supervisees may have different ideas of what should be included in the sergeant's role definition does not in itself create a problem. The problem arises when the groups are unable to compromise, and self-interest takes precedence over the common good of developing an adequate role definition. If, for example, department administrators want to maintain complete control over the role definition and job description in order to facilitate the desires of special-interest groups, or if the line officers want to dictate via their union what latitude the sergeant should have when monitoring and disciplining his people, then self-interest becomes dysfunctional. Each group should have input but not total control; otherwise, the process of role definition will either fail or be merely cosmetic, with no real meaning.

Step 1: Information gathering. Before a role definition for the sergeant can be developed, information has to be gathered: the type of community that the sergeant operates in, the crime rates in various areas of the city, and data on relevant community service organizations that can supplement police services. Among the last-named are block organizations and other citizen groups whose existence the sergeant may not even be aware of if such information is not gathered, but whose interaction with his officers he will be expected to oversee.

[30]Christopher Sower et al., *Community Involvement* (New York: The Free Press, 1957).

Step 2: Analysis of the community. Police services are determined by community needs, and since the sergeant's role will be to see that these needs are fulfilled by his line officers within the legal framework of law-enforcement activities, it is necessary to analyze the community he will operate in—its history, its development, and its current politics and problems. All these factors will influence how the sergeant will carry out his role and how his time and effort should be allocated when supervising his officers.

The analysis of the community should include the following:

1. Economic base:
   a. Single-industry or business-center base
   b. Expansion plans
   c. Community attitudes toward expansion
   d. Labor–management crises
   e. Present and future job market
2. Cultural aspects:
   a. Single- or multicultural community
   b. Class lines and prior conflict, if any
   c. In multiculture community, nature of equilibrium or strife, if any
   d. Official response to cultural situation, in terms of favoritism, distribution of services, alignment of elected officials
   e. Mobility patterns
3. Social organization:
   a. Extent and nature of social, fraternal, and church organizations
   b. Conflict, cooperation, or coalition, if any, for common cause
   c. Political affiliations of organizations and attachments to particular social movements
   d. Existing social programs and projects
   e. Potential for creation of new organizations
4. Official functions:
   a. Punitive formal justice agencies
   b. Nonpunitive approaches created or supported by formal agencies
   c. History of attempts to create programs or supplement official crime-prevention programs
   d. Current coordination and planning—fragmented or centrally assumed
   e. Inter- and intra-agency conflict or cooperation; attitudes of formal justice and social agencies toward each other
5. Crisis handling:
   a. Natural disasters and social crises that have influenced attitude formation
   b. Racial strife and its resolution or nonresolution

c. Sensational crime, by neighborhood or area; presence of organized crime, if any

d. Public perceptions of adequacy of officials in responding to past crises, especially regarding major crime[31]

Obviously, communities differ in their makeup and needs, and even though the general principles of first-line police supervision can be identified, the specific role definition and ultimate job description will vary according to the community. A sergeant in a large metropolitan police department will have different responsibilities and authority from those of a sergeant in a small rural police department. Therefore, analysis of the community is mandatory for adequate role-definition development.

Step 3: Relevant-system identification. Before constructing a role definition that will include input from many different people, it is necessary to identify the relevant interest groups—*relevant systems.* The major relevant systems concerned with the sergeant's role definition would be the community residents, the police department administrators, the sergeants, and the line officers whom the sergeants supervise. If these groups or relevant systems agree on what the sergeant's job should be, then he can be an effective quality-control point to make sure the line officers do the job and do it right.

Step 4: Identification of leadership. Obviously, not every person associated with the four relevant systems can be involved in the process of the sergeant's role definition. From each of the four groups, a sample must be selected of people who are able to reflect the system's norms, values, and goals and know how it functions. Such leaders also exert considerable influence; their opinions and suggestions are respected by the groups they represent.

The selected representatives may hold formal positions in their relevant systems, like the president of the line officers' union or the president of a community block club; or they may be informal leaders. For example, in a large department, there is usually an organization for sergeants; a particular sergeant who does not hold an office in the organization may nevertheless be influential and highly respected by his peers.

These leaders are identified by sampling members of the relevant organizations and asking such questions as, "Whom do you or most of the people in the organization go to for advice on problem solving?" and, "Who in the organization is respected, has power and influence, and has the reputation for getting things done?" After the sampling process is completed, a list

[31]See further elaboration by Forrest M. Moss in *Community Based Crime Prevention*, Robert C. Trojanowicz, John M. Trojanowicz, and Forrest M. Moss (Santa Monica, Calif.: Goodyear, 1975).

is made of those names that have been mentioned most often as leaders.

The sampling process is important for leadership identification. It should not be assumed that the names of leaders are already known. Leadership is not static, and those who are assumed to be leaders because of their formal or informal position may not be the major sources of power or influence. The identification of true leadership is mandatory if the process of role identification is to be successful.

Step 5: Bringing leaders of relevant systems together. After leaders have been identified in each relevant system, the next step is to contact these people, tell them that they have been so identified, and bring them together for a meeting.

The initial meeting, usually comprising about 20 to 30 persons, will be somewhat unstructured. The meetings are chaired by a technical-assistance advisor, a neutral person who is not part of any relevant system—for example, a respected professional person in the community. The major objectives of the initial meetings will be to:

1. Facilitate the expression of feelings about the perceived duties and responsibilities of sergeants.
2. Encourage relevant systems to exchange perceptions about each other—for example, suspicions that may exist between the citizens and the line officers.
3. Produce an atmosphere conducive to dialogue, so that the misperceptions can be identified.
4. Identify self-interests, pointing out that from the self-interest standpoint of all systems, cooperative problem solving to identify the sergeant's role will benefit everyone. The community will ultimately be better served because the sergeant will be a more effective supervisor, and the sergeant will be comfortable with his role because he will have reference points with which to be judged and to supervise his people.

In relation to point 1 above, the representatives of the relevant systems will first get to know one another and one another's viewpoints. The department administrators, for example, will give their ideas about what duties sergeants should perform, the priorities they give those duties, and the amount of authority they think should be vested in sergeants. Likewise, the other relevant-system representatives will express their opinions, ideas, and feelings about the factors to be included in role definition for sergeants.

Point 2 is necessary because when diverse interest groups assemble, they often have biased opinions, misinformation, and negative perceptions about one another. If they can be brought to exchange their perceptions of one another in an atmosphere of freedom of expression, defensiveness can be reduced and future cooperation increased. As an added bonus, involvement in this exchange by the police elements present may reduce future labor–management hostility during contract negotiations.

The technical-assistance advisor can play an important part in these early stages. He can help control the meetings so they are not monopolized by any one group, and so that expression of feelings does not become so strong as to disrupt the meeting. And he can also help clarify the issues, maintain order, and furnish insight into any problems that might arise.

The communication between the relevant systems should be open and straightforward. This will not be easy: Not only will the participants not always agree on the elements to be included in the sergeant's role definition; in some cases, they will be reluctant to discuss openly the factors that are critical to its development. The police participants may feel that civilians should not be a part of the process because they do not understand police work. Department administrators may resent the line officers and sergeants for "usurping management prerogatives." Sergeants may not care for the idea that line officers are helping to define the role of their immediate supervisors.

As the meetings progress, however, there will be increased understanding and positive communication between the relevant systems, and areas of agreement will emerge. This will help reduce suspiciousness and provide each of the systems with new insights into the thinking of the other groups and the rationale for their areas of input, thus establishing a basis for future understanding and cooperation.

The first few meetings are usually typified by (1) the unstructured expression of feelings and perceptions, (2) the discussion of the constellation of factors that should be included in role definition, (3) the facilitation of understanding, and (4) increased positive communication. The sessions then begin to take a more focused and structured orientation. If the initial meetings have achieved their objectives, the stage is set for the next phase of the process.

Step 6: The identification of areas of agreement and disagreement. In this stage of the process, the matrix method (see Table 9-3) is utilized for the identification of areas of agreement and disagreement. In dealing with this kind of methodology, Ladd has made an important contribution.[32] He obtained the following kinds of information for each of the major roles of the small society that he studied. This same information will be helpful in understanding the perceptions of the relevant systems when constructing the sergeant's role definition.

[32]John Ladd, *The Structure of a Moral Code* (Cambridge, Mass.: Harvard University Press, 1957).

TABLE 9-3

Diagram of the Matrix Method for Development of the Sergeant's Role

Norms and Behavior Perceptions Held by:	Norms and Behavior Perceptions Held About:			
	Sergeants	*Department Administrators*	*Department Line Officers*	*Community Residents*

Sergeants	*Self-Concept*
	
	1. Perceived norms and expected behavior as it relates to the sergeant's role
	2. Description of actual behavior
	3. Defined as:
	  a. Normative
	  b. Deviant
	4. Statement of alternatives for role definition
	5. What criteria should be used when evaluating sergeants?
		1. Perceived norms and expected behavior as it relates to the sergeant's role
		2. Description of actual behavior
		3. Defined as:
		  a. Normative
		  b. Deviant
		4. Perception as to what alternatives the other systems will select for role development
		5. What criteria should be used when evaluating sergeants?
			*	*

		Self-Concept		Self-Concept

Department Administrators	1. Perceived norms and expected behavior as it relates to the sergeant's role
	2. Description of actual behavior
	3. Defined as:
	  a. Normative
	  b. Deviant
	4. Perception as to what alternatives the other systems will select for role development
	5. What criteria should be used when evaluating sergeants?
		1. Perceived norms and expected behavior as it relates to sergeant's role
		2. Description of actual behavior
		3. Defined as:
		  a. Normative
		  b. Deviant
		4. Statement of alternatives for role definition
		5. What criteria should be used when evaluating sergeants?
			*	*

Department Line Officers	*	*	*Self-Concept*	*
Community Residents	*	*	*	*Self-Concept*

*Use the same criteria that are presented in the cell showing the Sergeant's perception of department administrators.

1. What are the prescriptions of expected behavior?
2. Who makes these prescriptions?
3. To what extent is there consensus about the prescriptions?
4. Who enforces them?
5. What are the rewards for compliance?
6. What is the punishment for deviance?

As illustrated in Table 9-3, this kind of information and others can be assembled into a matrix pattern for the analysis of the information obtained from the relevant systems concerning the sergeant's role definition. This method serves as a vehicle for visually and objectively comparing the perceptions among and between relevant systems. For example, the perception the sergeant has of his role (self-concept) can be compared with the perception community residents have of that role. Such comparisons can be made among all the relevant systems—administrators' with sergeants', line officers' with administrators', and so on. (As Table 1-2 in chapter 1 illustrated, the 300 interviewed line officers, department administrators, and sergeants themselves were able to list and rank what they felt were important traits of an effective sergeant.)

The perceptions of what the role should be (number 1 in Table 9-3) and the traits of the effective sergeant as viewed by all the relevant systems can then be compared with the sergeant's present or actual behavior (number 2). An evaluation can be made of whether the sergeant's behavior is congruent (number 3a) or incongruent (3b) with what is expected of him. If the sergeant is not functioning according to the expectations of the majority of those in the relevant systems, alterations in his role will be necessary. In addition, the relevant systems may wish to delete some of his duties or add some to make the role more adaptable to their community.

After comparing the perceptions of the relevant systems and comparing their suggested alternatives (number 4) for role identification, it may be apparent that there is little disagreement about what the role of the sergeant should be. In other words, the factors that the relevant systems include in the role-definition construction may be very similar and congruent. For example, all relevant systems may feel that the role definition should include a statement about the sergeant's involvement in employee grievance procedures. In many departments, the sergeant has minimal latitude in this area; he is limited to processing the grievance to a higher level. In business and industry, the first-line supervisor has an important responsibility in grievance settlement, and there may be almost total agreement that the sergeant's role should include grievance handling and settlement. A clear role definition of the sergeant's responsibility in this area will provide reference points for him.

As just pointed out, the fourth area of information in Table 9-3 asks relevant systems to suggest *alternatives* for role definition, both from their own viewpoint (self-concept) and those they feel the other systems will select.

For example, in the interviews with the 300 officers, the question was asked, "What alternatives will the sergeants suggest to improve their effectiveness?" The responses, given in Table 9-4, are from line officers, department administrators (lieutenants and above), and sergeants themselves (self-concept). The matrix chart (Table 9-3) has a fourth category, community residents, which ideally should be included in the construction of the sergeant's role definition. Community residents were, not part of the 300 interviews in the example shown in Table 9-4.

It is relatively easy to see and compare what the relevant systems see as possible alternatives for problem solving. Even though the question asked each of the three systems what it thought the *sergeant would say* he needs to improve his effectiveness, the suggested alternatives also reflect each system's own opinions.

As Table 9-4 shows, many of the suggested alternatives are congruent between relevant systems. The role definition of the sergeant then becomes more manageable, because the matrix method (Table 9-3) allows for visual comparison, incorporating into the sergeant's role those suggested alternatives on which there is agreement and discussing further and eventually compromising on those on which there is disagreement.

Another question that was asked of the 300 officers that has relevance to the role definition is the one asked under number 5 in Table 9-3: "What criteria should be used when evaluating sergeants"? Table 9-5 shows a great deal of agreement between the relevant systems regarding such criteria. In any meaningful role-development process, evaluation criteria will have to be discussed and developed so that realistic reference points can be established.

Identifying areas of agreement and disagreement by using the matrix method (Table 9-3) facilitates visually comparing (1) perceived norms and expected behavior of the four relevant systems as it relates to the sergeant's role; (2) the description of the sergeant's actual behavior; (3) whether the sergeant's behavior is perceived as *normative* (acceptable according to the standards of the four relevant systems) or *deviant* (not acceptable according to those standards); (4) the alternatives for role development; and (5) criteria to be used when evaluating sergeants.

The matrix method (Table 9-3) is not a magical process. It involves a great deal of time and the solicitation of input from the four relevant systems. And there will not always be agreement; for example, each of the four systems may have a different view of what should be considered normative

TABLE 9-4

What Alternatives Will the Sergeants Suggest To Improve Their Effectiveness?

Patrolmen	Sergeants (Self-Concept)	Lieutenants	Command
Uniform	*Uniform*	*Uniform*	*Uniform*
1. More authority and backing	1. More authority	1. Support and backing	1. More authority
2. More leeway in decision making	2. A better role definition	2. Better role definition	2. More training
3. Cooperation, communication, and understanding from administration	3. More backing	3. Involvement in decision making	3. More backing
4. A clearer role definition	4. More input into policy and decision making	4. More trust from the administration	4. More information
5. More input into decision making	5. More training and in-service schools	5. More direction and guidance	5. More equipment
6. The administration doesn't want sgts. who make decisions	6. More feedback and understanding from administration	6. Have the administration "get off their backs"	*Investigative*
7. Less paperwork	7. Relief from paperwork	7. More authority	1. More manpower
8. More training	8. More men and resources	8. More training	2. Better direction
9. Have administration "get off my back"	9. Reduce administration scapegoating	*Investigative*	3. More authority
10. More work to do	10. Have administration recognize contributions	1. More manpower	4. Less caseload
11. More responsibility	11. Let sgt. see the "big picture"	2. More equipment	*Special*
12. More manpower	12. More independence	3. More responsibility	1. More resources and supplies
13. More versatility	*Investigative*	4. Less paperwork	2. Better working conditions
14. Let them discipline the officers	1. More manpower	*Special*	3. Increased rank
15. More respect from administration	2. More latitude to run squad	1. They don't need anything	4. More training
Investigative	3. More money and equipment	2. Better role definition	
1. More manpower	4. More authority	3. Career advancement	
2. More freedom to operate	5. Better training	4. Equipment	
3. Equipment and facilities to operate	6. Less paper work	5. Manpower	
	7. Let sgt. be more of a supervisor and less of a paper shuffler		
	8. More cooperation from rest of Criminal Justice system		

4. Better coordination between units
5. More authority
6. Better reports from patrol
7. Less paperwork
8. Fewer lieutenants—reduce the chain of command
9. "Leave us alone"
10. Better cooperation and understanding from administration
11. Better information flow
12. More training
13. More follow-up of cases
14. More responsibility

Special
1. More manpower
2. More resources
3. They have what they want and need
4. More understanding from other units
5. More authority and backing
6. A better delineation of lines of authority
7. Assistance with paperwork
8. Better cooperation with media
9. Less politics in their operation
10. Less paperwork
11. More background knowledge in their area
12. Freer rein

9. More input into decision making
10. Better communication between units
11. More feedback
12. Better reports from patrol
13. Better physical facilities
14. More knowledgeable and competent officers

Special
1. More equipment and resources
2. More freedom and leeway
3. They don't need anything
4. More independence and support from the administration
5. Better understanding from other units in the department
6. Help with administration duties
7. More decision making
8. More praise and recognition of their expertise

Note: Responses are listed in the order of importance as stated by the particular group of respondents.

TABLE 9-5

What Criteria Should Be Used When Evaluating Sergeants?

Patrolmen	Sergeants	Lieutenants	Command
How well he gets along with others	Job knowledge	How well he takes care of his officers	The way his officers function—productivity and efficiency
Ability to communicate	How well his officers function	How he handles officers	How the officers look—appearance
Ability to make decisions	His overall performance and functioning	Morale of his officers	How the sergeant's reports look
Job knowledge	Ability to make decisions	How well he knows the strengths and weaknesses of his officers	Aggressiveness and capability in decision making
Ability to handle and treat men fairly	Leadership by example	The efficiency of his operation	Responsiveness to men
How helpful he is when he is called by his officers	How he handles stress and delicate situations	By how many complaints his lieutenants get	The attitude of his officers
How effective a trainer he is	Ability to get along with men and administration—his attitude	How he accepts responsibility	Loyalty to his officers and the organization
Whether he "chews his officers out" in front of others	How well he controls his men, fair but firm	If his work is done properly	How the sergeant functions
Productivity of his officers	Ability to communicate	How well he makes decisions	Knowledge of the job
His leadership and command ability	Ability to dispatch and obey orders	His loyalty to the department	Initiative
The morale of his officers	The number of complaints by his men	How he gets along with his officers	His outlook and attitude about the job
How well he backs up his officers	How he reviews his officers' reports plus his own reports	How officers respond to him	His versatility
Availability when his officers need him	How he and his men take care of their equipment	His judgment	His ability to lead
The way he reviews reports	Complaints about him from his men and citizens	How he reviews reports	
How responsive he is to officers' needs	Availability	Personality, character, and attitude	
His appearance and physical shape	Community involvement	His command and leadership ability	
Ability to innovate—not a "company man"		Job knowledge—whether he can answer questions	
		How he deals with people	
		How he follows through	

How well he understands his officers' problems

How he uses his authority

How much his officers respect him

How receptive he is of others' ideas

Consistency of his behavior

How well he maximizes the skills of his officers

His relationship to his superiors

His enthusiasm for the job

His time in job

Whether he can discipline yet be tactful

How up to date his officers are

Ability to handle administrative aspects of his job

Past work record

How well the officers like him

Whether he makes input into the system

His moral character

His contribution to the department

His potential

Longevity and seniority

His past record

Whether his officers produce without being harassed

Willingness to tolerate differences

Closure rate of cases (Detective Sergeant)

How well his records are kept

Appearance

Whether he is dependable— punctual, etc.

His ability to accomplish a specific objective

How well he trains and develops his officers

If he follows up to see if his men did the job

If he takes responsibility for his men's actions

How often his officers call in sick

Whether he respects his officers' ability to make decisions

Whether he is a "nit picker"

How much education he has

His loyalty to the department and his officers

Ability to adapt

Whether he supervises

Whether he can take constructive criticism

Whether he can effectively supervise

Whether the officers seek him out

How his personnel adhere to new procedures and orders

Note: Responses are listed in the order of importance as stated by the particular group of respondents.

or deviant. When the process is completed and the perceptions compared, however, there is usually much more agreement between systems than would have been anticipated prior to the role-definition process.

Step 7: Role-definition implementation. After areas of agreement and disagreement have been identified, the sergeant's role definition will have incorporated the input and perceptions of all relevant systems. Even though not all the systems may have agreed on all aspects of what should be included, there will have been enough areas of agreement that when the final job description is put down on paper, it should be supported by all the relevant groups, because they have all had input into the process of role construction.

Step 8: Quality control and role updating. As with the development of any role definition, whether it be for the line officer or the sergeant, there is a need for constant quality control, to make sure that the sergeant is operating according to the role definition. There should also be meaningful feedback about how the sergeant is functioning in relation to the job description, to see if updating of the job description is needed, or whether alterations should be made.

Conclusion

An effective job description results only from cooperative firsthand experience of all relevant systems in the role-definition process. A maximum of active involvement and a minimum of shallow verbalization will facilitate cooperation and mutual understanding among the relevant systems.

The most effective means of motivating people is to transmit to them that their opinions will be valued, that they will have a voice in decision making, and that they will be involved in the role development process. The ultimate job description will be sponsored and supported if these criteria are adhered to, because the parties who make up the relevant systems have a personal investment in the process. Involved action by the relevant systems will be mutually beneficial; it will increase understanding and cooperation between them, the police department will be more effective, and the community better served.

SUMMARY

This chapter has discussed the need for department and community support and, most important, the need for a well-defined role definition for the sergeant that the department can ultimately put into a job description. A complete and inclusive job description, reflecting the needs of the community as well as the goals of the police department, will provide the sergeant with reference points that will facilitate the supervisory process. Ultimately it is the sergeant, as first-line supervisor and quality-control agent, who makes sure that community needs are met and department goals are accomplished.

A role definition whose construction involves and includes community residents, department administrators, line officers, and the sergeants themselves will have a good chance of being implemented via the supervisory process because all these relevant groups will have a stake in seeing that the role is workable within the context of the particular community where the sergeant is working. Although the formal construction of a role definition for the sergeant will not be the same as the informal community processes that were so effective in role definition in the past, it will be a step in the right direction. A comprehensive and workable role definition is the most important factor in *the environment of the first-line police supervisor.*

Appendix*

As mentioned early in the book, the basis for much of the discussion in it was research conducted in three midwestern police departments. Many of the comments came out of the interviews conducted and the observation of participants.

The following are the results of the questionnaires distributed to the officers. The analysis of variance statistical technique was used in analyzing the questionnaires. (See questionnaire at end of appendix).

Some of the questions were collapsed into a common category. For example questions 1, 2, 4, 6, 12, 25, 26, 27, 28, and 29 were combined into item 1, called "Organizational Role." Questions 3 and 8 were combined to make item 2, "Organizational Backing." Questions 5, 18, 23, and 24 make up item 3, "Mediator Role," and questions 9, 14, 15, 31, 32, 36, and 37 constitute item 4, "Fairness." The rest of the questions stand alone.

The last question, which asked the participants to rate the seven supervisory items by their importance, was taken from *Police Supervision* by Paul Wheisenand. These rank-ordered data were analyzed by using median scores.

The data on the perceptions of the sergeant's role were analyzed by *rank, age, education,* and *years of experience.* Each category is illustrated by a table to facilitate a visual comparison; an X signifies that the questionnaire item is significant at, at least, the .05 level. The particular group that rated

*For an expanded discussion see Robert C. Trojanowicz, "A Three Dimensional Analysis of the Role of the Sergeant," *Journal of Police Science and Administration* (December, 1979).

286

PERCEPTIONS OF THE SERGEANTS ROLE BY RANK*

Items from Questionnaire	Ptl.-Sgt. (N=189)(N=31) Signif. at .05 Level	Ptl. or Sgt. More Favorable	Ptl.-Lts. (N=189)(N=15) Signif. at .05 Level	Ptl. or Lt. More Favorable	Ptl.-Cmd. (N=189)(N=9) Signif. at .05 Level	Ptl. or Cmd. More Favorable	Det.-Sgt. (N=22)(N=31) Signif. at .05 Level	Det. or Sgt. More Favorable	Det.-Lts. (N=22)(N=15) Signif. at .05 Level	Det. or Lt. More Favorable	Det.-Cmd. (N=22)(N=9) Signif. at .05 Level	Det. or Cmd. More Favorable	Sgt.-Cmd. (N=31)(N=9) Signif. at .05 Level	Sgt. or Cmd. More Favorable
1. Orgon. Role	X						X							
2. Orgon. Back.	X	S			X	C						C		
3. Mediator	X	S		L	X	C	X	S						
4. Fairness	X	S		L	X	C		S			X	C		
7. Personal Decisions	X						X	S			X			
10. Const. Suggest.	X	S					X	S						
11. Procrastinates														
13. Interested Pers. Wel.	X	S					X	S					–	
16. Sub. Feel Inferior	X	S					X	S					X	
17. Disc. New Ideas	X	S		L				S						S
19. Unnecessary Paperwork	X	S			X		X	S						
20. Inconsistency	X	S					X							
21. Eliminate Weakness	X	S			X	C	X	S	X		X	C		
22. Reprimand Ideas	X	S					X	S	X	L				
30. Talk to Officers	X	S					X	S						
33. Takes Responsibility	X	S					X	S						
34. Defends Policies	X	S					X	S					X	S
35. Cooperates	X	S					X	S						
ROLE PERFORMANCE														
38. Interp. Situation	X	S			X	C	X	S			X	C		
39. Other Agencies	X	S												
40. New Methods	X	S		L			X	S						
41. Directing Work	X	S			X	C	X	S	X	L	X	C		
42. Cut Red Tape	X	S					X	S						
43. Comm. Depts. Obj.	X	S			X		X	S						
44. Imp. Inexp. Officers	X	S		L			X	S	X	L				
45. Upgrades Exp. Officers	X	S					X	S						
46. Provides Leadership	X	S		L		C	X	S			X	C		
47. Maintains Morale	X	S		L			X	S			X	C		
48. Revise Procedures	X	S					X	S						
49. Shift Running	X	S					X	S						
50. General Planning	X								X	L				
51. Knows St. & Wk. of Off.	X	S		L	X	C	X	S	X	L	X	C		
52. Coord. Activities	X	S												
53. Knows B.,P.,D. St.	X	S						S						
54. Listens	X	S		L	X	C	X	S	X	L	X	C		
55. Improves Proc.	X	S			X	C	X	S	X	L	X	C		
56. Goes to Bat	X	S		L	X	C	X	S	X	L				

*No significant relationship for the following groups: Ptl.–Det., Sgt.–Lt., and Lt.–Cmd.

NOTE: The majority of the relationships were significant at the .01 or better.

PERCEPTIONS OF THE SERGEANTS ROLE BY AGE

Items from Questionnaire	20 - 29 vs. 30 - 39 (N=110) (N=97)		20 - 29 vs. 40 and Over (N=110) (N=59)		30 - 39 vs. 40 and Over (N=97) (N=59)	
	Signif. at at Least .05 Level	20-29 or 30-39 More Favorable	Signif. at at Least .05 Level	20-29 or 40 and Over More Favorable	Signif. at at Least .05 Level	30-39 or 40 and Over More Favorable
1. Organ. Role			X	40+	X	40+
2. Organ. Back.			X	40+	X	40+
3. Mediator			X	40+	X	40+
4. Fairness	X	20 - 29	X	40+	X	40+
7. Personal Decisions	X	30 - 39				
10. Const. Suggest.					X	40+
11. Procrastinates	X	20 - 29			X	40+
13. Interested Pers. Wel.	X	20 - 29			X	40+
16. Sub. Feel Inferior	X	20 - 29			X	40+
17. Disc. New Ideas			X	40+	X	40+
19. Unnecessary Paperwork			X	40+	X	40+
20. Inconsistency	X	20 - 29			X	40+
21. Eliminate Weakness			X	40+	X	40+
22. Reprimand Ideas						
30. Talk to Officers	X	20 - 29	X	40+	X	40+
33. Takes Responsibility			X	40+	X	40+
34. Defends Policies						
35. Cooperates						

ROLE PERFORMANCE

Items from Questionnaire	Signif. at at Least .05 Level	20-29 or 30-39 More Favorable	Signif. at at Least .05 Level	20-29 or 40 and Over More Favorable	Signif. at at Least .05 Level	30-39 or 40 and Over More Favorable
38. Interp. Situation	X	20 - 29			X	40+
39. Other Agencies			X	40+	X	40+
40. New Methods			X	40+		
41. Directing Work			X	40+	X	40+
42. Cut Red Tape			X	40+	X	40+
43. Comm. Depts. Objectives			X	40+	X	40+
44. Imp. Inexp. Officers			X	40+	X	40+
45. Upgrades Exp. Officers			X	40+	X	40+
46. Provides Leadership	X	20 - 29	X	40+	X	40+
47. Maintains Morale	X	20 - 29	X	40+	X	40+
48. Revise Procedures			X	40+	X	40+
49. Shift Running	X	20 - 29			X	40+
50. General Planning	X	20 - 29			X	40+
51. Knows St. & Wk. of Off.			X	40+	X	40+
52. Coord. Activities			X	40+	X	40+
53. Knows B.P.D. St.	X	20 - 29			X	40+
54. Listens	X	20 - 29			X	40+
55. Improves Proc.			X	40+	X	40+
56. Goes to Bat			X	40+	X	40+

sergeants more favorably is also designated. The first 35 questions relate to the extent that first-line supervisors engage in the behaviors listed in the questions. Questions 38 thru 56 asked the respondents to rate the sergeants on their actual role performance.

COMPARISONS BY RANK

There is reasonable congruence between the perceptions the sergeants have of themselves and the perceptions the command officers (captains and